Pompeis Difficile Est

Pompeis Difficile Est

Studies in the Political Life of Imperial Pompeii

James L. Franklin, Jr.

Ann Arbor

THE UNIVERSITY OF MICHIGAN PRESS

Copyright © by the University of Michigan 2001
All rights reserved
Published in the United States of America by
The University of Michigan Press
Manufactured in the United States of America
∞ Printed on acid-free paper

2004   2003   2002   2001   4   3   2   1

A CIP catalog record for this book is available from the British Library.

Library of Congress Cataloging-in-Publication Data

Franklin, James L.
    Pompeis difficile est : studies in the political life of imperial Pompeii /
James L. Franklin.
        p.   cm.
    Includes bibliographical references and index.
    ISBN 0-472-11056-X (cloth)
        1. Pompeii (Extinct city)—Politics and government—Sources.   2.
Elections—Italy—Pompeii (Extinct city)—Sources.   3. Upper class
families—Italy—Pompeii (Extinct city)—Political activity.   I. Title.

DG70.P7 F75   1999
320.937'7—dc21   99-052255

Acknowledgments

While I have for over twenty years been interested in the prosopography—the study of the inhabitants—of ancient Pompeii, this project saw its serious beginnings during the 1995–96 academic year, when I was granted a sabbatical leave from my teaching duties at Indiana University. I had admittedly before that begun to put my thoughts to paper, but that year's research and reflection convinced me that there was indeed this book for me to write. Likewise, final thoughts and changes were made possible thanks to a Summer Faculty Fellowship awarded me in 1998, again by Indiana University. For special support at this project's beginning and end, I therefore gratefully thank my home institution.

At Indiana I have enjoyed the loyal support of two individuals in particular: Eleanor Winsor Leach, colleague and fellow "Pompeianista," and James Werner Halporn, who even since his retirement has regularly prodded me forward. Almost before the project began, Lawrence Richardson, jr, my former teacher and internalized mentor, read a rambling, short typescript and pointed me in more productive, organized directions. To these people in particular I owe great debts of gratitude. The end result, of course, remains entirely my responsibility; in this world, alas, good counsel is as often rejected as taken.

Grateful acknowledgment is also made to Caratzas Publishing, Inc., for permission to include as the first chapter here a revised version of an article, "Augustans at Pompeii," from *The Shapes of City Life in Rome and Pompeii: Essays in Honor of Lawrence Richardson, jr on the Occasion of His Retirement,* edited by H.B. Evans and M.T. Boatwright (New Rochelle 1996). Ayer Company Publishers has permitted as figure 18 here reproduction of the illustration, "Façade of the house of Epidius Rufus, restored," from August Mau's *Pompeii: Its Life and Art,* translated by F.W. Kelsey, second edition (New York 1902). My analysis of the career of Alleius Nigidius Maius earlier appeared as the article "Cn. Alleius Nigidius Maius and the Amphitheatre: *Munera* and a Distinguished Career at Ancient Pompeii" in *Historia* 46 (1997): 434–47, and thanks are due Franz Steiner Verlag Wiesbaden GmbH for permission to reproduce it in part here. Finally, Liselotte Eschebach and Jürgen Müller-Trollius have graciously granted me permission to reproduce the overall plan of Pompeii as well as twenty-five detailed plans of city blocks from their recent volume *Gebäudeverzeichnis und Stadtplan der antiken Stadt Pompeji* (Cologne 1993), which includes Müller-Trollius' updated version of the master plan of Pompeii by Hans Eschebach.

Contents

Abbreviations

Abbreviations of titles of journals and standard reference works follow the *American Journal of Archaeology* 95 (1991) 1–16. In addition, the following short references are used:

Andreau, *Jucundus*   J. Andreau, *Les affaires de Monsieur Jucundus,* Collection de l'École Française de Rome, 19. Rome 1974.

Andreau, "Remarques"   J. Andreau. "Remarques sur la société pompéienne." *Dialoghi di Archeologia* 7 (1973) 213–54.

Apochae   Corpus Inscriptionum Latinarum. Vol. 4, supp. 1, pt. 1, *Tabulae Ceratae Pompeis Repertae Annis MDCCCLXXV et MDCCCLXXXVII.* Ed. Carolo Zangemeister. Berlin 1871.

Castrén   P. Castrén. *Ordo Populusque Pompeianus: Polity and Society in Roman Pompeii,* Acta Instituti Romani Finlandiae 8. Rome 1975.

Conway   R.S. Conway, *The Italic Dialects.* Cambridge 1897.

D'Ambrosio and De Caro   A. D'Ambrosio and S. De Caro. *Un impegno per Pompei: Fotopiano e documentazione della Necropoli di Porta Nocera.* Milan 1983.

D'Arms, "Pompeii and Rome"   J.H. D'Arms. "Pompeii and Rome in the Augustan Age and Beyond: The Eminence of the *Gens Holconia.*" In *Studia Pompeiana et Classica in Honor of Wilhelmina F. Jashemski,* ed. R.I. Curtis, 2 vols., 1:51–74. New Rochelle 1988.

De Caro, "Scavi"   S. De Caro. "Scavi dell' area fuori Porta di Nola a Pompei." *Cronache Pompeiane* 5 (1979) 61–101.

De Caro, "Sculptures"   S. De Caro. "The Sculptures of the Villa of Poppaea at Oplontis: A Preliminary Report." In *Ancient Roman Villa Gardens,* ed. E.B. MacDougall, Dumbarton Oaks Colloquium on the History of Landscape Architecture 10, pp. 79–133. Washington, D.C. 1987.

de Franciscis   A. de Franciscis. "La casa di C. Iulius Polybius." *Rivista di Studi Pompeiani* 2 (1988) 15–36.

Della Corte   M. Della Corte. *Case ed abitanti di Pompei.* Ed. P. Soprano. 3d ed. Naples 1965. (Unless otherwise specified, references are to section numbers, not pages.)

De' Spagnolis Conticello   M. De' Spagnolis Conticello. "Sul rinvenimento della villa e del monumento funerario dei Lucretii Valentes." *Rivista di Studi Pompeiani* 6 (1993–94) 147–66.

Dobbins, "Chronology"   J. Dobbins. "Problems of Chronology, Decoration, and Urban Design in the Forum of Pompeii." *American Journal of Archaeology* 98 (1994) 629–94.

Dyson, *Community*   S.L. Dyson. *Community and Society in Roman Italy*. Baltimore and London 1992.

Eschebach   H. Eschebach. *Die städtebauliche Entwicklung des antiken Pompeji*. Mitteilungen des Deutschen Archäologischen Instituts, Römische Abteilung, Supplemental Volume 17. Heidelberg 1970.

Eschebach and Müller-Trollius   L. Eschebach and J. Müller-Trollius, *Gebäudeverzeichnis und Stadtplan der antiken Stadt Pompeji*. Cologne 1993.

Fiorelli, *Descrizione*   G. Fiorelli. *Descrizione di Pompei*. Naples 1875.

Franklin, "Augustans"   J.L. Franklin, Jr. "Augustans at Pompeii." In *The Shapes of City Life in Rome and Pompeii, Essays in Honor of Lawrence Richardson, jr. on the Occasion of His Retirement*, ed. H.B. Evans and M.T. Boatwright, 71–89. New Rochelle 1996.

Franklin, *Electoral*   J.L. Franklin, Jr. *Pompeii: The Electoral Programmata, Campaigns, and Politics*, A.D. 71–79. Papers and Monographs of the American Academy in Rome 28. Rome 1980.

Franklin, "Maius"   J.L. Franklin, Jr. "Cn. Alleius Nigidius Maius and the Amphitheatre: *Munera* and a Distinguished Career at Ancient Pompeii." *Historia* 96 (1997) 434–47.

Franklin, "Pantomimists"   J.L. Franklin, Jr. "Pantomimists at Pompeii: Actius Anicetus and His Troupe." *American Journal of Philology* 108 (1987) 95–107.

Franklin, "*Scriptores*"   J.L. Franklin, Jr. "Notes on Pompeian Prosopography: *Programmatum Scriptores*." *Cronache Pompeiane* 4 (1978) 54–74.

Franklin, "Valens"   J.L. Franklin, Jr. "Notes on Pompeian Prosopography: Two Non-existent Ancients and the DD. Lucretii Valentes." *Parola del Passato* 34 (1979) 405–14.

Fröhlich   T. Fröhlich. *Lararien- und Fassadenbilder in den Vesuvstädten: Untersuchungen zur "volkstumlichen" pompejanischen Malerei*. Mitteilungen des Deutschen Archäologischen Instituts, Römische Abteilung, Supplemental Volume 32. Mainz 1991.

Giordano, "Polibio"   C. Giordano. "Iscrizioni graffite e dipinte nella Casa di C. Iulio Polibio." *Rendiconti dell' Accademia di Archeologia, Lettere e Belle Arti, Napoli*, n.s., 49 (1974) 21–28.

Giordano and Casale   C. Giordano and A. Casale. "Iscrizioni pompeiane inedite scoperte tra gli anni 1954–1978," *Atti della Accademia Pontaniana*, n.s., 39 (1990) 273–378. (Unless otherwise specified, references are to entry numbers, not pages.)

Giornale   *Giornale degli scavi di Pompei*.

Hänlein-Schäfer   H. Hänlein-Schäfer. *Veneratio Augusti: Eine Studie zu den Tempeln des ersten römischen Kaisers*. Rome 1985.

Helbig   W. Helbig. *Wandgemälde der vom Vesuv verschütteten Städte Campaniens*. Leipzig 1868.

Kockel   V. Kockel. *Die Grabbauten vor dem Herkulaner Tor in Pompeji*. Beiträge zur Erschliessung hellenisticher und kaiserzeitlicher Skulptur und Architektur 1. Mainz 1983.

Łoś, "Affranchis"   A. Łoś. "Les affranchis dans la vie politique à Pompei." *Mélanges de l'École Française de Rome, Antiquité* 99 (1987) 847–73.

Łoś, "Remarques"   A. Łoś *"Quibus patet curia municipalis:* Remarques sur la structure de la classe dirigente de Pompei." *Cahiers du Centre Gustave Glotz* 3 (1992) 259–97.

Magaldi, "Echi"   E. Magaldi. "Echi di Roma a Pompei." *Rivista di Studi Pompeiani* 2 (1936) 25–100.

Magaldi, "Echi II"   E. Magaldi. "Echi di Roma a Pompei II." *Rivista di Studi Pompeiani* 2 (1936) 129–209.

Magaldi, "Echi III"   E. Magaldi, "Echi di Roma a Pompei III." *Rivista di Studi Pompeiani* 3 (1939) 21–60.

Mau, *Pompeii.*   A. Mau. *Pompeii: Its Life and Art.* Trans. F.W. Kelsey. 2d ed. New York 1902.

Michel, *Cei*   D. Michel. *Casa dei Cei.* Deutsches Archäologisches Institut: Häuser im Pompeji 3. Munich 1990.

Moeller, "Maius"   W. Moeller. "Gnaeus Alleius Nigidius Maius, Princeps Coloniae." *Latomus* 32 (1973) 515–20.

Mouritsen, *Elections*   H. Mouritsen. *Elections, Magistrates and Municipal Élite: Studies in Pompeian Epigraphy.* Analecta Romana Instituti Danici, supp. 15. Rome 1988.

Mouritsen and Gradel   H. Mouritsen and I. Gradel. "Nero in Pompeian Politics: *Edicta Munerum* and Imperial Flaminates in Late Pompeii." *Zeitschrift für Papyrologie und Epigraphik* 87 (1991) 145–55.

Rawson, "Properties"   E. Rawson. "Ciceronian Aristocracy and Its Properties." In *Studies in Roman Property,* ed. M.I. Finley, 85–102. Cambridge 1976.

Richardson, *Architectural*   L. Richardson, jr. *Pompeii: An Architectural History.* Baltimore and London 1988.

Ruesch   A. Ruesch. *Guida del Museo Nazionale di Napoli.* 2 vols. Naples 1911.

Sabbatini Tumolesi   P. Sabbatini Tumolesi. *Gladiatorum paria: Annunci di spettacoli gladiatorii a Pompei.* Tituli: Pubblicazioni dell' Instituto di Epigrafia ed Antichità Greche e Romane dell' Università di Roma 1. Rome 1980.

Schefold   K. Schefold. *Die Wände Pompejis: Topographisches Verzeichnis der Bildmotive.* Deutsches Archäologisches Institut. Berlin 1957.

Väänänen   V. Väänänen. *Le latin vulgaire des inscriptions pompéiennes.* 2d ed. Abhandlungen der Deutschen Akademie der Wissenschaften zu Berlin, Klasse für Sprachen, Literatur und Kunst, Jahrgang 1958, no. 3. Berlin 1959.

Van Buren, "Maius"   A.W. Van Buren. "Cnaeus Alleius Nigidius Maius of Pompeii." *American Journal of Philology* 68 (1947) 382–93.

Van Buren, "Poppaea"   A.W. Van Buren, "Pompeii, Nero, Poppaea." In *Studies Presented to David Moore Robinson,* ed. G.E. Mylonas and D. Raymond, 2 vols., 2:970–74. St. Louis 1952.

Varone, *Erotica*   A. Varone. *Erotica Pompeiana.* Rome 1994.

Varone, "Tituli"   A. Varone. "Nuovi *tituli picti* pompeiani." *Rivista di Studi Pompeiani* 1 (1987) 91–106.

Vetter   E. Vetter. *Handbuch der italischen Dialekte.* Vol. 1. Heidelberg 1953.

Zanker, *Images*   P. Zanker. *The Power of Images in the Age of Augustus.*
  Jerome Lectures, 16. Ann Arbor 1988.
Zanker, *Pompeji*   P. Zanker. *Pompeji: Stadtbilder als Speigel von Gesellschaft
  und Herrschaftsform.* Mainz 1987.

Figures

Introduction

Idem Cicero alias facilitatem Caesaris in adlegendo senatu inrisit
palam. Nam, cum ab hospite suo P. Mallio rogaretur ut
decurionatum privigno eius expediret, adsistente frequentia dixit:
"Romae, si vis, habebis; Pompeis difficile est."[1]

[Likewise on another occasion Cicero openly mocked Caesar's
ease in placing men in the Senate. For when, with a crowd
standing round, he was asked by his friend Publius Mallius to
expedite his stepson's advance to decurion, he said, "At Rome if
you want it you shall have it; at Pompeii it's difficult."]

Writing centuries after the fact, Macrobius unintentionally preserved for
generations to come one of the few references to ancient Pompeii in the
larger Roman record, and since the rediscovery of the city with its thousands of electoral programmata, or campaign posters, in the eighteenth
century, his report of Cicero's jest has been taken as proof of the intensity of competition in Pompeian politics well into those imperial times
from which the posters survive. Yet even given the programmata, it has
hitherto proved possible to do little more than compose lists of men
known to have been politically active in a set span of years and then to
extrapolate from those lists overall trends in the city's political life. The
dynamics—the detailed interactions and interconnections—of Pompeian politics seemed to have escaped the record, to have been confined
to another, somewhat cryptic statement of Cicero, that after the arrival
of the Sullan colony, locals complained about walking, apparently cam-
paigning, and their voting rights.[2]

---

1. Mac. 2.3.11.
2. Cic. *Sul.* 61: *de ambulatione ac de suffragiis suis.* On the series of efforts
to understand *ambulatio,* see Mouritsen, *Elections* 202 n. 347. Setting the comment in its historical perspective, see Dyson, *Community* 74–76; R. Stewart,

No one, however, has undertaken to study in detail the families and factions of political life in ancient Pompeii. There are extant today over eleven thousand pieces of writing from this site, everything from shipping labels to scurrilous graffiti, from the well-known campaign posters to stone-cut inscriptions of the sorts commonly found elsewhere.[3] Even fragments of business records on wax tablets, the *apochae* of Caecilius Iucundus, have been found in the course of the excavations.[4] The lack of any substantial piece of continuous writing may have disappointed students of ancient literature, but the material at hand for the student of the political scene is abundant—and has remained largely neglected.[5]

This neglect has at least in part resulted because the key to understanding what has been recovered lies in a thorough knowledge of the topography of the site itself. Few scholars have had the opportunity to pass the years necessary in walking the ground and correlating with their walks the more than two hundred years' worth of excavation reports. Lacking the insights such experience offers, one cannot even ask the correct questions of this evidence but must turn to the sort of cataloguing that has characterized earlier work. Yet if we are ever to develop a detailed picture of political life outside Rome itself, it must be through analysis of this corpus, for in all the Roman world, it alone is sufficiently ample to allow meaningful exploration.

"Catiline and the Crisis of 63–60 B.C.: The Italian Perspective," *Latomus* 54 (1995) 62–78.

3. The count is that of Mouritsen (*Elections* 9) and does not take into account conflated graffiti and election notices mistakenly counted as single inscriptions in the various publications.

4. The tablets recovered at nearby Agro Murecine in 1959 record matters relating to Puteoli across the Bay, rather than Pompeii; on these, see F. Sbordone, "Preambolo per l'edizione critica delle tavolette cerate di Pompei," *RAAN*, n.s., 51 (1976) 145–68. For analysis of the legal processes attested in the tablets, see the studies of Lucio Bove, *Documenti processuali dalle Tabulae Pompeianae di Murecine* (Naples 1979) and *Documenti di operazioni finanziarie dall' archivio dei Sulpicii* (Naples 1984).

5. Pace A. Mau (*Pompeii* 491): "Taken as a whole, the graffiti are less fertile for our knowledge of Pompeian life than might have been expected." See H. Tanzer, *The Common People of Pompeii,* Johns Hopkins University Studies in Archaeology 29 (Baltimore 1939) 6, on Mau's nonegalitarian biases.

The Writing and Its Study

Over the course of the years, nearly all of the writing from Pompeii has faded and crumbled off the walls or been carted to museum storerooms, as attempts at in situ preservation have focused instead on paintings that cannot be transcribed or properly understood apart from their physical surrounds. In consequence, the student must turn to the publications, especially to the *Corpus Inscriptionum Latinarum (CIL)*, the complex organization of which raises problems of its own. In the *CIL*, the writing is catalogued according to type: parietal inscriptions— everything written rather than carved—appear in *CIL* IV and its three supplements; inscriptions on stone, in *CIL* X. Unfortunately, neither work is current. The final fascicle of the third supplement to *CIL* IV, which records inscriptions found only through 1956, appeared in 1970 and without an index; the last addition to *CIL* X, in 1899.[6] Parietal inscriptions found after 1956 and stone-cut inscriptions found after 1899, therefore, must be traced in archaeological and learned journals. All must then be checked against more recent work, annually compiled in the journal *L'Année épigraphique*.

The parietal material is further subdivided by type. There are professionally painted inscriptions *(pictae)*, in turn subdivided into announcements of games *(edicta munerum)* and newer *(recentiora)*, older *(antiquiora)*, and very old *(antiquissima)* political posters *(programmata)*. Graffiti scratched with a point *(graphio exaratae)* form a separate category, as do alphabets and masons' marks. Writing found on amphorae and other containers is subdivided into that written with brush, charcoal, or pen (likely to prove to be labels); that scratched with a point (likely to prove casual); and that written in Greek. Unfortunately there

---

6. The initial issue of *CIL* IV was compiled from over 130 earlier sources by Carl Zangemeister and contains many variant and often conflated readings. The first supplement to this collection, produced by Zangemeister in 1871, was the edition of the *apochae* of Caecilius Iucundus. The second supplement was again of written inscriptions in general and was prepared by August Mau in 1909; it is the most magisterial and reliable of the volumes. The third supplement, started by Matteo Della Corte, began appearing in fascicles in 1952; following Della Corte's death, it was completed by Fulcher Weber in 1970. *CIL* X was updated only by M. Ihm, in "Addimenta ad corporis vol. IX et X," *EphEp* 8 (1899) 1–221; pages 86–90 pertain to Pompeii.

is some confusion of these types; professional letterers, for example, occasionally painted comments that, because they were painted, were
classified as *pictae* rather than as the graffiti that they in fact are. Business records found on wax tablets are separately treated, and of course
there are suspect and false inscriptions. Some entries have been erroneously transcribed, and others contain two or more conflated readings; to distinguish conflations and to specify subdivisions of lengthy
inscriptions, lowercase italicized letters are added to the *CIL* entry numbers.

Within their divisions, painted inscriptions, graffiti, alphabets, and
stone-cut inscriptions are catalogued by their locations at the site. Amphorae were collected in *magazzini* before publication, so that often—
as with other movable finds at this site—an exact provenience is unknown, although as archaeological methods improved, so did record
keeping.

The initial issue of *CIL* IV was keyed to the plan of Pompeii published
with that volume. Later volumes were keyed to the master plan of the
site first drawn under the supervision of Giuseppe Fiorelli, in which the
system of numbering by *regio, insula,* and *ianua* was developed, so that
a property and its entrances—for example, the Casa del Chirugo at
VI.1.9,10,23—could be precisely located. Between editions, however, the
regio or *insula* numbers of fourteen *insulae* were changed; thirteen of
these were correlated by Hans Eschebach in the introductory matter to
his, the most recent, plan of the site,[7] but the change of the final supplement's *insula* I.11 to his I.19 escaped even his list. Doorways, too, frequently had their numbers changed or regularized over the course of
time. Since the city is still under excavation, blocks that have not been
entirely excavated are connoted by numbers in parentheses—for example, IX.(14)—and doorway numbers on those blocks that will be
changed as excavation proceeds are indicated by letters rather than
numbers. Every entry in Zangemeister's volume and large numbers
of those in subsequent supplements therefore must be carefully correlated with the plan of Eschebach, which is here reproduced (fig. 1), although not in its detailed version. Long considered standard and now
updated by Jürgen Müller-Trollius, this plan has recently been reissued
in Liselotte Eschebach's impressive bibliographic survey of the site,

---

7. Eschebach 115.

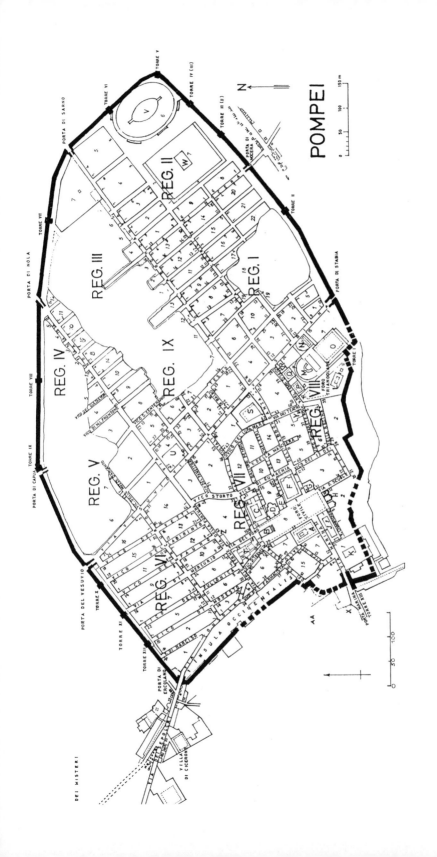

POMPEI

Gebäudeverzeichnis und Stadtplan der antiken Stadt Pompeji,[8] and
from it come the plans of the various houses I will be discussing.

Assembling the writing found on one wall or in one room requires
diligence and skill but is only preliminary to analysis. Thanks to his long
years and intimate knowledge of the site, Matteo Della Corte was able
to examine the evidence house-by-house in his pioneering identifications of individual properties and inhabitants of the city, *Case ed abitanti di Pompei.* While one may at times disagree with his conclusions
and admittedly must use his work with caution, his opinions must always be consulted. When I here cite his work positively, the reader can
rest assured that I have reviewed the evidence and am in agreement
with Della Corte's identifications; disagreements are regularly noted
and explained.

The degree of abbreviation in the political posters is surprising; the
Latinity of the graffiti, provincial and sometimes uneducated. Herein
abbreviations are regularly expanded but, even so, will become readily
apparent to the attentive reader; Latin inscriptions of all sorts are heavily formulaic. The peculiarities of the Latin generated at Pompeii and
preserved on its walls have been studied by Veikki Väänänen; anyone
working with these documents will frequently consult his *Le latin vulgaire des inscriptions pompéiennes.* Here the reader will most often
confront the interchangeability of *c* and *g,* as in the family name *Cellius*
for *Gellius,* and of *q* and *c,* as in *pequnia* for *pecunia.* Pompeians regularly contracted *-ii* in both the genitive singular and nominative plural
of second declension family names ending in *-ius;* in inscriptions this is
let stand without comment, but in the text the double *i* is standard. The
contracted form of the perfect tense appears in a number of inscriptions,
as in *curarunt* for *curaverunt,* herein again without comment.

Although they are generally anonymous and only occasionally of interest here, literary quotations and references form a fascinating subdi-
vision of the graffiti. Marcello Gigante has recently reexamined this material, and readers wearied by the banality important to these studies
will find *Civiltà delle forme letterarie nell' antica Pompei* (Naples, 1979)
a welcome corrective. More useful for these studies is Patrizia Sabbatini
Tumolesi's important recent edition of the notices of games, *Gladiato-*

---

8. Further on the lineage of plans of the site, see Müller-Trollius in Eschebach and Müller-Trollius 1–4.

rum paria: Annunci di spettacoli gladiatorii a Pompei, from which come all such texts herein cited.

Foremost, this is a study of men, families, and connections. One begins such a study of Pompeii with Paavo Castrén's *Ordo Populusque Pompeianus: Polity and Society in Roman Pompeii* close at hand and turns to its catalogue of known Pompeians often. Slightly less valuable because it deals with a more restricted group of men is Jean Andreau's *Les affaires de Monsieur Jucundus.* In his recent studies, *The Economy and Society of Pompeii* (Amsterdam 1988), Willem Jongman has again demonstrated the importance of family and connections in ancient Pompeii.

The student of the electoral programmata must now consult the careful catalogue of Henrik Mouritsen in his *Elections, Magistrates and Municipal Élite: Studies in Pompeian Epigraphy.* Mouritsen's opinion of the work of Della Corte, however, is overly dark, and as we shall see, his hesitancy to date more than a few of the *programmata recentiora* to times earlier than the earthquake is mistaken.[9]

Methods of Approach

At first glance the methodology of the studies in the following chapters is straightforward and traditional: strands of interconnecting evidence are gathered to weave a tapestry, albeit worn and ragged, that preserves a picture of an era or an aspect of political life. Yet underlying all of the chapters is the principle that the context of this evidence is as revelatory as its content. Writing does not appear on walls or objects at random, and the proper analysis of any piece of writing should include considerations of why it was produced where it was produced by its writer.

Stone-cut inscriptions of the sorts commonly found elsewhere label buildings and present what were intended to be official or carefully edited records and careers. They are our most valuable and reliable sources of information, limited in the matter they convey, yet not infrequently attesting the enduring human emotions. Chiseled into stone, they were meant to stand the test of time unquestioned.

Programmata, Pompeii's famous political posters, reveal the enthu-

---

9. On the work of Della Corte, see Mouritsen, *Elections* 13–27. Discussion of the dating of the programmata (contra Sabbatini Tumolesi 113–16) is at 32–37, with conclusions restated at 107–8.

siasms and often the identities of the inhabitants of the property on which they were recovered. Some, it is true, were painted ostensibly to sway an inhabitant, while others appear to have been posted merely because there was space available. All, however, were posted to be seen and, thanks to their recurring format, are easily read. In its simplest form, this format begins with the candidate's name—sometimes simply his initials—in the accusative case along with the office for which he was standing. Later, the verb *rogat* or the phrase *oro (ut) vos faciatis* or *oro ut faciatis,* "I ask that you elect," most often abbreviated as *o v f,* appears, so that the candidate's name is revealed as the direct object of the phrase. Both individual and group recommenders, *rogatores,* sometimes added their names, and occasionally recommendations, such as *iuvenem probum,* "upright young man," were appended, but all such additions hang on the simple, basic formula, making straightforward translation easy.

Labels on amphorae and other containers help with the identification of a property's inhabitants and their trade connections; although rarely providing a full name, they often confirm more explicit evidence. Moreover, study of the quality of the products the containers held can add a valuable factor to the analysis of the lifestyle of those who purchased and consumed the contents.

Graffiti were written by people with time, interest, and opportunity—all factors that can offer insight into a person, pursuit, or property. Graffiti also tend to cluster, because one writer produced more than one graffito, because one graffito elicited another—or a modification—from a second writer, or because the location itself inspired the writers. Graffiti therefore must be studied in light of the ambience in which they were found and with reference to any others found with them. Clusters of similar graffiti from distant properties, moreover, can illuminate each other, providing deeper understanding than that which results from analysis of a single wall.

Heretofore, study of this material has tended to center on a single property or to consider writing on a specific topic gathered from the entire site. The emphasis has been on content, the context being either that of a carefully circumscribed property or that of the entire city. Each of the following chapters attempts to consider context as well as content, adding an additional factor to the analysis. It thus is often possible to focus on social units larger and more diverse than the individual household yet smaller and more restricted than the whole population.

The Political Structure

Throughout these studies, the focus is on the political elite, who strove for municipal offices, as established with the constitution of the Roman colony, *colonia Cornelia Veneria Pompeianorum,* following the Social War in about 80 B.C.[10] A man began his career by standing for *duovir,* or *aedilis, viis aedibus sacris publicisque procurandis.* This was the lower level annual magistracy, commonly termed simply *aedile,* of two men who primarily saw to the physical upkeep of the city. The successful aedile next stood for *duovir iure dicundo,* commonly termed simply *duovir.* This was the higher annual magistracy, again of two men, that handled local law cases and presided at the meetings of the local senate, the *ordo decurionum.* The successful duovir could stand for *duovir iure dicundo quinquennalis,* commonly termed simply *quinquennial.* This was the highest elected office and was filled by two men every fifth year in lieu of the simple duovirate.[11] Its holders revised the *ordo* by naming new members, decurions, to replace those who had died or been eliminated since the last reconstitution, and they let major contracts in addition to their regular duties as duovirs. Normally election as aedile earned a man membership in the *ordo,* but exceptional men—talented or rich—could be named directly by the quinquennials in the process of *adlectio.*

Naturally, special circumstances occasionally arose. There was, for example, provision for appointing a *praefectus iure dicundo* when, as an act of respect, an emperor or member of his family had been elected duovir and it was necessary to appoint a local representative, a prefect, to act in his stead.[12] Such an appointment obviously argues great distinction for the Pompeian chosen to represent the ruling dynasty. In addition, when for some reason regular duovirs could not be elected, extraordinary prefects, *praefecti iure dicundo ex decreto decurionum*

---

10. On the establishment of the colony and on possible early variations in its government, see Castrén 49–55; on preceding forms of government, C. Gatti, "Sull' ordinamento istituzionale di Pompei dopo la conquista romana," *AttiC-ItRom* 6 (1974–75) 165–78. On the precise name of the colony and on possible elements of its founding constitution, see P. Ciprotti, "Il nome e la legge di Pompei colonia romana," *CronPomp* 2 (1976) 21–28.

11. Quinquennial years at Pompeii were calculated by Mau (*CIL* X, p. 92); they fell on the fives and tens, e.g., A.D. 65 and 70.

12. The procedure is attested in the *lex municipalis Salpensana* (24–25).

lege Petronia, could be appointed by the local *ordo* in accordance with
the *lex Petronia.* At Pompeii only the eldest C. Cuspius Pansa is known
to have held this office, apparently following the earthquake of A.D. 62.[13]

Regular elections were held in March, and the newly elected admin-
istrators took office on 1 July, their incumbencies stretching through
parts of two calendar years.[14] This can naturally lead to some confusion
for the modern student, and herein dates are as specific as possible; a
man's incumbency is referred to as, for example, A.D. 78–79, but particular instances in his career are given the most specific dates known. For
easy consultation, all the dated magistracies of Pompeii's history as well
as references to the documents that date them are presented in tabular
format in the appendix.

Elsewhere in the Roman world, *augustales,* wealthy freedmen organized into an *ordo* of their own, grew in importance in the early imperial years. At Pompeii, unfortunately, only a dozen are known,[15] and
of them only C. Calventius Quietus and C. Munatius Faustus seem to
have developed into persons of standing; each was awarded the right
of a *bisellium,* the double-sized, cushioned seat of a member of the *ordo
decurionum,* by decree of the decurions.[16] To judge from the richness of

---

13. On the *lex Petronia,* see G. Rotondi, *Leges Publicae Populi Romani* (Mi-
lano 1912; reprint, Hildesheim 1962) 439; on Cuspius Pansa, see *CIL* X.858; Castrén 112; and below, chap. 5.

14. The times of elections and taking office were calculated by Mommsen at
CIL X, pp. 90–91.

15. As Łoś ("Remarques" 289 n. 152) observes, this may well be due simply
to our lack of funerary inscriptions for those *augustales* who were still alive
when Pompeii was destroyed. Indeed, only two of the inscriptions naming
augustales (D'Ambrosio and De Caro 23OS and *CIL* X.1034) date earlier than
A.D. 50.

16. *CIL* X.1026: *C(aio) Calventio Quieto / augustali / huic ob munifi-
cent(iam) decurionum / decreto et populi conse(n)su biselli(i) / honor datus est.*
CIL X.1030: *Naevoleia L(uci) lib(erta) / Tyche sibi et / C(aio) Munatio Fausto
aug(ustali) / et pagano / cui decuriones consensu populi / bisellium ob merita
eius / decreverunt / hoc monumentum Naevoleia Tyche / libertis suis / liber-
tabusq(ue) et C(ai) Munati / Fausti viva fecit.* The "tombs" of Calventius and
Munatius outside the Porta di Ercolano on the Via dei Sepolchri from which
these inscriptions come are cenotaphs; Munatius was actually buried outside
the Porta di Nocera (D'Ambrosio and De Caro 9ES), while the burial spot of
Calventius remains unrecovered. On the tomb of Calventius (Kockel S20), see
Kockel 90–97; on that of Munatius (S22), Kockel 100–109.

his house, the well-known Casa dei Vettii, the *augustalis* A. Vettius Conviva may have been of similar powerful standing when Pompeii was overwhelmed.[17]

Of priesthoods of political significance, there were flamens of the various emperors (as well as the heir apparent Nero),[18] whose cults were successively housed in the building today known as the Temple of Vespasian, on the east side of the forum.[19] These priests appear to have been appointed for life, since with the exception of Holconius Celer, who replaced his deceased father, Holconius Rufus, as flamen of Augustus, we know of only two other men who served in these offices—one for Nero, the other for Vespasian—and all these flamens became major figures of their days.[20] To Castrén, an imperial flaminate marked the zenith of a

---

17. On the Vettii, see Castrén 240; on the owners of the house, Della Corte 89–90. On the Casa dei Vettii, see now Richardson, *Architectural* 324–29.

18. Under Augustus the title *sacerdos* seems to have been interchangeable with *flamen,* but thereafter the latter term became standard. The most recent survey of the evidence for the various religious offices at Pompeii from the time of the colony to the eruption is that of Castrén (68–78). *CIL* X.961*a* has been restored to suggest that there may have been a cult of Augustus' wife Livia at Pompeii: *Vibiae C(ai) f(iliae) S[abinae] / [sacer]doti Iu[liae Augustae].* However, it is too highly restored to be secure, and the stone itself may not actually have come from Pompeii. Zangemeister notes at the *CIL* entry: "Pompeis tribuit Fiorelli coniectura. Est Napoli in museo."

19. On the history and rededications of this temple, originally erected by the priestess Mamia to the *genius Augusti* (*CIL* X.816), see Richardson, *Architectural* 191–94. Recently I. Gradel ("Mamia's Dedication: Emperor and Genius, the Imperial Cult in Italy and the Genius Coloniae in Pompeii," *AnalRom* 20 [1992] 43–58) has challenged the traditional restored reading of Mamia's dedicatory inscription, preferring *genius coloniae* to *genius Augusti,* and arguing for the removal of the cult of the *genius coloniae* to the nearby Santuario dei Lari Pubblici. But see the convincing objections of Dobbins ("Chronology" 663), who notes especially the "potent Augustan imagery" of the altar. Arguing from the design of the building but without inscriptional evidence, Zanker (*Pompeji* 687–88) has suggested that the Santuario dei Lari Pubblici, rather than the Temple of Vespasian, was the seat of imperial cult at Pompeii. For a detailed discussion of the history of these and other buildings along the east side of the forum, see Dobbins, "Chronology."

20. Following R. Étienne, *Le culte impérial dans la péninsule ibérique d' Auguste a Dioclétien, BEFR,* 191 (Paris 1958) 237, however, Mouritsen and Gradel (149) argue that these were annual offices. Yet it is impossible to believe that these flaminates, broadly announced by those who clearly held them, were of such insignificance to others that they went entirely unmentioned in the

man's career;[21] it also seems to have been able to be awarded early to
men of great promise. The flamens appear to have been assisted by the
ministri Augusti, who were recruited from both slaves and freedmen.
Separate were the *ministri Fortunae Augustae,* again both slaves and
freedmen, but attached to the Temple of Fortuna Augusta at the corner
of the Via del Foro / Via di Mercurio and the Via della Fortuna.

For a woman, great distinction came as a priestess of the local cults
of Venus and Ceres, *sacerdos publica Veneris* or *sacerdos publica
Cereris,* later combined as *sacerdos publica Veneris et Cereris.* Little
more than the title is known, but only female members of the city's most
powerful families gained the priesthood.

Some families were able to play a role in local politics over a period
of several generations. They were, however, few, and the more typical
pattern is that of a family that rose to the *ordo* for a generation or perhaps two before sinking out of sight. Yet, to a degree, this rapid rise and
fall of families may represent inherent limitations of the documents
themselves. For the period of the early Julio-Claudian empire, the evidence is the funerary and honorific inscriptions that were not salvaged
after the eruption of A.D. 79. For the middle years of the dynasty, the
apochae of Caecilius Iucundus are the primary source, while for the late
Neronian and early Vespasianic years, the electoral programmata and
graffiti are central. Each of these is a distinct variety of evidence, limited
in how it can be mined for information; and the seam of evidence gives
out far more often than it leads to further deposits. Still, recent study has
shown that at Rome senatorial families of this era disappeared at a rate
of 75 percent per generation, a rate that tends to confirm the rapid
turnover at Pompeii.[22]

---

honorary and funerary inscriptions of the men who must have held them if they
were annual offices, and some of these inscriptions (especially from the years of
Augustus and Nero) must be among those recovered. On the special title *perpetuus* in the case of D. Lucretius Satrius Valens, see chap. 4, n. 99.

21. Castrén 68–69. Further on the extraordinary status of priests in Roman
society in the Augustan era, see Zanker, *Images* 120: "Some felt driven to sui-
cide when they were removed from one of these coveted priesthoods. The frequent public appearances of the priests and the special privileges attached to
their office, such as places of honor in the theater, were constant reminders to
the general public of their status in society."

22. P. Garnsey and R. Saller, *The Roman Empire: Economy, Society, and Cul-
ture* (Berkeley and Los Angeles 1987) 143.

The Historical Record

In the history of the early empire, as in that of other eras, Pompeii is rarely mentioned in the historical record, centered as it is on Rome. Yet Tacitus recorded that in A.D. 59 there was a riot in the amphitheater that caused such grief to the neighboring Nucerians that they protested all the way to Rome.[23] The matter was passed back and forth between Nero and the Senate, and finally the Senate forbade gladiatorial games at Pompeii for ten years.[24] Then, on 5 February A.D. 62, a severe earthquake struck the region, badly damaging the city.[25] In fact, repairs of damage incurred then (and, quite possibly, in subsequent, lesser seismic activity)[26] were still being carried out when Vesuvius erupted on 24 and 25 August A.D. 79.[27] Both the riot and the earthquake are frequently referred to in the following pages; significant enough to attract attention in Rome, both had serious repercussions in Pompeii's social and political life.

Presentation

In essence, the following chapters are searches for patterns in the evidence. Each of the chapters 1–6 seeks to reveal a separate pattern; the

---

23. Tac. *Ann.* 14.17.

24. Actual causes of the riot are debated. M. Della Corte (*Iuventus* [Arpino 1924] 36–41) identified the *iuvenes Venerii Pompeiani,* the local *collegium iuventum,* as the culprits. L. Richardson, jr. (*The Casa dei Dioscuri and Its Painters, MAAR* 23 [Rome 1955] 88–93) blamed the *Campani* (named at *CIL* IV.1293), an illegal organization of the youth of descendants of the older, Samnite inhabitants of the city, in contrast to the legal, Roman *collegium iuventum.* W.O. Moeller ("The Riot of A.D. 59 at Pompeii," *Historia* 19 [1970] 94) believed that the riot resulted from a meeting of the *collegia iuvenum* of Pompeii and Nuceria and that only public meetings of those groups were prohibited. In an earlier work (Franklin, "Pantomimists") I have faulted gladiator fan clubs similar to the pantomimists' fan clubs I there identified (106–7).

25. Sen. *Nat.* 6.1.1–2. On the correct calculation of the date of the earthquake, see G.O. Onorato, "La data del terremoto di Pompei 5 febbraio 62 d.C.," *RendLinc,* 8th ser., 4 (1949) 644–61.

26. The case for subsequent activity is strongly argued by P. Allison, in "The Distribution of Pompeian House Contents and Its Significance" (Ph.D. Diss., University of Sydney, 1992) 7–12.

27. On the strength and effects of the earthquake, see Richardson, *Architectural* 18–22.

final chapter, to draw them all together in a coherent form. Yet patterns can only be based on the solid evidence of the writing itself, and so that writing is featured prominently in the text. To focus discussion, summaries of the important features and statements of the significance of each entry immediately precede or follow, while for the Latinless reader interested in further detail, literal translations are included. Except where noted, the translations are my own. Words enclosed within parentheses are readily supplied from the context, lacunae are marked with brackets as in the inscriptions themselves, and indecipherable letters are italicized within brackets.

In editing inscriptions, I have attempted diligently to follow the "Leiden system" as elaborated by S. Dow,[28] the basics of which are straightforward: abbreviations are expanded within parentheses, ( ); restorations are enclosed in brackets, [ ]; excess letters are marked with braces, { }; and editorial additions are enclosed in pointed brackets, ⟨ ⟩. Lacunae of whatever length are indicated by three dashes enclosed in square brackets, [---], and ligatures are indicated by curving lines above the letters conjoined in the original. Words that were erased—here to ease the memory of Caligula or to observe the *damnatio memoriae* of Nero—are enclosed in double brackets, [[ ]]. To emphasize the name of the candidate advertized, programmata regularly employed different sizes of letters in the same inscription, so that there is often even confusion over appropriate line divisions, and in the case of graffiti especially, personal judgment of appropriate editing is regularly necessary. The attentive Latinist will even notice that Pompeii's letterers and stonecarvers varied between writing and abbreviating duovir as one or two words. However, no inscription is here published for the first time, and the more curious reader is encouraged to explore the sources further. I here focus on the matter the inscriptions present rather than the presentation itself.

Proper nomenclature, a major feature of the inscriptions, included praenomen, nomen, paternity, tribe, and cognomen,[29] although the tribe was rarely included except in funerary inscriptions. Native-born

28. S. Dow, *Conventions in Editing, GRBSA* 2 (Durham, N.C. 1969).

29. As Mouritsen (*Elections* 75–76) observes, regular use of cognomina by most Pompeians seems to have begun early in the Augustan era. We in fact know of no cognomina for three important Augustans, L. Ceius, A. Veius, and M. Tullius. On the development of cognomina at Pompeii in general, see P. Castrén, "Le aristocrazie municipali ed i liberti dalla guerra sociale all' epoca flavia: Contributi onomastici," *OpInstRomFin* 1 (1981) 15–24.

Pompeians were all members of the *tribus Menenia*. Although a son occasionally bore exactly the same name as his father, at Pompeii in these years a man of standing traditionally passed on his praenomen and nomen to his eldest son, who was distinguished from his father by his cognomen.[30] So, for example, Q. Postumius Modestus fathered Q. Postumius Proculus. Cognomina sometimes skipped generations as fathers named sons after their grandfathers. So L. Albucius Celsus was father of L. Albucius Iustus and grandfather of a second L. Albucius Celsus. Occasionally, if the mother came from a distinguished family, her son's cognomen preserved her family name, as in the case of M. Holconius Gellius, son of an M. Holconius and Gellia or Cellia, daughter of the prominent Augustan L. Cellius; a similar case is that of L. Obellius Lucretianus. One family even passed the same name on for three generations, apparent testimony to the distinction of its original holder, C. Cuspius Pansa.

Adoption was generally indicated by the adjectival form of the original family name inserted between nomen and cognomen, as in M. Lucretius Decidianus Rufus, who was born Decidius Rufus and adopted by an M. Lucretius. Occasionally both nomina were preferred, as in D. Lucretius Satrius Valens; this seems to indicate that the son was adopted at an adult age when his own personality, in this case as a Satrius, had already been publicly established.[31]

To help the reader track these ponderously named Pompeians and their generations, stemmata tracing direct ancestors and descendants of each era's notables are appended to each chapter, insofar as they can be devised. Men, however, do not conveniently pass away in pace with their emperors, and so several reappear in the discussion of multiple chapters, although they are included in the stemmata only of the first

---

30. In fact, J.P.V.D. Balsdon (*Romans and Aliens* [Chapel Hill 1979] 147) observes, "It seems likely that, if the first son died, his next eldest brother then assumed his (and the father's) *praenomen*." In contrast, freedmen tended to pass along the nomina and cognomina of their former owners, changing only the praenomina, although there were of course variations; on naming patterns at Pompeii, see Andreau, *Jucundus* 161–62.

31. On the adoption of D. Lucretius Satrius Valens, see Franklin, "Valens." Cf. also, e.g., M. Stlaborius Veius Fronto, who identified himself as both Stlaborius and Veius after his adoption (see chap. 2), and Q. Coelius Caltilius Iustus (see chap. 3). On the difficulties imposed on the modern scholar because of adoptive name changes, see Andreau, *Jucundus* 135–37.

chapter in which they appear. In every case, the highest honor, office, or candidacy the man is attested to have held is noted; a name alone indicates that the man can be demonstrated to have been alive during the years covered in that chapter.

Throughout the Roman world, official inscriptions were eponymously dated by the inclusion of the current consuls in Rome. Dates for inscriptions that may seem miraculously to appear here are owed to this system. As the consulship became increasingly honorific, it was held by additional men, *consules suffecti*, who regularly took office on 1 July in the period under study here[32] (whereas normal taking of office in Rome was 1 January), and it is often therefore possible to date an inscription more narrowly to a period of months rather than to an entire year.

Buildings for which the ancient name is known are referred to in English translation or in Latin. Names in Italian represent modern titulature in common use but unattested in the ancient evidence.

I begin with the beginning of the imperial age, the era of Augustus, and proceed through the final, Flavian years of Pompeii.

---

32. On the development of this system, see the recent work of D.A. Phillips, "The Conspiracy of Egnatius Rufus and the Election of Suffect Consuls under Augustus," *Historia* 46 (1997) 103–12.

Chapter 1

Augustans

For ancient Pompeii—indeed, for all the Roman world—the Augustan Age must have been uniquely demanding. Rome had for generations proved an awkward bedfellow, but as Octavian metamorphosed into Augustus, entirely new rules and protocols had to be developed and then hedged. There was scant precedent for such delicate political maneuvering, and it was by no means evident that this new government would prove any more successful than its disastrously outdated predecessor. There had besides been the city's supporters of Antony.[1] Yet from the first, Pompeians seem to have discerned the future in Augustus; certainly by the time of his death, they had enthusiastically embraced the concept and cult of emperor.

In early days, Marcellus, the nephew and son-in-law of Augustus, had been named *patronus coloniae* to represent the city in Rome, and a statue was dedicated in his honor in the Foro Triangolare.[2]

1:

M(arco) Claudio C(aii) f(ilio) Marcello
patrono.[3]

[To Marcus Claudius Marcellus, son of Gaius, patron.]

But Marcellus died in 23 B.C., severing this most obvious tie to Rome and its leader.

With the metamorphosis of Augustus, however, came that of Rome's

---

1. Zanker, *Images* 45–46: "An engraved stone from a ring, found at Pompeii, shows that there were statues of him [Antony] of this type [modeled as Hercules] and that his followers gladly carried such an image of their hero on a ring and used it as a seal." The ring is illustrated in Zanker's fig. 35.
2. On the unlikely possibility that Marcellus served rather as *patronus iuventutis*, see D'Arms, "Pompeii and Rome" 54, following Della Corte 513*b*.
3. *CIL* X.832.

government, and among new provisions developed for Italy, Suetonius reports an equestrian military rank awarded to distinguished local men on the recommendation of the populace of their hometowns.[4] Although he fails in further specifics, it has become clear that this office was *tribunus militum a populo* and that it was awarded to men thoroughly committed to implementing the Augustan regime.[5] Six men—M. Holconius Rufus, L. Cellius, A. Clodius Flaccus, A. Veius, M. Tullius, and M. Lucretius Decidianus Rufus—are known to have held this title at Pompeii, forming the core of the Augustan faction in local politics.

Unfortunately, we can identify the houses of none of these men, as might well be expected since they lived so many years before the city's end. We must therefore in this chapter turn solely to the inscriptional record, although as we shall see, these Augustans proved remarkably active and resourceful, leaving the city adorned and embellished in honor of their new leader in Rome. And despite the lack of such personal details as can often be coaxed from houses and graffiti, the inscriptions both present us with personable characters and preserve surprising familial details.

M. Holconius Rufus

While the gens Holconia appears to have been long established at Pompeii—even to have bred the best Campanian vine, *Horconia,* or *Holconia, vitis*[6]—to our knowledge Holconii entered the political fray only in Augustan times, in the person of the first citizen of the day, M. Holconius Rufus.[7] His accomplishments were recorded in an inscription iden-

---

4. Suet. *Aug.* 46: *Ac necubi aut honestorum deficeret copia aut multitudinis suboles, equestrem militiam petentis etiam ex commendatione publica cuiusque oppidi ordinabat, at iis, qui e plebe regiones sibi revisenti filios filiasve approbarent, singula nummorum milia pro singulis dividebat.*

5. See C. Nicolet, "Tribuni Militum a Populo," *Mel Rom* 79 (1967) 29–76. On the office at Pompeii, see Castrén 98–99 and now especially D'Arms, "Pompeii and Rome" 56–58.

6. Plin. *Nat.* 14.2.35; Col. 3.2.27.

7. On the Holconii, see Castrén 176, to which now add Varone, "Tituli" 1 (pp. 91–92), a programma supporting the Flavian Holconius Priscus for aedile; on M. Holconius Rufus, see D'Arms, "Pompeii and Rome"; Castrén 97.

tifying his statue in the Ianus Holconiorum, the tetrapylon honoring the family at the corner of the Via dell' Abbondanza and the Via Stabiana.[8]

2:

M(arco) Holconio M(arci) f(ilio) Rufo
trib(uno) mil(itum) a popul(o) II vir(o) i(ure) d(icundo) V
quinq(uennali) iter(um)
Augusti Caesaris sacerd(oti)
patrono coloniae.[9]

[To Marcus Holconius Rufus, son of Marcus, military tribune by (choice of) the people, five times duovir *iure dicundo,* twice as quinquennial, priest of Caesar Augustus, patron of the colony.]

According to a second, dated inscription recording the naming of *ministri Augusti,* Holconius was duovir for the fourth time in 2–1 B.C.[10] That inscription dates his career to Augustan days, but the title *tribunus militum a populo* alone attests his Augustan floruit.

As the presumed replacement of Marcellus as patron of the colony, he represented Pompeii's interests in Rome, and given such status and access, he doubtless served as unofficial leader of the Augustans at Pompeii. He was involved in building at the Temple of Apollo,[11] and recent study has shown that he remodeled the Teatro Grande at Pompeii to recall the Theater of Marcellus in Rome and to commemorate the Senate's bestowal of the title *pater patriae* on Augustus.[12] It is therefore no surprise that Holconius had also been named priest of the cult of Augus-

---

8. On the statue (*MusNazNap* 6233), see P. Zanker, "Das Bildnis des M. Holconius Rufus," *AA* (1981) 349–61.

9. *Cil* X.830.

10. *Cil* X.890.

11. *Cil* X.787: *M(arcus) Holconius Rufus d(uo) v(ir) i(ure) d(icundo) tert(ium) / C(aius) Egnatius Postumus d(uo) v(ir) i(ure) d(icundo) iter(um) / ex d(ecreto) d(ecurionum) ius luminum / opstruendorum HS ↀ ↀ ↀ / redemerunt parietemque / privatam Col(oniae) Ven(eriae) Cor(neliae) / usque ad tegulas / faciundum coerarunt.*

12. D'Arms, "Pompeii and Rome" 54–58. On the diffusion of theatres throughout the Roman world during the Augustan years, see G. Bejor, "L'edificio teatrale nell' urbanizzazione augustea," *Athenaeum,* n.s., 57 (1979) 126–38. On the interrelationships of theaters and imperial cult, see P. Gros,

tus; an Augustan through and through, his reading of the political lay of the land had proved perspicacious, and his loyalties were beyond question.[13]

M. Holconius Celer

Holconius Rufus, however, must have died before Augustus himself, for he was consistently termed *Augusti Caesaris sacerdos* or *flamen*. In contrast, a second Holconius, M. Holconius Celer, was termed both *Augusti sacerdos* and *divi Augusti sacerdos*.

3:

M(arco) Holconio Celeri
d(uo) v(iro) i(ure) d(icundo) quinq(uennali) designato
Augusti sacerdoti.[14]

[To Marcus Holconius Celer, duovir *iure dicundo,* quinquennial duovir designate, priest of Augustus.]

4:

M(arco) Holconio M(arci) f(ilio) Celeri
sacerdoti divi Augusti.[15]

[To Marcus Holconius Celer, son of Marcus, priest of the divine Augustus.]

Apparently the son of Holconius Rufus,[16] Celer was also associated with him in the remodeling of the Teatro Grande, especially of the

---

"Théâtre et culte impérial en Gaule narbonnaise et dans la pénisule ibérique," in *Stadtbild und Ideologie: Die Monumentalisierung hispanischer Städte zwischen Republik und Kaiserzeit,* ed. W. Trillmich and P. Zanker, *AbhMünch,* n.s., 103 (1990) 381–90.

13. The exact title of this priesthood is uncertain. *CIL* X.830 and 837 read *sacerd(os),* but 838 and 947 read *flamen.*

14. *CIL* X.840.

15. *CIL* X.945.

16. Contra Franklin, "Augustans," where, following Castrén 176, Celer was identified as the brother of Rufus.

vaulted corridor *(cryptam)* under the upper-level seats and of the platforms *(tribunalia)* above the entrances to the orchestra.

5:

> M(arcus) M(arcus) Holconii Rufus et Celer cryptam tribunalia
> thea[trum] s(ua) p(ecunia).[17]

[Marcus Holconius Rufus and Marcus Holconius Celer (built) the vaulted passageway, platforms, and theater with their own money.]

Presumably the reference to Holconius Celer as quinquennial designate dates the first of these inscriptions to March–June A.D. 15, when he had been elected quinquennial duovir but was yet to assume office. Augustus, however, had been officially divinized on 17 September A.D. 14, so that by March A.D. 15 Holconius should already have been *sacerdos divi Augusti,* as one additional stone also attests him later to have been.

6:

> [M(arco) Holconio] Celer[i]
> sacerdoti div[i Augusti]
> IIvir(o) i(ure) d(icundo) quinq[uennali].[18]

[To Marcus Holconius Celer, priest of the divine Augustus, quinquennial duovir *iure dicundo.*]

Probably the discrepancy is owed to lassitude and habit on the local level, although it has been suggested that Celer was somehow specially appointed quinquennial designate in conjunction with the general census of A.D. 14 before the death and divinization of Augustus, rather than elected according to procedure later.[19] At any rate, Celer clearly served

---

17. *CIL* X.833. *CIL* X.834 is a near duplicate: *M(arcus et) M(arcus) Holco[nii] Rufus et Celer [cryp]tam tribunalia theatrum s(ua) p(ecunia);* 835 can also be so restored: *[M(arcus) et M(arcus) Holcon]ii Rufus [et Celer] / [cryptam tri]bunal(ia) thea[trum] / coloni(ae).*

18. *CIL* X.946.

19. Castrén 104. Mommsen (*CIL* X.840), followed by Mouritsen (*Elections* 102), notes the discrepancy but fails to explain it. Contra Franklin, "Augustans," Holconius Celer did not take office in A.D. 14, which is not a quinquennial year.

as quinquennial duovir, and since one could presumably not have been elected quinquennial without having served as regular duovir, he must be credited also with at least one term as duovir that is otherwise unattested.

The Holconius of the next generation, M. Holconius Gellius, duovir in A.D. 22,[20] leads to the most interesting relationships of this family. His name is unusual, and his second nomen, *Gellius,* standing for a cognomen, must reveal a connection between his family and the Gellii (or, as locally pronounced, the Cellii), a connection that his family was pleased to trumpet.[21]

L. Cellius

In the preceding generation, an L. Cellius had been elected duovir and, like Holconius Rufus, had been named *tribunus militum a populo,* although this is known only from his funerary inscription.[22]

7:

L(ucio) Cellio L(ucii) f(ilio)
Men(enia tribu) IIvir(o) i(ure) d(icundo) tri(buno)
mil(itum) a populo
ex testam(ento).[23]

[To Lucius Cellius, son of Lucius, tribe Menenia, duovir *iure dicundo,* military tribune by (choice of) the people, in accordance with his will.]

There will have been a Cellia—probably daughter of this second *tribunus militum a populo*—married to Holconius Celer, and it must have been this further Augustan connection that was underscored in naming their son, Holconius Gellius.[24] This is but the first intermarriage we can trace among these families; the Cellii also intermarried with the family

---

20. *CIL* X.895.

21. On *Gellius* for *Cellius,* see Castrén 171; on the confusion of *c* and *g* in general at Pompeii, see Väänänen 52–54.

22. On Cellius, see Mouritsen, *Elections* 101.

23. D'Ambrosio and De Caro 4EN, not included in the *CIL.*

24. Castrén (97 and 104) observed that there were connections between the families.

discussed next, the Clodia, although no such naming pattern trumpeted the fact.

A. Clodius Flaccus

The only other Cellius of significance, L. Cellius Calvus, apparent son of L. Cellius, brother of Cellia, and uncle of Holconius Gellius,[25] was connected—doubtless by marriage—to the gens Clodia, with whom he shared the family tomb.[26]

8:

L(ucius) Cellius L(ucii) f(ilius)

Men(enia tribu) Calvos *[sic]*

decurio

Pompeis.[27]

[Lucius Cellius Calvus, son of Lucius, tribe Menenia, decurion at Pompeii.]

His apparent father-in-law, the well-known A. Clodius Flaccus, who was buried in the same tomb, was a distinguished Pompeian, serving as duovir three times (once as quinquennial) and—again—as *tribunus militum a populo.*[28] Again, therefore, we see two descendants of powerful Augustans married, although probably in a childless union, since no further Gellii are attested. Although Clodius' funerary inscription continues to describe his three terms as duovir in great detail (which I shall examine shortly), the essential items are contained in the first three lines.

9:

A(ulus) Clodius A(uli) f(ilius)

Men(enia tribu) Flaccus IIvir i(ure) d(icundo) ter(tium)

quinq(uennalis)

trib(unus) mil(itum) a populo.

---

25. So Castrén 97, contra Franklin, "Augustans," where Calvus is identified as brother of the *tribunus militum.*

26. On the Clodii, see Castrén 154–55.

27. *CIL* X.1074e.

28. On Flaccus, see Mouritsen, *Elections* 99.

Primo duomviratu Apollinarib(us) in foro pompam
tauros taurocentas succorsores pontarios
paria III pugiles catervarios et pyctas ludos
omnibus acruamatis pantomimisq(ue) omnibus et
Pylade et HS N CCIƆƆ in publicam pro duomviratu.
Secundo duomviratu quinq(uennali) Apollinaribus in foro
pompam tauros taurarios succorsores pugiles
catervarios poster die solus in spectaculis athletas
par(ia) XXX glad(iatorum) par(ia) V et gladiat(orum) par(ia) XXXV et
venation(em) tauros taurocentas apros ursos
cetera venatione varia cum collega.
Tertio duomviratu ludos factione prima
adiectis acruamatis cum collega.[29]

[Aulus Clodius Flaccus, son of Aulus, tribe Menenia, three times duovir *iure dicundo,* (once as) quinquennial, military tribune by choice of the people.

During his first duovirate, for the *ludi Apollinares,* he provided in the forum a parade, bulls, bullfighters and their aides, three pairs of skirmishing gladiators, group boxers, and boxers in the Greek style. He also provided for all plays and musical pantomimes featuring Pylades; and for the privilege of holding the duovirate, he paid ten thousand sesterces to the public coffers.

During his second duovirate, his quinquennial, for the *ludi Apollinares,* he provided in the forum a parade, bulls, bullfighters and their aides, and group boxers. On the following day, in the amphitheater, he alone provided thirty pairs of athletes and five pairs of gladiators, and together with his colleague, he provided thirty-five pairs of gladiators, a hunt, bulls, bullfighters, boars, bears, and other hunting variations.

During his third duovirate, he provided, together with his colleague, a production by a foremost troupe, with musical accompaniment.]

Clodius Flaccus appears to have been the son of A. Clodius M. f., whose tribe was the Roman Palatine, and of a Lassia, *sacerdos publica*

---

29. *CIL* X.1074d.

(public priestess) of Ceres.[30] His daughter, Clodia A. f., also served as *sacerdos publica* of Ceres, and she erected the tomb for her family.

10:

> Clodia A(uli) f(ilia)
> sacerdos
> publica
> Cereris d(ecreto) d(ecurionum).[31]

[Clodia, daughter of Aulus, public priestess of Ceres, by decree of the decurions.]

11:

> Clodia A(uli) f(ilia) hoc monumentum sua impensa
> sibi et suis.[32]

[Clodia, daughter of Aulus, (built) this monument at her own expense for herself and her relations.]

Her marriage to Cellius Calvus and Flaccus' lack of a recorded wife—apparently long expired by the time this tomb was built and so buried elsewhere—explain the men's inclusion in the group; the odd detail that Cellius Calvus served as decurion perhaps reveals Clodia's attempt to add distinction to her rather unaccomplished husband in the presence of her remarkably distinguished father.

Both parents of Flaccus also shared the tomb, and as his tribe indicates, Clodius the father had been a newcomer to Pompeii, a scribe, and *magister pagi Augusti Felicis Suburbani,* that is, magistrate of the suburban settlement called Augustus Felix.[33]

---

30. So Castrén 154–55 and 181; but Lassia cannot have been the wealthy Sorrentine he suggests, for she would surely have been a Pompeian to hold the position of *sacerdos publica* (and see further on the family fortunes the discussion that follows in text).

31. *CIL* X.1074a.

32. *CIL* X.1074f.

33. Castrén (94) wrongly created a nonexistent, second A. Clodius to serve as *magister pagi Augusti Felicis Suburbani.*

12:

A(ulus) Clodius
M(arci) f(ilius) Pal(atina tribu) scriba
magist(er) pag(i) Aug(usti)
Fel(icis) Sub(urbani).[34]

[Aulus Clodius, son of Marcus, tribe Palatine, scribe, magistrate of the suburban settlement Augustus Felix.]

The office of *magister pagi* must have come relatively late in Clodius' life, for the *pagus* had by then adopted the title "Augustus." Indeed, his incumbency probably reflects the high degree to which his son was perceived as a proponent of the new regime; Flaccus had become so prominent that his father was a politically shrewd—perhaps unavoidable—choice as magistrate of the "Augustan" suburb.

As attested by the office *tribunus militum a populo,* the Augustan politics of these interrelated men are beyond question. It will therefore have been of great significance that Clodius Flaccus and Holconius Rufus were recalled to the duovirate, the former for the third time and the latter for the fourth, in 2–1 B.C., just after the Senate at Rome had granted Augustus the title *pater patriae,*[35] and as the Holconii were initiating the remodeling of the Teatro Grande.

A. Veius

Of A. Veius *tribunus militum a populo,* nothing is known apart from his funerary inscription, recovered on a semicircular schola tomb along the Via dei Sepolchri just outside the Porta di Ercolano. From it, however, it is clear that Veius served twice as duovir (on the second occasion as quinquennial) and was honorably buried by order of the decurions.

13:

A(ulo) Veio M(arci) f(ilio) II vir(o) i(ure) d(icundo)
iter(um) quinq(uennali) trib(uno)
milit(um) ab popul(o) ex d(ecurionum) d(ecreto).[36]

---

34. *CIL* X.1074c.
35. *CIL* X.890. On the bestowal of the title, see Dio Cass. 55.10.
36. Kockel S2 = *CIL* X.996; on the tomb, see Kockel 51–53. On the Veii in general, see Castrén 235; on A. Veius himself, Mouritsen, *Elections* 103.

[To Aulus Veius, son of Marcus, twice duovir *iure dicundo,* (once as) quinquennial, military tribune by (choice of) the people, in accordance with a decree of the decurions.]

As we shall see in chapter 2, a Veius Fronto was adopted by M. Stlaborius and rose to be quinquennial duovir in A.D. 25–26; as there are no other attested Veii from whom he could have descended, he will have been the son of the Veius attested here and is indicated as such in the stemmata that follow this chapter. Moreover, we know that the apparent freedman of the Veius attested here, A. Veius Phylax, had been named a *minister Augusti* in 2–1 B.C.,[37] when Holconius Rufus and Clodius Flaccus were duovirs in what must have been perceived as an especially Augustan administration, as we have just seen.

M. Tullius

M. Tullius proves far more interesting, although the two *cippi* bearing the same, simple inscription that apparently marked his tomb outside the Porta di Stabia reveal even less than usual.[38]

14:

M(arco) Tullio
M(arci) f(ilio)
ex d(ecreto) d(ecurionum).[39]

[To Marcus Tullius, son of Marcus, in accordance with a decree of the decurions.]

Tullius, however, had built the earliest known Temple of Fortuna Augusta on his own property at the corner of the Via del Foro/Via di Mercurio and the Via della Fortuna and with his own money, as stones there testified.[40]

---

37. *CIL* X.890.
38. On the Tullii, see Castrén 231–32; on M. Tullius, Mouritsen, *Elections,* 103.
39. *EphEp* 8.330.
40. On the temple, see Hänlein-Schäfer 105–7.

15:

    M(arcus) Tullius M(arci) f(ilius) d(uo) v(ir) i(ure) d(icundo)
    ter(tium) quinq(uennalis) augur tr(ibunus) mil(itum)

a pop(ulo) aedem Fortunae August(ae) solo et peq(unia) sua.[41]

[Marcus Tullius, son of Marcus, duovir *iure dicundo* three times,
(once as) quinquennial, augur, military tribune by (choice of) the people, (built) the building of Fortuna Augusta on his own property and
with his own money.]

16:

    M(arci) Tulli M(arci) f(ilii)
    area privata.[42]

[Private property of Marcus Tullius, son of Marcus.]

Not only was he *tribunus militum a populo,* but he also served three
times as duovir (once as quinquennial) and was one of only two augurs
known at Pompeii.[43] The building of the temple, too, can be closely
dated; it is likely just to have been finished in A.D. 3, when the first *ministri Fortunae Augustae* were named.

17:

    Agathemerus Ve[tti]
    Suavis Caesiae Primae
    Pothus Numitori
    Antheros Lacutulani
    minist(ri) prim(i) Fortun(ae) Aug(ustae) iuss(u)
M(arci) Stai Rufi Cn(aei) Melissaei d(uo)v(irorum) i(ure) d(icundo)
P(ublio) Silio L(ucio) Volusio Saturn(ino) co(n)s(ulibus).[44]

---

41. *CIL* X.820.

42. *CIL* X.821.

43. Also augur was M. Stlaborius Veius Fronto (*CIL* X.806), on whom see
chap. 2, under "A.D. 25–26."

44. *CIL* X.824. In the *CIL,* line 1 is restored with the nomen *Vettius* as likely;
it is only possible and is so edited here.

[Agathemerus (slave) of Vettius, Suavis (slave) of Caesia Prima, Pothus (slave) of Numitor, and Antheros (slave) of Lacutulanus (are named) the first attendants of Fortuna Augusta by order of Marcus Staius Rufus and Cnaeus Melissaeus, duovirs *iure dicundo*, Publius Silius and Lucius Volusius Saturninus (being) consuls (at Rome).]

Unfortunately, it is uncertain when Tullius presented games advertised in three *edicta munerum*, although the lack of reference to the temple perhaps indicates that they belong earlier in his career.[45] Featuring a hunt and twenty pairs of gladiators, they were scheduled for 4, 5, 6, and 7 November of an unspecified year.

18:

Venat(io) et glad(iatorum) par(ia) XX M(arci) Tulli
pug(nabunt) Pom(peis) pr(idie) non(as) non(is) VIII, VII idu(s)
novembr(es).[46]

[(There will be) a hunt, and twenty pairs of gladiators of Marcus Tullius will fight at Pompeii on the day before the nones, on the nones, and on the eighth and seventh days before the ides of November.]

M. Lucretius Decidianus Rufus

Later prominent at Pompeii were two major branches of the Lucretii, the Marci and the Decimi, but the earliest known Lucretius is M. Lucretius Decidianus Rufus.[47] He was born L. Decidius Rufus[48] and adopted by an otherwise unknown M. Lucretius, as was recorded on a stone recov-

---

45. On the *edicta,* see Sabbatini Tumolesi 22–24; Sabbatini Tumolesi, however, hesitates to identify the M. Tullius of the notices with the only M. Tullius known at Pompeii, the *tribunus militum a populo.*

46. Sabbatini Tumolesi N. 3 = *CIL* IV.9980. Near duplicates (texts of Sabbatini Tumolesi Nn. 2 and 4) are *CIL* IV.9979: *Venat(io) et glad(iatorum) par(ia) XX / M(arci) Tulli pugn(abunt) Pom(peis) pr(idie) non(as) novembres / VII idus nov(embres);* and *CIL* IV.9981a: *Venat(io) [et] gladiat(orum) [par(ia) XX] M(arci) Tulli pug(nabunt) [Pom(peis) pr(idie) non(as), non(is)], VIII, VII eidus* [sic] *novembr(es).*

47. On the Lucretii, see Castrén 185–86 and Della Corte 163a. On M. Lucretius Decidianus Rufus, see Mouritsen, *Elections* 102.

48. On the Decidii, see Castrén 162.

ered long ago in the construction of the Sarno Canal, the digging for which actually precipitated the discovery of Pompeii.

19:
  M(arcus) Lucretius L(uci) f(ilius) Dec[i]d(ianus) Rufus dec(reto)
  dec(urionum).[49]

[Marcus Lucretius Decidianus Rufus, son of Lucius, by decree of the decurions.]

He was elsewhere consistently termed *praefectus fabrum,* or military aide-de-camp, as well as *tribunus militum a populo,* and his career is remarkably well attested.[50] He had been duovir and quinquennial duovir when a stone recovered in block VIII.2 was carved.

20:
  M(arcus) Lucretius L(uci) f(ilius) Dec(idianus) Rufus
  IIvir iter(um) quinq(uennalis)
  trib(unus) milit(um) a populo
  praefect(us) fabr(um).[51]

[Marcus Lucretius Decidianus Rufus, son of Lucius, twice duovir, (once as) quinquennial, military tribune by (choice of) the people, military aide-de-camp.]

Later he again served as duovir, was named a pontifex—unfortunately unspecified—and by decree of the *ordo decurionum* was honored with a statue in the forum after his death.

---

49. *CIL* X.952.

50. On the development of the office *praefectus fabrum,* see J. Suolahti, *The Junior Officers of the Roman Army in the Republican Period,* Annales Academiae Scientiarum Fennicae, ser. B, 97 (Helsinki 1955) 205–9; B. Dobson, "The *Praefectus Fabrum* in the Early Principate," in *Britain and Rome: Essays Presented to Eric Birley on His Sixtieth Birthday,* ed. M.G. Jarret and B. Dobson (Kendal 1965) 61–84. The post is intriguingly difficult to define, being a personal one to the commander and of declining military importance by the time of Claudius. Further, as Dobson notes (68), when no military posts are included in a man's *cursus,* "either the post was completely honorary or if any duties were exercised they were not of a military nature."

51. Reported at *NSc* (1898) 171 and not entered in the *CIL.*

21:

M(arco) Lucretio Decidian(o)
Rufo II vir(o) III quinq(uennali)
pontif(ici) trib(uno) mil(itum) a populo
praef(ecto) fabr(um) ex d(ecreto) d(ecurionum)
post mortem.[52]

[To Marcus Lucretius Decidianus Rufus, three times duovir, (once as) quinquennial priest, military tribune by (choice of) the people, military aide-de-camp, in accordance with a decree of the decurions after his death.]

He left at his death at least six bequests, which were honored by similar inscriptions on four herms and two plaques found erected at various locations around the city: near the Via dei Sepolchri, in the Temple of Isis, in the Teatro Grande (twice), in the chalcidicum of the Building of Eumachia, and in the Foro Triangolare.[53]

22:

M(arcus) Lucretius Rufus
legavit.[54]

[Marcus Lucretius Rufus bequeathed.]

Then much later, following the earthquake of A.D. 62, his memory was restored by M. Decidius Pilonius Rufus, who replaced two inscriptions—one on the base of a second statue in the forum,[55] the second and more complete in the Temple of Isis.

23:

M(arcus) Lucretius Decid(ianus)
Rufus II vir III quinq(uennalis)
pontif(ex) trib(unus) mil(itum)

---

52. *CIL* X.789.

53. For the locations, see *CIL* X.815; "tertium et quartum in theatro minore *nella grada dietro il corridoio*," however, can only mean along the ramp leading from the upper levels of the Teatro Grande to the Via Stabiana (VIII.7.21).

54. *CIL* X.815. These inscriptions actually take two forms; the two plaques were inscribed on a single line.

55. *CIL* X.788.

a populo praef(ectus) fab(rum)
M(arcus) Decidius Pilonius
Rufus reposuit.[56]

[Marcus Lucretius Decidianus Rufus, three times duovir, (once as) quinquennial, priest, military tribune by (choice of) the people, military aide-de-camp. Marcus Decidius Pilonius Rufus reset (this inscription).]

M. Decidius Pilonius Rufus is otherwise unknown, but it is clear that he was eager to keep the name of his adopted gens, the Decidia, as familiar to the public as possible; through it he was claiming relation to the far more powerful gens Lucretia.

M. Lucretius Decidianus Rufus in fact appears to have been the second most powerful man of his age at Pompeii, only slightly less distinguished than M. Holconius Rufus, whose career ran roughly parallel to his own. In contrast to Holconius, however, Lucretius began his career in the military, serving as *praefectus fabrum,* in which office his administrative skills will have been early recognized and fostered. He was thus prepared to serve three times as duovir (once as quinquennial) on his return to Pompeii. He had also been soon nominated by the city as one of its premier citizens to serve as *tribunus militum a populo,* which attests his strong Augustan sympathies. Holconius had become *Augusti Caesaris sacerdos,* and the pontificacy of Lucretius may well also have been tied to imperial concerns. Holconius was responsible for the remodeling of the Teatro Grande to recall the Theater of Marcellus at Rome and to commemorate the granting of the title *pater patriae* to Augustus. The discovery of two herms marking the bequests of Lucretius in the ramped corridor leading from the upper levels of the theater to the Via Stabiana ties him also to that structure, its program, and the era. Moreover, in the Foro Triangolare, near the statue honoring Marcellus as patron, an area that must have been perceived as rededicated in the Augustan mode just as the theater to which it was attached, was another of the herms honoring a bequest of Lucretius. Given such firm foundations, there is little surprise that both the gens Holconia and the gens Lucretia flourished politically in the years to come.

---

56. *CIL* X.851.

Roughly contemporary with Lucretius Decidianus Rufus, his relative L. Obellius Lucretianus entered politics. He was apparently son of a Lucretia married to the first Obellius known at Pompeii, and like that of Holconius Gellius, his cognomen underscores the importance of his mother's gens, the Lucretia, in these years.[57] Of him we know only that he served as aedile in A.D. 1–2.[58] Then the gens Obellia disappears from the record until the last years of the city, when M. Obellius Firmus rose to prominence.[59]

In the next generation Cn. Lucretius Decens became aedile in A.D. 22, when the Holconius of that generation, Holconius Gellius, was serving as duovir.[60] Both Holconii and Lucretii continued to appear in the *alba* of Pompeii—but already with Decens and Gellius, we are beyond the Augustan era. The original M. Lucretius Decidianus Rufus, *tribunus militum a populo,* however, leads to a further important family of the day.

Eumachia, *sacerdos publica*

One other inscription marking a bequest of Lucretius was found in the chalcidicum of the Building of Eumachia, or properly the Porticus Concordiae Augustae Pietatique.[61] Erected to recall the Porticus Liviae at Rome (just as the remodeling of the Teatro Grande by the Holconii was designed to recall the Theater of Marcellus), it featured a statuary area (chalcidicum) and covered passageway *(crypta).* Its dedication, "To Augustan Harmony and Respect," reflects the political programs of Livia and Tiberius from 7 B.C. to A.D. 12, firmly tying Eumachia—who built it with her own funds and dedicated it in both her own name and that of her son (N. Numistrius Fronto)—to Augustan times.[62]

---

57. Contra Franklin, "Augustans," where Lucretianus is identified as an adopted son. On the Obellii, see Castrén 198.

58. *CIL* X.891.

59. On M. Obellius Firmus, see chap. 5.

60. *CIL* X.895.

61. On the porticus and their program, see L. Richardson, jr, "Concordia and Concordia Augusta: Rome and Pompeii," *PP* 33 (1978) 260–72.

62. The presence of the plaque attesting the bequest of Lucretius demonstrates that he was still alive when the chalcidicum and hence the entire structure was erected, a further argument for a late Augustan date.

24:
Eumachia L(ucii) f(ilia) sacerd(os) publ(ica) nomine suo et
N(umeri) Numistri Frontonis fili chalcidicum cryptam porticus
Concordiae
Augustae Pietati sua pequnia fecit eademque dedicavit.[63]

[Eumachia, daughter of Lucius, public priestess, built in her own
name and in that of her son, Numerius Numistrius Fronto, the chalcidicum, crypt, and porticus to Augustan Harmony and Respect with
her own money and dedicated the same.]

Here the chalcidicum included not only statues of local worthies but
also a small set of busts, *tituli,* and *elogia* of the *summi viri* from the Forum Augusti in Rome.[64] Lucretius was probably connected with these
latter—either as the original donor or with a bequest for maintenance.

N. Numistrius Fronto, Eumachia's husband, after whom their son
was named, served as duovir in A.D. 2–3, when *ministri Augusti*—one
even a freedman of the birth family of Lucretius Decidianus Rufus—
were named. Thanks to the building and dedication of the porticus, Numistrius' and Eumachia's Augustan leanings are secure.[65]

25:

Messius Arrius
Silenus
M(arcus) Decidius M(arci) M(arci) l(ibertus)
[F]austus ung(uentarius)
min(istri) Augusti
M(arco) Numistrio Frontone

---

63. *CIL* X.810. Following Mau (*Pompeii* 111) and now D'Arms ("Pompeii
and Rome," 63 n. 12), I read both *Concordiae Augustae* and *Pietati* as datives
dependent on *dedicavit* in the inscription and take *porticus* as the plural noun.

64. *Elogia* for Aeneas and Romulus (*CIL* X.808, 809) were found in situ at
Pompeii; for the *elogia* of the Forum Augusti and elsewhere, see A. Degrassi,
"Elogia," *Inscriptiones Italicae* 13.3, especially 68–70.

65. On the gens Eumachia, see Castrén 165–66; on the Numistria, 197–98.
Only one other Eumachius, L. Eumachius Fuscus, aedile in A.D. 32, is known to
have played a role in Pompeian public life (*CIL* X.899, 900).

Q(uinto) Cotrio Q(uinti) f(ilio) d(uo) v(iris) i(ure) d(icundo)
M(arco) Servilio L(ucio) Aelio
Lamia co(n)s(ulibus).⁶⁶

[Messius Arrius Silenus and Marcus Decidius Faustus the perfumer, freedman of the Marci Decidii, (are named) attendants of Augustus, Marcus Numistrius Fronto and Quintus Cotrius, son of Quintus, (being) duovirs *iure dicundo,* and Marcus Servilius and Lucius Aelius Lamia (being) consuls (at Rome).]

No more is known of Numistrius Fronto, and judging from another stone apparently naming a Gratus, slave of Lucius Caesar, as an unspecified *minister,* he died in office, for only his colleague Cotrius was there named.

26:

a a p r d d
Gratus Caesar(is)
L(uci) minist(er) iussu
Q(uinti) Cotri d(uo) v(iri) i(ure) d(icundo)
C(ai) Anni Maruli
D(ecimi) Alfidi Hypsa[e]i
d(uo) v(irorum) v(iis) a(edibus) s(acris) p(ublicisque) p(rocurandis)
M(arco) Servilio L(ucio) Aelio
co(n)s(ulibus).⁶⁷

[[a a p r d d] Gratus (slave) of Lucius Caesar (is named) attendant by order of Quintus Cotius, duovir *iure dicundo,* and Gaius Annius Marulus and Decimus Alfidius Hypsaeus, duovirs *viis aedibus sacris publicisque procurandis,* Marcus Servilius and Lucius Aelius (being) consuls (at Rome).]

Perhaps his death explains the unusual concern of Eumachia to establish their son Numistrius *filius* in the dedicatory inscription to the Por-

66. *CIL* X.892.
67. *EphEp* 8.316; the significance of line 1 of this inscription remains uncertain.

ticus Concordiae Augustae Pietatique; he, however, also sadly disappears from the record after his mention in the inscription.

Mamia, *sacerdos publica*

Immediately north of the Porticus Concordiae Augustae Pietatique stands the building today generally called the Tempio di Vespasio.[68] According to an inscription preserved there, however, it was originally dedicated to the *genius Augusti* by the public priestess Mamia and was built on her own property and with her own funds,[69] and it will have been the temple in which the Holconii exercised their duties as *sacerdotes Augusti.*

27:
   M[a]mia P(ublii) f(ilia) sacerdos public(a) Geni[o Augusti s]olo et
   pec[unia sua].[70]

[Mamia, daughter of Publius, public priestess, to the *genius Augusti,* on her own land and with her own money.]

Little more is known of either Mamia or her family; a relative was aedile in republican times, and her own schola tomb stands on land given by the decurions just outside the Porta di Ercolano, to the west, near the tomb of Veius.

28:
   Mamiae P(ublii) f(iliae) sacerdoti publicae locus sepultur(ae) datus
   decurionum decreto.[71]

[To Mamia, daughter of Publius, public priestess, (this) place of burial was given by decree of the decurions.]

---

68. The title is owed to Mau's analysis, published first in *RendNap* 15 (1891–93) 181ff. and then in *Pompeii* 106–9. On the temple, see Hänlein-Schäfer 57–59.

69. See introd., n. 19.

70. *CIL* X.816.

71. Kockel S4 = *CIL* X.998. On the tomb, see Kockel 57–59; Kockel prefers the spelling *Mammia* and so restores it in the funerary inscription.

Nevertheless, it is clear that Mamia can be termed an Augustan; like M. Tullius, she built for the city an Augustan monument on her own property with her own money. The building, moreover, seems to have stood as the seat of the cult of all succeeding emperors, eventually earning its title as the Temple of Vespasian.[72]

Ministri Augusti, ministri Fortunae Augustae

Many other Pompeians must also have considered themselves Augustans, although unlike Eumachia or Mamia, they were unable to leave such physically impressive proof of their leanings. Of these there are, of course, few traces. Yet those gentes willing to allow their slaves and freedmen to become *ministri Augusti* or *ministri Fortunae Augustae* in these years surely can be considered supporters of the new regime, even if, of the *ministri Augusti* especially, specific duties remain unknown.[73] In toto, five inscriptions name these *ministri,* who carry the names Arrius, Arruntius, Caecilius, Caesius, Decidius, Lacutulanius, Lollius, Mescinius, Numitorius, Popidius, Stallius, Veius, and Vettius.[74] Of these thirteen gentes, two—the Decidia and Veia—have already been connected to Augustan figures. Only five—the Caecilia, Lollia, Numitoria, Popidia, and Vettia—were sufficiently vital still to be active in the last decade of Pompeii's existence. Yet the Mescinii—and, as we shall see from related evidence, the Staii—demonstrate how powerfully gentes struggled to establish themselves in these new times, applying themselves—like A. Veius and his freedman Phylax or like Clodius Flaccus and his father—on several Augustan commissions.

Gens Mescinia. T. Mescinius Amphio was named *minister Augusti* in 2–1 B.C., when Holconius Rufus and Clodius Flaccus, *tribuni militum a populo,* together shared the duovirate, and when the Holconii began their remodeling of the Teatro Grande, incumbencies of obvious Augustan reverberations, as we have already observed.

---

72. On the rededications, see Richardson, *Architectural* 194. Arguing from its advanced architectural form, Zanker, (*Pompeji* 28) has suggested that later imperial cult at Pompeii was located in the Santuario dei Lari Pubblici. No finds, however, support the suggestion.

73. For a summary of the case of the *ministri Augusti,* see Castrén 75; of the *ministri Fortunae Augustae,* 76–78.

74. *CIL* X.824, 884, 890, 891, 892.

29:

> A(ulus) Veius Phylax
> N(umerius) Popidius Moschu(s)
> T(itus) Mescinius Amphio
> Primus Arrunti M(arci) s(ervus)
> min(istri) Aug(usti) ex d(ecreto) d(ecurionum) iussu
> M(arci) Holconi Rufi IV
> A(uli) Clodi Flacci III
> d(uo) v(irorum) i(ure) d(icundo)
> P(ubli) Caeseti Postumi
> N(umeri) Tintiri Rufi
> [d(uo)]v(irorum) v(iis) a(edibus) s(acris) p(ublicisque) p(rocurandis)
> [Imp(eratore) Cae]sare XIII
> [M(arco) Plautio Si]lvano co(n)s(ulibus).[75]

[Aulus Veius Phylax, Numerius Popidius Moschus, Titus Mescinius Amphio, and Primus, slave of Marcus Arruntius, (are named) attendants of Augustus in accordance with a decree of the decurions by the order of Marcus Holconius Rufus and Aulus Clodius Flaccus, (respectively for the) fourth and third times duovirs *iure dicundo,* and of Publius Caesetius Postumius and Numerius Tintirius Rufus, duovirs *viis aedibus sacris publicisque procurandis,* Caesar (being) imperator for the thirteenth time, Marcus Plautius Silvanus (being) consul (at Rome).]

Distinguished Pompeians and powerful Augustans themselves, it is highly likely that Holconius and Clodius approved only likewise committed men and that members of the gens Mescinia qualified. Indeed, five years earlier a Princeps Mescinii had established the Augustan leanings of the gens when he had been named one of the four original *ministri pagi Augusti Felicis Suburbani.*

30:

> Dama Pup(i) Agrippae
> Manlianus Lucreti
> Anteros Stai Rufi
> Princeps Mescini

---

75. *CIL* X.890.

ministri pagi
Aug(usti) Fel(icis) Sub[urb]an(i)
primi posie[run]t [*sic*]
Ti(berio) Claudio Nerone iter(um)
Cn(aeo) Calpurnio Pisone co(n)s(ulibus).[76]

[Dama (slave) of the boy of Agrippa, Manlianus (slave) of Lucretius, Anteros (slave) of Staius Rufus, and Princeps (slave) of Mescinius, first magistrates of the suburban settlement Augustus Felix, placed (this inscription), Tiberius Claudius Nero—for the second time—and Cnaeus Calpurnius Piso (being) consuls (at Rome).]

Being among the first *ministri* of the newly named suburb must have been a distinct honor—especially when the office was shared with a slave of the gens Lucretia and of the five-year-old Agrippa Postumus, here styled pupus, "boy," of Agrippa, as he was known before his adoption by Augustus.[77] Unfortunately, we know nothing of T. Mescinius, owner of this slave Princeps and patron of his freedman Amphio; on the basis of his slave's and freedman's activities, however, he can clearly be identified as a committed, if obscure, Augustan.

Gens Staia. The *minister* preceding Princeps on this last stone, Anteros Stai Rufi, also leads to another—this time distinguished—Augustan, M. Staius Rufus. Along with approving Anteros' role as *minister,* Staius had served as duovir when the first *ministri Fortunae Augustae* were named on the establishment of the temple in A.D. 3, doubtless taking prominent part in the inauguration ceremonies.[78] Here we again see efforts on two distinct levels, that of a duovir and that of his slave.

Staius' colleague in office was Cn. Melissaeus Aper, the first known prominent member of another gens that, as we shall see, likewise worked hard to establish itself as an imperial proponent slightly later, in the early Julio-Claudian years.[79] Unfortunately, neither gens, Mescinia or Staia, later played an elected role in Pompeian politics, although both

---

76. *CIL* X.924.

77. See *CIL* X.924 and likewise *CIL* II.1528.

78. *CIL* X.824 (inscription 17).

79. Further on Staius Rufus and Melissaeus Aper, see chap. 2. On the gens Melissaea, see Castrén 190. Three Melissaei—two slaves and one freedman—were named *ministri Fortunae Augustae* in A.D. 22–23 (*CIL* X.827), 31–32 (*CIL* X.895), and 39–40 (*CIL* X.899).

gentes' efforts at establishing themselves, which continued throughout Tiberian days,[80] are clear.

In fact, as interesting as the successes of the Holconii and Lucretii—successes not without significant stumbles in the next imperial era—is the disappearance of the majority of these other Augustan gentes, even those who held the *tribunus militum a populo*. Following the funerary inscription of Clodia, only freedmen and slaves of the Clodii are known. No Tullii or Cellii rose to political prominence, and only one, adopted Veius, M. Stlaborius Veius Fronto, represents the end of that line.

Indeed, the major reasons for political and social decline seem again to have been at work: lack of progeny—in the cases of the Cellii and, as we shall see, the Staii, lack of male progeny—and dwindling resources. The Holconii appear to have survived throughout the imperial period, but the Lucretii managed only through adoption, the convention that had also produced the first significant member of their line, M. Lucretius Decidianus Rufus.[81] Augustus was not the only leader who struggled for a successor.

Loss of fortunes seems equally apparent.[82] Tullius, Eumachia, and Mamia each single-handedly took on the building of a major edifice, Tullius and Mamia even providing the land from their own holdings. A glance back at the funerary inscription of the Clodii raises sincere questions about the expenses of public office, especially for the incautious man seeking first to establish his gens in the public eye. By his third duovirate, Clodius Flaccus would appear to have faced declining financial resources head-on. And his daughter, Clodia, seems perhaps defensively proud of her ability to erect the family monument, entombing her father without—oddly—the cooperation of the *decuriones* that marks most major burials at Pompeii.

Augustans

Nevertheless, these *tribuni militum a populo* allow us to gauge as never before the eagerness with which the Pompeians embraced the new

---

80. See chap. 2.

81. For the possibility that the Holconii of later years represented a freedman's line of the family, see D'Arms, "Pompeii and Rome" 61–62.

82. On various temptations to loss, see Dyson, *Community* 78–79: "Emulation of the lifestyles of the Roman elite could rapidly exhaust local incomes" (78).

regime. These six Augustans were elected duovir or quinquennial duovir an astonishing seventeen times, and to that total can be added the minimal two additional incumbencies of Holconius Celer, *divi Augusti flamen,* and of M. Numistrius Fronto, both undoubted Augustans. In addition, other Clodii, Veii, and Lucretii held lesser Augustan offices. Nor did Augustan penetration stop at the political level; on the religious front two powerful public priestesses, Eumachia and Mamia, threw their considerable clout behind the new Augustan government. We have seen cooperation between individuals, and the intermarriages on which I have remarked in passing become significant when one examines the stemmata that follow this chapter. These families cooperated on several fronts.

The Holconii remodeled the theater area in the new Augustan mold. M. Tullius presented the new Temple of Fortuna Augusta to the city. Through his bequests M. Lucretius Decidianus Rufus was associated with activity in the Via dei Sepolchri, the Temple of Isis, the Teatro Grande, the chalcidicum of the Porticus Concordiae Augustae Pietatique, and the Foro Triangolare. Eumachia offered the new Porticus Concordiae Augustae Pietatique themselves; Mamia, the Templum Genii Augusti. The city can never before have seen such major additions to its public fabric in such a short time, and the tomb inscription of Clodius Flaccus suggests with what sumptuous attractions the populace was entertained: "During his first duovirate, for the *ludi Apollinares,* he provided in the forum a parade, bulls, bullfighters and their aides, three pairs of skirmishing gladiators, group boxers, and boxers in the Greek style. He also provided for all plays and musical pantomimes featuring Pylades; and for the privilege of holding the duovirate, he paid ten thousand sesterces to the public coffers.[83]

I must also remark on the coordination of several of these activities with building and happenings in the city of Rome. As we have seen, it appears that the building of the Theater of Marcellus and the Porticus Liviae at Rome stimulated respectively at Pompeii the rededication of the Theatro Grande and the building of the Porticus Concordiae Augustae Pietatique. Of events, the renaming of the apparent Sullan Pagus Felix Suburbanus as the Pagus Augustus Felix Suburbanus came in

---

83. *CIL* X.1074d (inscription 9). On Pylades, see *PIR* 3.110 and *RE,* s.v. "Pylades," 2; on Pylades and other pantomimists at Pompeii, Franklin, "Pantomimists."

7 B.C., the year in which Augustus established the fourteen new *regiones*
in the capital city.[84] The common concern for urban organization is obvious. Then, Holconius and Clodius served their final, extraordinary
terms as duovirs—Holconius for the fourth time and Clodius for the
third—in 2–1 B.C., their elections having taken place in March, just following the granting of the title *pater patriae* to Augustus on 5 February
2 B.C.[85] No two men could better represent the Augustan era at Pompeii,
and to celebrate the occasion, it was during this term of office that the
Holconii remodeled the theater, prominently referring to the new title
of the emperor.[86]

31:

[Imp(eratori) Caesari] Augusto Patri

[patriae imp(eratori) XIV co(n)]s(uli) XIII pontif(ici) max(imo)
trib(unalicia)

[pot]est(ate) XXII.[87]

[To the imperator Caesar Augustus, father of his country, imperator
for the fourteenth time, consul for the thirteenth time, *pontifex max-
imus,* with the tribunician power for the twenty-second time.]

Moreover, all this activity seems to be owed to local inspiration; there is
no indication, such as we shall see in later Flavian times, of interference
from Rome. Certainly the approach to Marcellus to request his service
as *patronus coloniae* will have come from below, and we have, after all,
been studying men nominated as *tribuni militum* by the populace, not
set over it as Castrén once argued.[88] Both Cellius and Clodius, whose
tomb inscriptions have been recovered, were members of the tribe
Menenia, a sign of local birth. The Holconii, given their deep connection
with the land, can be assumed to be of local blood, as can Lucretius Decidianus Rufus, whose birth family had enough prominence also in Augustan times to record at least one freedman, M. Decidius Faustus, es-

---

84. On the first *ministri* of the renamed *pagus,* see *CIL* X.924 (inscription 30);
on the new *regiones* in Rome, Dio Cass. 55.8.
85. Dio Cass. 55.10.
86. See D'Arms, "Pompeii and Rome" 55.
87. *CIL* X.842.
88. See also Mouritsen, *Elections* 121, contra Castrén 96; Castrén sees it all as
"instigated by Augustus."

tablished in the perfume trade and named *minister Augusti* in A.D. 2–3 before Numistrius Fronto died during his term in office.[89] Of the women we have highlighted, Eumachia and Mamia, there can be no doubt of local origins either.

The timing of the completion of a building is difficult, and it is therefore likely that A.D. 3, the completion date of the Temple of Fortuna Augusta, is less significant than the date of its inception, which remains unknown to us. Nevertheless, in A.D. 3 Augustus' powers were renewed for a fourth ten-year period, and according to Dio, in that year a strange upswing occurred in the Roman populace's concern for Julia. When Augustus stated that it was no more likely that she would be recalled from banishment than that fire and water would be mixed, torches were thrown into the Tiber, apparently in an attempt to modify his judgment.[90] Taken together, this is a significant cluster of events, revealing a concern for the *domus Augusti* now known to have been fostered by Augustan coinage and to have developed into cult at Rome by A.D. 19, when it is mentioned in conjunction with the death of Germanicus.[91] At Pompeii, this had earlier been reflected by the establishment of the first known Temple of Fortuna Augusta, where the identification of Augustus' line with the life of the country was again emphasized.

32:

[Augu]sto Caesari
[---] parenti patriae.[92]

[To Augustus Caesar, [---] parent of his country.]

---

89. See *CIL* X.892 (inscription 25).

90. Dio Cass. 55.13.1.

91. On the coinage, see M.D. Fullerton, "The *Domus Augusti* in Imperial Iconography of 13–12 B.C.," *AJA* 89 (1985) 483: "What emerges is not a series of coin types with disparate messages, but a unified scheme which expresses a single idea: the *gens Iulia* brought peace and prosperity to the world through Augustus, and this favorable state of affairs could only persist with the continued leadership of the *gens Iulia*—through the *domus Augusti*." On the cult of *domus Augusti,* mentioned at Rome in the *tabula Siarensis,* see J. Gonzâlez, "Tabula Siarensis, Fortunales Siarenses et Municipia Civium Romanorum," *ZPE* 55 (1984) 55–100, especially 63–64.

92. *CIL* X.823. The title *parens patriae* here, rather than *pater patriae,* is paralleled elsewhere (*BMC* 397–402; *ILS* 101), although as E.S. Ramage ("Augus-

It had been, after all, with the emperor's line in the person of Marcellus that Pompeii had entered the Augustan Age.

In fact, with the appointment of Marcellus, the nephew and son-in-law of Augustus, as patron sometime before 23 B.C., Pompeii had begun to align itself with the victor in Rome. Presumably replacing Marcellus as *patronus coloniae,* M. Holconius Rufus headed a coalition that not only dominated Pompeii's politics but also brought to the city a series of buildings and events carefully coordinated with buildings and events in Rome itself.

We shall see similar patterns in the Neronian and Flavian years as well. First, however, we must explore the intervening years, when the dangers inherent in too ready an alignment with an emperor also become visible.

---

tus' Treatment of Julius Caesar," *Historia* 34 [1985] 227) observes, Augustus preferred *pater* in distinction to Caesar's *parens.*

Augustans

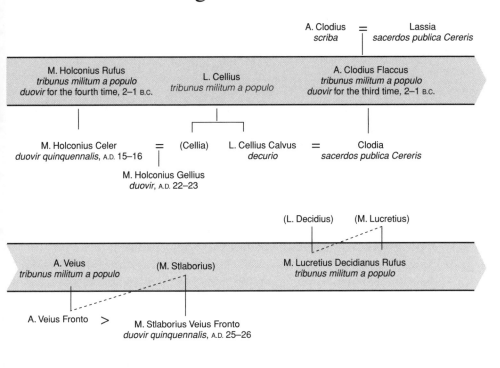

A. Clodius = Lassia
scriba | sacerdos publica Cereris

M. Holconius Rufus
tribunus militum a populo
duovir for the fourth time, 2–1 B.C.

L. Cellius
tribunus militum a populo

A. Clodius Flaccus
tribunus militum a populo
duovir for the third time, 2–1 B.C.

M. Holconius Celer = (Cellia)
duovir quinquennalis, A.D. 15–16

L. Cellius Calvus = Clodia
decurio *sacerdos publica Cereris*

M. Holconius Gellius
duovir, A.D. 22–23

(L. Decidius) (M. Lucretius)

A. Veius
tribunus militum a populo

(M. Stlaborius)

M. Lucretius Decidianus Rufus
tribunus militum a populo

A. Veius Fronto >
M. Stlaborius Veius Fronto
duovir quinquennalis, A.D. 25–26

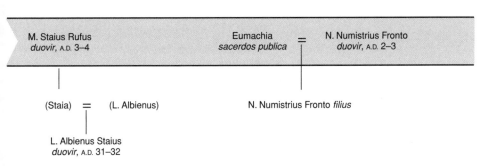

M. Staius Rufus
duovir, A.D. 3–4

Eumachia = N. Numistrius Fronto
sacerdos publica *duovir*, A.D. 2–3

(Staia) = (L. Albienus)

N. Numistrius Fronto *filius*

L. Albienus Staius
duovir, A.D. 31–32

Chapter 2

Early Julio-Claudians

Our knowledge of the years of Tiberius and Caligula at Pompeii is slim and hangs from a very few inscriptions, mostly stones recording the naming of *ministri Augusti.* For this era it is therefore easiest to proceed chronologically, examining the five electoral years for which we have evidence.[1] The overall picture that results from these is admittedly less developed, although detailed for the individual years for which we have stones; dominated by families that had gained firm footing in the Augustan era, it is supplemented also by rising new lines. Yet despite paucity of evidence and apparent steady regularity, unexpected developments can also be traced.

A.D. 22–23

The earliest document from this period, a record of the appointment of new *ministri Augusti,* dates to A.D. 22–23.

33:

Inventus Dentat(i) Daph(ni)
Felix Melissaei Faust(i)
Nymphodotus Helvi
Speratus Caesiae Mus(ae)
min(istri) Aug(usti) (ex) d(ecreto) d(ecurionum) iussu

---

1. For his own reasons, Castrén (77) assigns to this era (specifically to A.D. 39–40) another inscription, *CIL* X.827, the date of which is insecure since the date of the consulships of Futius and Calvisius by which it is dated remains uncertain. Cf., however, *PIR*[2] 2.80 (n. 344), which I follow: "C Vibius . . . cum vix diversus sit a C. Vibio Secundo duoviro a. 56/57 (X.826), consulatus Futii et Calvisii probabiliter attribuendus est uni ex annis praecedentibus, sed excluduntur anni 52/53 et 55/56." Mouritsen (*Elections* 108) notes that "a dating of X 827 to c. 50–54 AD seems plausible." The inscription belongs to Claudian times; see below, chap. 3, under "L. Numisius Rarus."

M(arci) Holconi Gelli L(uci) Aeli Tuber(onis) d(uovirorum) i(ure)
d(icundo)
C(aii) Vergili Salinatoris Cn(aei) Lucreti
Decentis ⟨d(uovirorum)⟩ v(iis) a(edibus) s(acris) p(ublicisque)
p(rocurandis)
C(aio) Asinio C(aio) Antistio co(n)s(ulibus).[2]

[Iuventus (slave) of Dentatius Daphnus, Felix (slave) of Melissaeus
Faustus, Nymphodotus (slave) of Helvius, and Speratus (slave) of
Caesia Musa (are named) attendants of Augustus in accordance with
a decree of the decurions and by order of Marcus Holconius Gellius
and Lucius Aelius Tubero, duovirs *iure dicundo,* and of Gaius
Vergilius Salinator and Gnaeus Lucretius Decens, duovirs *viis aedibus sacris publicisque procurandis,* Gaius Asinius and Gaius Antistius (being) consuls (at Rome).]

We have earlier met one of the duovirs of this year, Holconius Gellius,
scion of the gentes Holconia and Gellia, and descendant of two of Pompeii's *tribuni militum a populo.* Lucretius Decens, one of the aediles of
the year, must somehow be related to Lucretius Decidianus Rufus, *tribunus militum a populo,* although he is the only Gnaeus Lucretius
known; what is important, however, is the continued role of both the
Holconii and Lucretii well into the time of Tiberius. Of the families of
the remaining magistrates of the year, Aelius Tubero and Vergilius Salinator, little is known, and these men appear to be their only politically
distinguished members.[3]

Similarly, among the lines of the slaves named *ministri* in this inscription, two sorts can be distinguished. The Melissaei had risen to
duoviral rank in Augustan days in the person of Cn. Melissaeus Aper,
although he had not been so conspicuous as the men and women discussed in chapter 1.[4] Nevertheless, he had held the duovirate together
with the more distinguished M. Staius Rufus (apparently both men
serving for the second time) in A.D. 3–4,[5] when the most noteworthy

2. *CIL* X.895.
3. Attested later in the Neronian era is an Aelius Magnus, on whom see
chap. 4, n. 69. On the Aelii in general, see Castrén 130–31; on the Vergilii, 237.
4. On the Melissaei, see Castrén 190.
5. *CIL* X.824, 893. *Iterum* appears in 817 and 893 "ita collocato ut ad
utrumque pertineat" (Mommsen at *CIL* X.824).

monument of their careers, the large marble *labrum* in the Terme del
Foro, was set up. On its lip was a long inscription formed from inset
bronze letters that recorded the expense of 5,250 sesterces of public
money for its purchase and installation. Unfortunately, the names of
Melissaeus and Staius were by mistake thrown into the dative case, although the nominative case was called for. Its meaning nevertheless
stands clear.

34:
Cn(aeo) Melissaeo Cn(aei) f(ilio) Apro M(arco) Staio M(arci)
f(ilio) Rufo IIvir(is) iter(um) i(ure) d(icundo) labrum ex d(ecreto)
d(ecurionum) ex p(ecunia) p(ublica) f(aciundum) c(uraverunt).
Constat HS IƆƆCCL.[6]

[Gnaeus Melissaeus Aper, son of Gnaeus, and Marcus Staius Rufus,
son of Marcus, duovirs *iure dicundo* for the second time, saw to the
setting up of this *labrum* out of public money in accordance with a
decree of the decurions. It cost 5,250 sesterces.]

Melissaeus Aper is the only member of his family known to have been
elected to public office[7]—Melissaeus Faustus, owner of the slave Felix
who was now named *minister Augusti,* presumably being his freedman. In A.D. 31–32 another slave of Faustus was named to the same
office of *minister Augusti,* so that we have in this family a gens moving

---

6. *CIL* X.817.
7. Later there may have been an M. Melissaeus who stood for office, but he
must be dated long before the city's destruction, since only one programma securely records his name (*CIL* IV.208: *M(arcum) Melissaeum et Igium Fuscum*).
Unfortunately, *Igius* must be a corruption of the second candidate's name,
which was perhaps *Nigidius* (see L. Richardson, jr, *Pompeii: The Casa del
Dioscuri and Its Painters, MAAR* 23 [1955] 84). Castrén also records *CIL* IV.394,
3342, 3344, and 7116. All are highly fragmentary, 3342 read through overlying
whitewash (*latet sub tectorio recentiore*) and 7116 read *cum periit tectorium . . .
programmatis antiquissimi vestigia apparuere.* From 394 Castrén argues that
Melissaeus' candidacy was for quinquennial, but only the final four letters of
the name, *-aeum,* were clear, and it must be remembered that Veranius Hypsaeus, to whom the notice may just as well refer, securely stood for quinquennial. Mouritsen (*Elections* 143) notes that a Melissaeus of unknown praenomen
is apparently named in *CIL* IV.1175c.

forward in Tiberian days just as we saw the Clodii, Mescinii, and Staii do in Augustan times.

Of the other lines represented by these new *ministri* (inscription 33), the Helvii were eventually to produce several candidates for elected office in Claudian through Flavian days.[8] The Dentatii and Caesii, however, were not important in imperial Pompeii, although a Suavis, slave of Caesia Prima, had been one of the first *ministri Fortunae Augusti* named in A.D. 3.[9] Interestingly, both Suavis and now Speratus were slaves owned by female members of this family.

A.D. 25–26

The quinquennial year 25–26 proves more interesting, for in a fragmentary inscription dated to it, a family that remained prominent throughout Pompeii's history, the Alleia, was first attested.[10]

35:

[---]
[ex d(ecreto) d(ecurionum)] iussu
M(arci) Allei Lucci Libell(ae)
M(arci) Stlabori Fronton(is)
IIvir(orum) i(ure) d(icundo) quinq(uennalum)
Q(uinti) Pompei Maculae
M(arci) Fulvini Silva[ni]
d(uo) v(irorum) v(iis) a(edibus) s(acris) p(ublicisque) p(rocurandis)
C(aio) Calvisio Cn(aeo) [Lentulo]
co(n)s(ulibus)[11]

[[---] in accordance with a decree of the decurions and by order of Marcus Alleius Luccius Libella and Marcus Stlaborius Fronto, quinquennial duovirs *iure dicundo,* and of Quintus Pompeius Macula and Marcus Fulvinus Silvanus, duovirs *viis aedibus sacris publi-*

---

8. See Castrén 173–74.

9. See *CIL* X.824 and above, chap. 1, "*Ministri Augusti, ministri Fortunae Augustae.*" On the Dentatii, see Castrén 163; on the Caesii, 146. An L. Caesius had been duovir in republican times; on his tomb, see D'Ambrosio and De Caro 29OS.

10. On the Alleii, see Castrén 133.

11. *CIL* X.896.

cisque procurandis, Gaius Calvisius and Gnaeus Lentulus (being) consuls (at Rome).]

Alleius Luccius Libella, an adopted son, is the earliest known member of his gens. From his tombstone, it is known that previous to serving as quinquennial in A.D. 25–26, he had been both duovir and *praefectus iure dicundo* (replacing an emperor named duovir) at earlier, unspecified dates. His wife, Alleia Decimilla—to judge from her name, the daughter of Alleius' adoptive father—served as the public priestess of Ceres,[12] and they produced a son, M. Alleius Libella. When the younger Libella died at seventeen, he had already been named a decurion, and he shared with his father the tomb built by his mother on publicly donated land outside the Porta di Ercolano.[13] Providing a quinquennial duovir, a public priestess, and a son early named decurion, this was patently an important family, whose earlier members, albeit untraceable, themselves will have been powerful.

36:
M(arco) Alleio Luccio Libellae patri
aedili II vir(o) praefecto quinq(uennali) et
M(arco) Alleio Libellae f(ilio) decurioni vixit
annis XVII locus monumenti
publice datus est. Alleia M(arci) f(ilia)
Decimilla sacerdos publica
Cereris faciundum curavit viro
et filio.[14]

[To Marcus Alleius Luccius Libella the father, aedile, duovir, prefect, quinquennial, and Marcus Alleius Libella the son, decurion, (who) lived seventeen years, the location of this monument was publicly given. Alleia Decimilla, daughter of Marcus, public priestess of Ceres, saw to its erection for her husband and son.]

Outside the Porta di Stabia, another Alleius, M. Alleius Minius, who had served simply as duovir, was buried in a tomb also built on publicly do-

---

12. Castrén 133.
13. On the tomb, Kockel N37, see Kockel 166–68.
14. *CIL* X.1036.

nated land.[15] Both men must have seen Augustan times; to rise to quinquennial in A.D. 25–26, Alleius Luccius Libella will have begun his career some fifteen to twenty years earlier, and Alleius Minius was buried
in a schola tomb, a type that has itself been dated to the Augustan era.[16]

Serving as quinquennial duovir with Alleius Luccius Libella was
Stlaborius Fronto, who becomes more interesting when his full name,
M. Stlaborius Veius Fronto, is known. Adopted by M. Stlaborius,[17] he is
a descendant, probably the son, of A. Veius, *tribunus militum a populo,*
and his adoption marks the end of the line of another prominent Augustan. In fact, only freedmen and low-ranking members of either gens,
Veia or Stlaboria, are known later. According to another inscription
found in the basilica, Fronto also served as augur, probably having succeeded M. Tullius, *tribunus militum a populo,* in the office.[18]

Q. Pompeius Macula, one of the year's aediles, is the first known
magistrate of his family; although carrying a different cognomen, Sex.
Pompeius Proculus, duovir in A.D. 57–58 and *praefectus iure dicundo*
in A.D. 60, should have been a relation. Neither, however, is to be confused with the Pompeii Grosphi of Sicilian origins, duovirs when the ri-
ots erupted in the amphitheater.[19] Fulvinus, the colleague of Pompeius,
is the only known member of his family at Pompeii.[20]

In addition to marking the end of his birth line, M. Stlaborius Veius
Fronto introduces a slight problem that we shall meet again. He was apparently adopted late in life when his adult identity was fully established, and he therefore was known and officially identified both as
Stlaborius, as here, and as Veius, as in *CIL* X.901 of A.D. 33–34 (= inscription 39). The same is true of M. Lucretius Epidius Flaccus. In A.D.

15. The discovery of the tomb was reported at *NSc* (1889) 280; the inscription was added to the corpus at *EphEp* 8.318: *M(arco) Alleio Q(uinti) f(ilio)
Men(enia) Minio II vir(o) i(ure) d(icundo) locus sepulturae publice datus ex
d(ecreto) d(ecurionum).* On Alleius Minius, see Mouritsen, *Elections* 99.
16. Kockel 18–22.
17. On the Stlaborii, see Castrén 225. D. Falco Carozzi's article, "La gens
Stlaboria di Pompei" (*RendLinc* 72 [1939] 341–47) is a fanciful attempt to
demonstrate Etruscan origins for this family.
18. *CIL* X.806: *M(arco) Stlaborio Veio Frontoni aug(uri) d(uo) v(iro) i(ure)
d(icundo) iterum quinq(uennali).*
19. On the various lines of the Pompeii, see Castrén 205–6 and below,
chapt. 5.
20. Castrén 170.

33–34, he is identified with his full name, but in A.D. 40–41 (*CIL* X.904 = inscription 41) he is called simply M. Epidius Flaccus. In Lucretius' case, different space limitations on the different stones may help explain the name variation, while in Stlaborius' case, his slave may have continued to think of him as Veius Fronto even after adoption and so may have caused that name to be engraved on the second stone, which attests his naming as *minister*. However, the problem arises also with other men at Pompeii and seems ultimately to be owed to an adult adoption.[21]

A.D. 31–32

It is again a record of the naming of *ministri Augusti* in A.D. 31–32 that preserves the names of that year's magistrates.[22]

37:

Philippus Melissaei

Fausti

Ianuarius Piricati

Quartionis

Iucundus Holc[o]ni

Anterotis

Auctus Helvi

Nymphodoti

ministri Aug(usti)

iussu

M(arci) Lucreti Manliani L(uci) Albieni Stai II vir(orum) i(ure)
d(icundo)

L(uci) Eumachi Fusci N(umeri) Herenni Veri d(uo) v(irorum)

v(iis) a(edibus) s(acris) p(ublicisque) p(rocurandis)

Cn(aeo) Domitio Camillo Arruntio

co(n)s(ulibus).[23]

---

21. Cf. also Q. Coelius Caltilius Iustus, duovir in A.D. 52–53, discussed in chap. 3.

22. See also the highly fragmentary *CIL* X.900, on which the magistrates names can be easily restored, although not the names of the *ministri Augusti*.

23. *CIL* X.899.

[Philippus (slave) of Melissaeus Faustus, Ianuarius (slave) of Piricatius Quartio, Iucundus (slave) of Holconius Anteros, and Auctus
(slave) of Helvius Nymphodotus (are named) attendants of Augustus by order of Marcus Lucretius Manlianus and Lucius Albienus
Staius, duovirs *iure dicundo,* and of Lucius Eumachius Fuscus and
Numerius Herennius Verus, duovirs *viis aedibus sacris publicisque
procurandis,* Gnaeus Domitius and Camillus Arruntius (being) consuls (at Rome).]

Of these officials, Lucretius and Eumachius can quickly and securely
be linked to Augustan notables whom we have already met, although
in Lucretius Manlianus lurks a surprise. Nearly forty years earlier, the
same name elements had occurred when the original *magistri pagi Augusti Felicis Suburbani* were named in 7 B.C.[24] They were, however, in
a significantly different arrangement, for then a Manlianus, slave of a
Lucretius, was appointed to office. If the two Manliani are to be connected, it must be that the slave was later freed and that Lucretius Manlianus is his son. If so, this is unquestionably the earliest magistrate that
we can identify who was the son of a freedman, and this seems more
likely to have been the case when we consider that there are no other
known Manlii at Pompeii with whom Lucretius Manlianus could be
connected.[25] It is unlikely that a Lucretius would unthinkingly endow
his son with a name recently carried by a well-known slave. Lucretius
Manlianus must simply have been the son of a freedman. Himself freeborn and a man of obvious ability and presumably substantial wealth,
he will also have been greatly aided in escaping the taint of his freedman father by his connection with one of the grandest families of the
day, the gens Lucretia.

The Herennii had long been prominent at Pompeii,[26] although
Herennius Verus is only the second Numerius known; his father,
N. Herennius Celsus, had (like Lucretius Decidianus Rufus, *tribunus
militum a populo*) begun his career as *praefectus fabrum,* or military
aide-de-camp, and then twice served as duovir sometime in the Augus-

---

24. See *CIL* X.924 (inscription 30).
25. Only two later Manlii are known, a simple Manlius in the house of
M. Fabius Rufus, and A. Manlius Secundus, a witness in the wax tablets of Caecilius Iucundus. See Castrén 188.
26. On the Herennii, see Castrén 174–75.

tan Age, facts gleaned from the tomb inscription of his wife, Aesquillia
Polla, who had died early and been buried outside the Porta di Nola.[27]

38:

> N(umerius) Herennius N(umerii) f(ilius) Men(enia tribu)
> Celsus d(uo) v(ir) i(ure) d(icundo) iter(um) praef(ectus)
> fabr(um)
> Aesquilliae C(aii) f(iliae) Pollae
> uxori vixit annos XXII.
> locus sepulturae publice datus
> d(ecreto) d(ecurionum)[28]

[Numerius Herennius Celsus, son of Numerius, tribe Menenia,
duovir *iure dicundo* twice, military aide-de-camp, to Aesquillia
Polla, daughter of Gaius, his wife, (who) lived twenty-two years.
Place of burial publicly given by decree of the decurions.]

An Ma. Herennius was named in an Oscan inscription,[29] and Pliny the
Elder referred to an otherwise unknown M. Herennius, Pompeian decurion, who was struck by a lightning bolt at the time of the Catilinar-
ian conspiracy.[30] M. Herennius Epidianus had served as duovir in the
Augustan era, although he was not a prominent supporter of the regime
like the men and women mentioned in chapter 1.[31] Henceforward, however, N. Herennius Verus and his son, a second Celsus named for his
grandfather, represented the gens in electoral politics.

Of these magistrates, only Albienus Staius, the sole member of his
gens known at Pompeii, seems at first glance to lack significant antecedents.[32] As his cognomen proves, however, he will have been the

---

27. On dating this and other schola tombs to the Augustan era, see Kockel
18–22.

28. *NSc* (1910) 390.

29. Conway 64 = Vetter 30.

30. Pliny *HN* 2.137: *in Catilinariis prodigiis Pompeiano ex municipio M.
Herennius decurio sereno die fulmine ictus est.*

31. *CIL* X.802, 831, 939. The tomb inscription of Epidianus was found in
tomb 11ES of the Porta Nocera area, although it does not belong to that tomb:
*(M[arco] H)erennio / [A(uli) f(ilio) Epid]iano II vir(o) i(ure) d(icundo) /
[lo]cu[m] monumento / [h]onoris caussa [sic] / ex d(ecreto) d(ecurionum);* see
D'Ambrosio and De Caro 11ES.

32. Castrén 132.

son of a Staia, daughter of M. Staius Rufus, duovir in A.D. 3–4, who with Cn. Melissaeus erected the *labrum* in the Terme del Foro. Since no other family members are attested, Albienus Staius represents the end of not only the Albieni but also the Staii, yet another powerful Augustan gens.

The slaves who were named *ministri* this year for the most part also carried familiar names, including again a Melissaeus, a Holconius, and a Helvius, all slaves of freedmen, to judge from their names. An L. Piricatius twice served as duovir, although at unknown times, and probably belongs to this era.[33] Piricatius Quartio, owner of Ianuarius, the new *minister Augusti,* will then also have been a freedmen of a former duovir, as were, presumably, Melissaeus Faustus and Holconius Anteros, although we do not know of which prominent Holconius in the case of Anteros.

A.D. 33–34

In A.D. 33–34, again according to an inscription naming new *ministri Augusti,* Caius Caesar, soon to become the emperor Caligula, was honored by being named duovir at Pompeii. His duties were performed by another distinguished—again, adopted—Lucretius, the prefect M. Lucretius Epidius Flaccus, demonstrating the continued political dominance of the gens Lucretia. Later, presumably after his assassination, Caligula's name was erased from the stone, although not from a more fragmentary near duplicate, which allows secure reconstruction here.[34] M. Vesonius Marcellus, the second duovir of the year, is the only distinguished member of his family known,[35] suggesting that Lucretius Epidius Flaccus intended to dominate this year with little interference from his colleague—or competition from a stronger colleague. As Lu-

---

33. So Castrén 204. For the tomb inscription of Piricatius, see *NSc* (1900) 344: *L(ucius) Piricatius L(uci) f(ilius) / Men(enia tribu) d(uo) v(ir) i(ure) d(icundo) iter(um) sibi et suis.* On Piricatius, see Mouritsen, *Elections* 102.

34. *CIL* X.902. The significant lines follow: *[Marci L]ucre[ti] Epidi Flac[ci praef(ecti) i(ure) d(icundo)] / C(ai) Caesaris / L(uci) Albuci Celsi D(ecimi) Lucreti Valentis / IIvir(orum) v(iis) a(edibus) s(acris) p(ublicisque) p(rocurandis) / Paullo Fabio L(ucio) Vitellio co(n)s(ulibus).*

35. On the Vesonii, see Castrén 238. There is no firm evidence attesting a stand for quinquennial duovir by Vesonius Marcellus, as suggested by Castrén; *CIL* IV.3528 supports him for duovir, there is no office specified in 4012, and 7283 more likely supports Veranius Hypsaeus, a certain candidate for quinquennial.

cretius Decidianus Rufus had aligned himself with Augustus, Lucretius
Epidius Flaccus was aligning himself with the rising emperor, Caligula.

39:
> [Phroni]mus Messi Fausti
> [Pl]acidus Vei Frontonis
> A(ulus) Arellius Graecus
> min(istri) Aug(usti) ex d(ecreto) d(ecurionum) iussu
> [[C. Caesaris]] M(arci) Vesoni Marcelli
> II v(irorum) i(ure) d(icundo)
> M(arci) Lucreti Epidi Flacci
> praefecti
> L(uci) Albuci D(ecimi) Lucreti II vir(orum) v(iis) a(edibus) s(acris)
> p(ublicisque) p(rocurandis)
> Paullo Fabio L(ucio) Vitellio
> co(n)s(ulibus).[36]

[Phronimus (slave) of Messius Faustus, Placidus (slave) of Veius
Fronto, and Aulus Arellius Graecus (are named) attendants of Augustus in accordance with a decree of the decurions and by order of
Gaius Caesar and Marcus Vesonius Marcellus, duovirs *iure dicundo,*
of Marcus Lucretius Epidius Flaccus, prefect, and of Lucius Albucius
and Decimus Lucretius, duovirs *viis aedibus sacris publicisque procurandis,* Paullus Fabius and Lucius Vitellius (being) consuls (at Rome).]

Also, a second Lucretius, D. Lucretius Valens, in this year made his de-
but in elected politics, serving as aedile with L. Albucius, actually L. Albucius Celsus, the first known member of a family that was to continue
its prominence in Neronian and Flavian times.[37] Of this Lucretius Valens,
a great deal has recently been learned from his family tomb, found on
their estate, now buried under modern Scafati.[38] His name was lacking
from a fallen, fragmentary inscription, but it must refer to him;[39] although he himself was not buried here, since he will have been given a

---

36. *CIL* X.901.

37. For the full names of D. Lucretius Valens and L. Albucius Celsus, see *CIL*
X.902 (quoted above, in n. 34). On the Albucii, see Castrén 132.

38. For details of the location, see De' Spagnolis Conticello 147.

39. So also De' Spagnolis Conticello 164: "Essa non può pertanto che referirsi
a quel D. Lucretius Valens, edile nel 33–34. . . ."

prominent, although still unrecovered, tomb elsewhere at public expense, the family nevertheless wanted his accomplishments recorded where his descendants were to lie.

40:

> [D(ecimo) Lucretio D(ecimi) f(ilio) Men(enia tribu) Valenti ---]
>
> [equo pub]lico honorato a Ti(berio) Claudio Caesare Aug[usto]
>
> ann(is) VIII in ordinem decurionum gra[ti]s adlecto m[---].
>
> Hic cum patre gladiatorum XXXV paria c[um ---]
>
> legitima venatione dedit huic ordo de[curion]um [ob liberalitatem funera et]
>
> locum sepulturae et [dari] laudarique publice eum et statuam equestrem poni pecunia public(a).
>
> Censuit item augustales [paga]ni statuas pedestres et ministri eorum et nates et scabiliar(i)
>
> et fore⟨n⟩ses clupeos censuerunt. Vi[xit a]nnis [---]⁴⁰

[To Decimus Lucretius Valens, son of Decimus, tribe Menenia, [---] honored by Tiberius Claudius Caesar Augustus with equestrian rank, named gratis to the *ordo decurionum* at age eight [---]. This man, with his father, gave thirty-five pairs of gladiators with [---] a real hunt. To this man, on account of his generosity, the *ordo decurionum* decreed that his funeral and place of burial be given, that he be praised publicly, and that an equestrian statue of him (be erected, all) with public money. Likewise, the *augustales* of his suburb decreed standing statues, and their attendants and the cushion sellers, pantomime players, and *forenses* decreed shields. He lived [---] years.]⁴¹

D. Lucretius Valens was obviously an up-and-coming man when elected aedile, and we shall meet him repeatedly in the following chapters as his career develops. He had already been named to the *ordo decuri-*

---

40. Text of De' Spagnolis Conticello 161.

41. The shields referred to here are presumably *imagines clupeatae,* portraits embossed on shields, as in the funerary inscription of M. Obellius Firmus (see chap. 5). I vary in translation slightly from De' Spagnolis Conticello (164), who thinks the *nates* and *scabilliarii* "associazioni di venditori"; to her the *foreses* represent the "corporazioni dei *forenses*" without further specification. On the problem of the *forenses,* see Castrén 80–81 and Mouritsen, *Elections* 67–68; both Castrén and Mouritsen think them dwellers around the forum.

onum at age eight, doubtless in respect for his father, and the games that he and his father produced probably date to this, his aedilician, year. The award of equestrian rank by Tiberius is unparalleled to our knowledge, and Valens will have been one of the most important Pompeians of his generation. It is sad to know that his two children, a daughter and a homonymous son, also buried in the family tomb, died young.[42] He, however, turned to the expedient of adoption, and his adopted son soon underscored his prominence: D. Lucretius Satrius Valens, named *flamen Neronis Caesaris Augusti filii perpetuus*, was a central figure of the Neronian age at Pompeii, and he is a main character of my chapter 4. As we shall see, M. Lucretius Epidius Flaccus, *praefectus iure dicundo* in A.D. 33–34, was soon to disappear from the electoral whirl, but it is certainly worth observing that at this point the Lucretii were dominant enough to supply two lines, both the Marci and the Decimii, to the political scene.

Named as new *ministri Augusti* this year were a slave of Stlaborius Veius Fronto, quinquennial duovir of A.D. 25–26, and a slave of a Messius and an Arellius, neither of which was an important family at Pompeii.[43]

---

42. Contra De' Spagnolis Conticello (164), who thinks the unnamed female (burial 1) and first D. Lucretius Valens (burial 2) were children of the son of Lucretius Satrius Valens. The burials here appear to proceed in order, from right to left, along the north wall of the enclosure. First come two unnumbered and unidentified burials of the Augustan Age; then come, their urns sharing a pit, a daughter of the Lucretius Valens under discussion here and his homonymous son *(D(ecimo) Lucretio / D(ecimi) f(ilio) Men(enia tribu) Valenti)*, whose death forced the adoption of Lucretius Satrius Valens. Next (burial 3) follows a previously unknown son of Lucretius Satrius Valens, Iustus, named after his mother, Iusta *(D(ecimo) Lucretio D(ecimi) f(ilio) / Men(enia tribu) Iusto / in ordinem decurion(um) / adlecto gratis / vixit annis XIII)*. Finally (burial 4) comes the grandson of Lucretius Satrius Valens and homonymous son of his son Lucretius Valens, the Flavian candidate for aedile *(D(ecimo) Lucretio / D(ecimi f(ilio) Valenti / vixit an(nis) II)*. Apart from these children, along the east wall of the enclosure was the burial of Lucretius Satrius Valens *(D(ecimo) Lucretio D(ecimi) f(ilio) Men(enia tribu) / Satrio Valenti)*. Further on these confusing, homonymous men, see chap. 4.

43. Castrén 191 and 137, respectively.

A.D. 40–41

Finally, there is one fragmentary inscription from the last, portentous year of Caligula's reign, when as emperor he was again named duovir, this time quinquennial duovir, at Pompeii.

41:

[---]
[---]s Adeptus
[---]sius Felicio
[[C(aio) Caesare]] M(arco) Epidio Flacco
quinq(uennalibus) M(arco) Holconio Macro
praef(ecto) i(ure) d(icundo) L(ucio) Licinio C(aio) Adio
[II] vir(is) v(iis) a(edibus) s(acris) p(ublicisque) proc(urandis).[44]

[[---] Adeptus and [---] Felicio, Gaius Caesar and Marcus Epidius Flaccus (being) quinquennials, Marcus Holconius Macer (being) prefect *iure dicundo,* and Lucius Licinius and Gaius Adius (being) duovirs *viis aedibus sacris publicisque procurandis.*]

This year M. Lucretius Epidius Flaccus served in office with Caligula rather than replacing him; M. Holconius Macer now served as prefect. Both of these men came from families now very familiar, and Lucretius Epidius Flaccus, once Caligula's prefect and now officially his colleague, was preeminent in these years. In contrast, the aediles of the year, a Licinius and an Adius, are of far lower standing. Later, apparently in the early sixties A.C., both a Licinus Faustinus and a Licinius Romanus stood for aedile, but the exact dates of those candidacies are unknown.[45] Only a G. Hadius Ventrio, *eques natu Romanus inter beta(s) et brassica(s),* apparently also represents the gens Adia at Pompeii.[46] A native-born Roman knight, he seems to have ironically borne his poverty "among the beets and cabbages."

---

44. *CIL* X.904.
45. See chap. 5.
46. *CIL* IV.4533. J. Day ("Agriculture in the Life of Pompeii," *YCS* 3 [1932] 189) considered this an invented name.

Early Julio-Claudians

Although this is the most poorly attested era in Pompeii's imperial history, we can nevertheless draw some valuable conclusions from these inscriptions. Most obvious are the three lines of continuity from Augustan days. First, descendants of families that were active in Augustan times, both as members of the powerful core and as contributors of lesser status, played important roles throughout Tiberian and Caligulan days. Lucretii and Holconii in particular have dominated this survey of the stones, and the Allei can be shown to have been active also under Augustus. Second, men who were not capable of sustained success—an Aelius, a Vergilius, and a Fulvinus, among others—appeared for the first and only time. Third, in these years, an up-and-coming family, the Albucii, made the first of what were to be several appearances as city magistrates.

Likewise, the slaves and freedmen named *ministri Augusti* came from three parallel kinds of lines. There were the well-established Melissaei, Veii, and Holconii. The Caesii, Piricatii, and Arellii appeared only now. And one family, the Helvia, was soon to climb to prominence. Taken together, both magistrates and *ministri Augusti* demonstrate continuity of power and of steady striving for power, albeit more often without than with success.

But let us return to the Albucii, who are interesting for yet another reason. In the person of L. Albucius Celsus, they appeared now in the record without any traceable antecedents. Yet they lived in the famous Casa delle Nozze d' Argento, a huge house containing the largest atrium yet known at the site, one of Pompeii's major properties (fig. 2).[47] Decorated in the Second Pompeian style, this house architecturally belongs to far earlier days,[48] and it is impossible that the Albucii could have escaped the earlier record had they been living in it all along. They must, in fact, have now moved to town and acquired the house. With wealth sufficient for such an acquisition behind them, we should expect the family to play a quite visible role in the eras to come, and indeed they will.

The family that disappeared—at least fell noticeably—when the Albucii took possession of the Casa delle Nozze d'Argento would be of

---

47. For identification of the house and its inhabitants, see Della Corte 150a–e.

48. Richardson (*Architectural* 155–59) classifies this as a house of the early Roman colony.

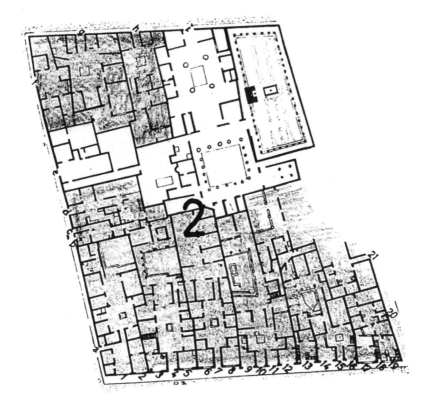

Fig. 2. Block V.2 and the house of L. Albucius Celsus

equal interest to us. Unfortunately, we cannot identify that family. In fact, the Albucii are the very first family to whom we can link a specific urban property, although as we have seen, the estate of the Decimi Lucretii, yet to be excavated, has now been found buried under modern Scafati. As our studies continue into later eras, properties will become increasingly valuable sources of information about Pompeii's leading men and their families. Here, lack of identifiable property for other families merely raises questions. Did they all die out and lose their property, like whoever originally owned the Casa delle Nozze d' Argento? Or were they, like the Decimi Lucretii, based on estates or in villas rather than in the city proper? In this light it certainly is worth observing that we have now seen the ends of the lines of four of the Augustan *tribuni militum a populo;* only the Holconii and Marci Lucretii survived through Caligulan times.

However, there is a related dynamic of perhaps even more interest. In M. Alleius Luccius Libella, quinquennial of A.D. 25–26, we first met a man who had served as *praefectus iure dicundo,* standing in for an emperor who had been named duovir. The exact date of Alleius' prefecture is unknown, but from his tombstone, on which his offices are listed chronologically, it is clear that it preceded his quinquennial year, and it probably will have been early in the reign of Tiberius, when the emperor was honored, both to draw his attention to Pompeii and to cement the city's connections with this first heir of Augustus. Castrén suggested that the year was in fact A.D. 20–21 and that with an eye on the future, the city so honored Drusus, who had recently become Tiberius' heir, rather than Tiberius himself.[49] Perhaps this is so, since, as we saw earlier in this chapter, Alleius' naming as prefect was soon followed by his service for the next heir, Caius Caesar, or Caligula. Most important to us, however, is the distinction that Alleius' prefecture added to the already established prominence of the gens Alleia, which was to remain among Pompeii's most powerful families until the very end.

The dangers involved in this very same process, however, can perhaps also be demonstrated in these years. In A.D. 33–34 Caligula was named duovir and was replaced in office by the prefect M. Lucretius Epidius Flaccus. The descendant of an old Pompeian family, and adopted by that of an Augustan *tribunus militum a populo,* Lucretius was, like Alleius, prominent even without this additional honor. Then, in A.D. 40–41, the honor was again extended to Caligula, and in his stead M. Holconius Macer, another man of highly distinguished family, functioned. His colleague was Lucretius Epidius Flaccus. However, Caligula was assassinated in 41, and the stain of his debacle as emperor seems to have reached as far as Pompeii, for both the Holconii and the Marci Lucretii now temporarily disappear from the lists of elected magistrates. The tradition of firm alignment with the ruling emperor, a strategy Pompeians apparently learned from Augustan successes, in this instance seems to have backfired. Both the Holconii and Marci Lucretii reappeared on the political scene only in Flavian times.

It would be wrong, however, to make too much of this development. While it appears that the Holconii and the Marci Lucretii lost popularity, presumably for identifying the city too strongly with Caligula, there is no evidence for what Castrén has called the "Claudian crisis," argu-

---

49. Castrén 104.

ing that the naming of Caligula as duovir indicated local crisis and that Pompeii lost its right of local government as a consequence of that crisis.[50] As we have seen, both Tiberius (perhaps Drusus) and Caligula had been named Pompeian magistrates earlier as a mark of honor, not as resolvers of local crisis. And as we shall see, local government continued as normal under Claudius.

The nature of the evidence misled Castrén.[51] So far, like him, I have been focusing on inscriptions carved into stone, which give out at approximately this point. For the remainder of this study, however, the more ephemeral writing of graffiti, electoral programmata, and the wax tablets of Caecilius Iucundus will serve as my primary sources, and with those sources we can trace even more varied and intriguing patterns of evidence.

---

50. Castrén 105–7.
51. So also Mouritsen, *Elections* 98.

Early Julio-Claudians

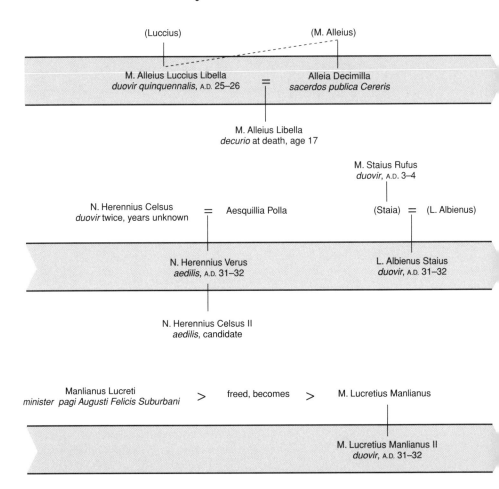

(Luccius)   (M. Alleius)

M. Alleius Luccius Libella
duovir quinquennalis, A.D. 25–26   =   Alleia Decimilla
sacerdos publica Cereris

M. Alleius Libella
decurio at death, age 17

M. Staius Rufus
duovir, A.D. 3–4

N. Herennius Celsus
duovir twice, years unknown   =   Aesquillia Polla   (Staia)   =   (L. Albienus)

N. Herennius Verus
aedilis, A.D. 31–32

L. Albienus Staius
duovir, A.D. 31–32

N. Herennius Celsus II
aedilis, candidate

Manlianus Lucreti
minister pagi Augusti Felicis Suburbani   >   freed, becomes   >   M. Lucretius Manlianus

M. Lucretius Manlianus II
duovir, A.D. 31–32

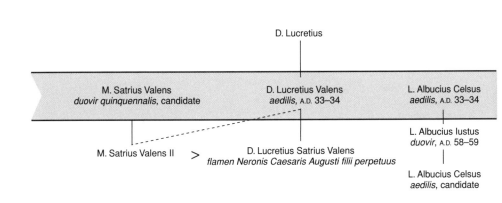

D. Lucretius

M. Satrius Valens
duovir quinquennalis, candidate

D. Lucretius Valens
aedilis, A.D. 33–34

L. Albucius Celsus
aedilis, A.D. 33–34

M. Satrius Valens II   >   D. Lucretius Satrius Valens
flamen Neronis Caesaris Augusti filii perpetuus

L. Albucius Iustus
duovir, A.D. 58–59

L. Albucius Celsus
aedilis, candidate

Chapter 3

Middle to Late
Julio-Claudians—Claudians

One of the best-known political posters from ancient Pompeii supported M. Pupius Rufus, "worthy of the state" [*dignum r(ei) p(ublicae)*],
for election as duovir.

42:
  M(arcum) Pupium Rufum II vir(um) i(ure) d(icundo) dignum r(ei)
      [p(ublicae)] o(ro) v(os) f(aciatis).
              Mustius fullo facit
          et dealbat scr(ibit) unicus
      s[in]e reliq(uis) sodalib(us) non(is).[1]

[I ask that you elect Marcus Pupius Rufus, a man worthy of the state,
duovir *iure dicundo*. Mustius the fuller is making (this notice), white-
washing (the space), and lettering it alone without any other helpers.]

The fuller Mustius painted this notice on the facade of the house belonging to him and his wife, Ovia at VI.15.3. Because he first white-
washed a section of the wall and then lettered the poster without assis-
tance, the notice has been used to illustrate by contrast the modus
operandi of Pompeii's professional letterers, or *scriptores,* who regularly worked with a team of skilled assistants.[2]

The candidate M. Pupius Rufus and his political life, however, have
merited little attention, and few details of his career are now recover-
able.[3] Yet starting from this poster, a general picture of the years of his

---

1. *CIL* IV.3529.
2. On Mustius the fuller and his wife, Ovia, see Della Corte 85–86. On the
Mustii, see Castrén 194; on the Ovii, 296. On letterers and their modus operandi,
see Franklin, "*Scriptores*."
3. On the Pupii, see Castrén 211.

activity, the forties and early fifties A.C., can be reconstructed.[4] These
years and many of the men who were active in them are meagerly attested and little studied, and as we have already seen in the preceding
chapter, a perceived paucity of evidence even led Castrén to postulate a
"Claudian crisis" during which the government was handed over to the
revived Nucerian league of pre-Roman days.[5] To the contrary, surprising details of a flourishing local scene can be assembled by tracing the
evidence from Pupius Rufus and his house, although only for Rufus can
we identify a property and much more than bare prosopographical
bones. Yet to these actual attestations can be added several men of high
accomplishments in later times who must have begun their careers in
this era. Our evidence thus falls into two categories: attesting first men
of moderate means who were able only briefly to establish themselves
in the political fray, and then those of considerable success whose families were active until the very end.

I

M. Pupius Rufus

The large house of M. Pupius Rufus has been securely identified at
VI.15.4,5,24,25 (fig. 3), to the immediate south of the shop and house of
Mustius, the fuller who lettered inscription 42.[6] There a graffito naming
the owner was recovered in the tablinum.

43:

M Pupius Ruphus[7]

Although his cognomen is here differently spelled, the variation is
obvious, and the graffito can name no one but the candidate M. Pupius
Rufus.[8]

---

4. In his arrangement of the evidence, Mouritsen (*Elections* 90–112) created
three large periods, 80–30 B.C., 30 B.C.–A.D. 40, and A.D. 50–79. He thus lost ten
years of the city's history and assigned most of the men of this chapter to the period A.D. 50–79. In fact, most began their careers in his lost decade or in the early
fifties A.C.

5. Castrén 105–7. The many problems with the thesis are decisively set forth
at Mouritsen, *Elections* 94–99: "To summarize, Castrén's theory of a period of
crisis without magistrates in the years 40–50 is untenable" (99).

6. See Mau at *CIL* IV.4615, followed by Della Corte (83a–c).

7. *CIL* IV.4615.

8. On the confusions of *f* and *ph* in the graffiti, see Väänänen 57.

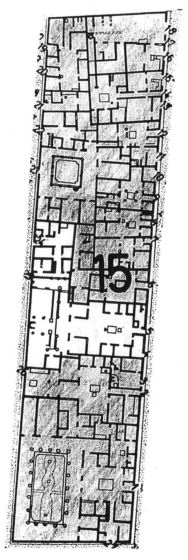

Fig. 3. Block VI.15 and the house of M. Pupius Rufus

Interestingly, references to Rufus do not end at his own walls but appear in his neighbors' houses as well. To the south, in VI.15.2, was another graffito, in which the prenominal initial was either incorrect or simply misread.[9]

44:

N Rufus[10]

On their house facade the owners of this second property, Appuleia and Narcissus[11]—along with Mustius the fuller, who was also their neighbor—posted a programma supporting Pupius for duovir; it and Pupius Rufus' physical proximity as their neighbor make it doubly likely that the graffito recovered inside their house refers to the candidate M. Rufus as well.

45:

Pupium IIvir(um) i(ure) d(icundo) o(rat) v(os) f(aciatis) Appuleia
cum Mustio vicino f[ullone]
et Narcissus vos roga(t)[12]

[Appuleia, along with Mustius the fuller, her neighbor, and Narcissus, asks you that you elect Pupius duovir *iure dicundo.*]

To the north, in VI.15.6, the house of A. Caesius Valens and N. Herennius Nardus, a graffito seems also to record another, more personable appearance of Rufus.[13]

46:

Cornelia Hele[na]
amatur ab Rufo.[14]

[Cornelia Helena is loved by Rufus.]

---

9. N. Rufus would appear to be N. Popidius Rufus (Mau at *CIL* IV.4608), who has no known connection with the property.

10. *CIL* IV.4608.

11. On the house and its inhabitants, see Della Corte 87–88.

12. *CIL* IV.3527.

13. So Mau, hesitatingly, at *CIL* IV.4637, followed by Della Corte (83*d*). On the house and its owners, see Della Corte 78–79.

14. *CIL* IV.4637.

In fact, references to Pupius Rufus and his career cluster around his house in block VI.15. As was clear from their physical appearance when they were found, the programmata supporting him for political office belong to an earlier period than the majority of those recovered,[15] and it is not surprising that these older posters were preserved near the candidate's property, where programmata were originally probably thickly posted, and where reminders of earlier support would have been appreciated.

In toto, seven programmata name M. Pupius Rufus. Four support him for duovir; one, for aedile.[16] In another, mention of no office survived, while the final notice was posted by Rufus himself in support of another man for aedile.

47:

[---] aed(ilem) i(uvenem) p(robum) d(ignum) r(ei) p(ublicae)
o(rat) v(os) f(aciatis) Pupius Rufus facit
idem probat.[17]

[Pupius Rufus asks that you elect, supports, and himself approves [---] an upright young man, worthy of the state, as aedile.]

The name of this candidate was unfortunately not preserved to attest Rufus' enthusiasm, and so his political connections can be traced in only more general fashion. Rufus' floruit, however, is by no means uncertain. He was the first witness to sign one of the wax tablets of Caecilius Iucundus, and with two exceptions the dates of these tablets belong to the years A.D. 52–62.[18] As J. Andreau has demonstrated, names in the tablets are listed generally by rank,[19] and therefore Pupius was the most senior and established man involved in witnessing the tablet he signed. By the time of his signature, he probably had served as duovir, or at least was

15. At CIL IV.3534: titulus antiquior; 3562: in tectorio antiquiore.
16. CIL IV.142, 302, 3527, 3529, 3534, 3537, 3562.
17. CIL IV.3537.
18. Apochae 109. On dates in the tablets, see Andreau, Jucundus 27. Apochae 1 was written sometime after A.D. 15; Apochae 2 in A.D. 27 (Mau at CIL IV, p. 277).
19. Andreau, "Remarques" 244–50 and Jucundus 170–76, but see H. Mouritsen, "A Note on Pompeian Epigraphy and Social Structure," C&M 41 (1990) 131–49, on inconsistencies and the impossibility of using the order of witnesses as absolute ranking of status.

well launched in politics; and he must have begun his career several
years earlier. M. Pupius Rufus was a man of the forties and fifties A.C.

L. Rusticelius Celer

At VI.13.21, on the block contiguous to that in which his own house
stood, one of the four programmata supporting Pupius Rufus for duovir
was recovered.[20]

48:
M(arcum) Pupium IIvir(um) i(ure) d(icundo) o(ro) v(os) f(aciatis).[21]

[I ask that you elect Marcus Pupius duovir *iure dicundo.*]

Painted up with it and belonging to the same period was a second notice, in support of a Rusticelius.[22]

49:
[---] Rusticelium II vir(um).[23]

[[---] Rusticelius as duovir.]

Only one Rusticelius, L. Rusticelius Celer, is known to have been active
in Pompeian politics; not only was he elected duovir as this programma
requests, but he also stood for the office a second time *(iterum)*, as is attested by another notice.

50:
L(ucium) Rusticelium Celerem IIvir(um) i(ure) d(icundo)
iter(um) d(ignum) r(ei) p(ublicae) o(ro) v(os) f(aciatis).[24]

---

20. The owner of this property remains unidentified, pace Della Corte (184),
who can muster only a Philippus, who in fact ran the shop at VI.13.1.
21. *CIL* IV.302.
22. On the Rusticelii, see Castrén 214. At *CIL* IV.301, 302: *eiusdem aetatis
utrumque.*
23. *CIL* IV.301.
24. *CIL* IV.3572.

[I ask that you elect Lucius Rusticelius Celer, a man worthy of the state, duovir *iure dicundo* for a second time.]

Seven programmata name Rusticelius, and of these, five were recovered in blocks VI.13 and VI.15,[25] as were the majority of those supporting Pupius Rufus. It is therefore likely that this is the area of town in which the house of Rusticelius is to be identified and that he and Pupius were in fact neighbors.

Inscription 49 has been dated to the same period as inscription 48, which supports Pupius Rufus, and it has been noted that inscription 50, which records the second stand of Rusticelius for duovir, was painted on plaster that predated the earthquake of A.D. 62.[26] Rusticelius and Pupius are likely to have been roughly coeval, active in the forties and fifties A.C.

L. Terentius Felix

Nearly opposite the main door of the house of Pupius Rufus stood, at VI.16.32–33, the small house and *caupona* of L. Aurunculeius Secundio and a second inhabitant of whom only the initials A.B.L. are known.[27] To the left of the doorway of this house, the two inhabitants posted a programma seeking the support of Pupius for a Terentius.

51:

Terentium
[a]edilem rogamus.
Dignus est. Pupi fac.[28]

[We ask Terentius for aedile. He is worthy. Pupius elect (him).]

---

25. In blocks VI.13 and VI.15: *CIL* IV.301, 329, 3511, 3569, 3572; elsewhere *CIL* IV.3815 (IX.9.e) and Varone, "Tituli" 5 (pp. 100–101) (IX.8.1–2).

26. Mau at *CIL* IV.3572: "in tectorii rudis parte antiquiore, quam anno 63 [sc. 62] anteriorem esse credibile est." On the correct date of the earthquake, see G.O. Onorato, "La data del terremoto di Pompei 5 febbraio 62 d.C.," *RendLinc*, 8th ser., 4 (1949) 644–61.

27. Della Corte 95.

28. *CIL* IV.6678.

Of the Terentii, only T. Terentius Felix is known to have played a role in Pompeian politics.[29] Like Pupius Rufus, he once signed as first witness on a tablet of Caecilius Iucundus and so also was well established by the fifties A.C.[30]

Six programmata attest his career—four recommending him for aedile, two lacking specification of an office.[31] Terentius, however, never stood for higher office, for he died young, never having climbed higher than aedile. His tomb inscription, belonging to tomb N2, was found just outside the Porta di Ercolano.[32]

52:

> T(ito) Terentio T(iti) f(ilio) Men(enia tribu)
> Felici maiori aedil(i).
> Huic publice locus
> datus et HS CIƆ CIƆ.
> Fabia Probi f(ilia) Sabina uxor.[33]

[To Titus Terentius Felix the elder, son of Titus, tribe Menenia, aedile. To this man space and two thousand sesterces were publicly given. Fabia Sabina, daughter of Probus, his wife.]

Terentius, who, as is indicated by the descriptive *maior* of line 2, had fathered a homonymous son (of whom nothing more is known) by his wife, Fabia Sabina, was honored both by the public bestowal of land for his tomb and by the expenditure of two thousand sesterces on his funeral. Although a number of Terentii appear in the records of Pompeii, no other ever rose to such distinction.

---

29. On the Terentii at Pompeii, see Della Corte p. 120 n. 1; Castrén 227–28; Castrén, however, mistakenly assigns the political career of Terentius to his son. On Terentius Felix, see Mouritsen, *Elections* 108–9.

30. *Apochae* 80.

31. Recommending T. Terentius Felix for aedile: *CIL* IV.697, 6629, 6678, 7980; for unspecified office: 808, 3370. *CIL* IV.7980, which recommends Terentius for aedile, seems also to recommend a Cn. Alleius; the scale and style of lettering (see *NSc* [1910] 408), however, vary between the lines, and in reality these are the remains of two programmata.

32. On the tomb, see Kockel 115–17.

33. Kockel N2 = *CIL* X.1019.

L. Numisius Rarus

On a column of the peristyle of the house of Pupius Rufus, a graffito naming a P. Numisius Hyla was recorded.

53:
P(ublius) Numisius Hyla[34]

Hyla himself appears to have been a freedman of the otherwise unknown P. Numisius. The Numisia was a small gens at Pompeii, and only one member of the family, L. Numisius Rarus, achieved any prominence.[35] Fourteen programmata recommended Rarus for office—eight specifically for aedile, six without an office specified.[36] Although then not a magistrate, he signed in a position of prominence on a wax tablet of Caecilius Iucundus in A.D. 56,[37] and a few years earlier two of his freedmen, L. Numisius Primus and L. Numisius Optatus, had been named *ministri Fortunae Augustae,* as attested in an as yet undated inscription.[38]

54:
L(ucius) Numisius Primus
L(ucius) Numisius Optatus
L(ucius) Melissaeus
Plocamus
ministr(i) Fortun(ae) Aug(ustae)
ex d(ecreto) d(ecurionum) iussu
L(ucii) Iuli Pontici P(ublii) Gavi Pastoris
d(uo) v(irorum) i(ure) d(icundo)
Q(uinti) Poppaei C(aii) Vibi aedil(ium)
Q(uinto) Futio P(ublio) Calvisio co(n)s(ulibus).[39]

---

34. *CIL* IV.4625.
35. On the Numisii, see Castrén 197.
36. Recommending L. Numisius Rarus for aedile: *CIL* IV.293, 838, 844*a* (cf. *Add.*), 883, 885, 3648, 3755, and probably 315 (cf. 885); for unspecified office: 287, 308, 511, 874 (cf. *Add.*), 3416.
37. *Apochae* 22; Numisius Rarus signed second, after Numitorius Bassus.
38. The date is insecure since the consulships of Futius and Calvisius remain undated, but see the discussion that follows in text under "C. Vibius Secundus." On Castrén's mistaken dating of this inscription (*CIL* X.827) to A.D. 39–40, see above, chap. 2, n. 1.
39. *CIL* X.827.

[Lucius Numisius Primus, Lucius Numisius Optatus, and Lucius Melissaeus Plocamus (are named) attendants of Fortuna Augusta in accordance with a decree of the decurions and by the order of Lucius Iulius Ponticus and Publius Gavius Pastor, duovirs *iure dicundo,* and of Quintus Poppaeus and Gaius Vibius, aediles, Quintus Futius and Publius Calvisius (being) consuls (at Rome).]

The prominence of Numisius Rarus, too, belongs to the forties and fifties A.C.

C. Vibius Secundus

Unfortunately, the consulships of Futius and Calvisius, which were used to date this inscription, remain themselves undated. However, the Vibius then serving as aedile must be C. Vibius Secundus, later duovir in A.D. 56–57.[40] His earlier career and this inscription therefore must be dated to these Claudian years.[41] Secundus' apparent son, C. Vibius Severus, was to stand for duovir in Flavian times;[42] a T. Vibius Verus had served as duovir in an unknown early year; and several Vibii of undistinguished rank are known. However, no property has ever been assigned the Gaii Vibii, and little more is known of them.

Q. Poppaeus

Of two of the three other men who served as magistrates with Vibius Secundus, again little is known. However, Q. Poppaeus, Vibius' colleague as aedile, is the only Poppaeus known to have served in elected office and was probably Q. Poppaeus Sabinus, owner of the famous Casa del Menandro.[43] As a relative of Poppaea Sabina, wife of Nero, Poppaeus will figure large in chapter 4. Given his imperial connections, further

---

40. *Apochae* 145, 149 and *CIL* X.826, on which see the discussion that follows in text under "C. Memmius Iunianus." On the Vibii at Pompeii, see Castrén 240–41.

41. Mouritsen, *Elections* 108: "a dating of X 827 to c. 50–54 AD seems plausible." An even earlier date seems likely, however, given the need for development of Vibius' career.

42. *CIL* IV.333, 888, 3831, 7291, and perhaps 739.

43. On the Poppaei at Pompeii, see Castrén 209 and below, chapter 4, n. 9.

elected office presumably did not interest him, but his beginnings, too, date to these Claudian years.

L. Iulius Ponticus

L. Iulius Ponticus is the only Lucius Iulius known.[44] Later the city was to be inundated with Gaii and Tiberii Iulii, obviously imperial freedmen and their descendants. In contrast, according to Castrén, L. Iulius Ponticus and an M. Iulius Simplex belong to local homonymous families.[45] We lose sight of Ponticus entirely after this one attestation.

P. Gavius Pastor

With Ponticus' colleague as duovir, P. Gavius Pastor, we meet the first attested member of what was to prove a disastrous line.[46] Pastor served now as duovir, and his son, P. Gavius Proculus, was to stand for aedile and sign a tablet of Caecilius Iucundus in the late fifties and early sixties A.C.[47] It will have been the son of Proculus and grandson of Pastor who was adopted by Cn. Pompeius Grosphus to become Cn. Pompeius Grosphus Gavianus (see stemmata in chapter 5). As we shall see, both father and adopted son were serving as duovirs when the riot erupted in the amphitheater; removed from office, neither they nor any other Publii Gavii again appeared in the public record.

Q. Appuleius Severus

Of his neighbors who posted programmata supporting Pupius Rufus, Appuleia, his neighbor and the wife of Narcissus (see inscription 45),[48] deserves closer study. Appuleia came from a small gens out of which only one member, Q. Appuleius Severus, rose to prominence.[49] Severus

---

44. On the Iulii at Pompeii, see Castrén 178–79.

45. Castrén 178.

46. On the Gavii, see Castrén 170–71.

47. *Apochae* 96. Four posters supported his stand for aedile (*CIL* IV.825, 895, 3564, 6686), three of which were conspicuously old (825: *antiquior,* 3564: *programma antiquior,* 6686: *apparuit delapso tectorio posteriore*).

48. *CIL* IV.3527.

49. On the Appuleii, see Castrén 136. Largely because of his cognomen (on which see I. Kajanto, *The Latin Cognomina* [Helsinki 1965] 68–69, 131), An-

signed sixteen of the wax tablets of Caecilius Iucundus, and of the seven
of these that carry a date, all belong to A.D. 55 or 56.[50] It also must be he
who was elected aedile and stood for duovir, although only his gentilicial attests his political career. One notice was even recovered at VI.15.1,
just two doorways from the programma in support of Pupius Rufus
posted by Appuleia, Narcissus, and Mustius.

55:

$$\text{Appuleium II vir(um) } \overline{\text{o(ro)}} \text{ v(os) f(aciatis)}.^{51}$$

[I ask that you elect Appuleius duovir.]

Only four programmata supporting Appuleius survive—three attesting his stand for duovir, one without an office specified.[52] Of the sixteen wax tablets he securely signed, his name is first in ten cases, second
in five, and third in one; to have earned such status, he had probably already served as duovir by the mid-fifties A.C., when he signed. His name
is preceded only by the names of a Cuspius, a Laelius, Caltilius, a Ti.
Claudius, and by an indistinct nomen;[53] Q. Appuleius Severus was another prominent man of his time, the forties and fifties A.C.

---

dreau, (*Jucundus* 174) was uncertain whether Appuleius Severus was freeborn
("probablement un fils d'affranchi ou même plutôt d'ingénu"), although he was
keenly aware of the precedence given his name throughout the tablets of Caecilius Iucundus. Appuleius was freeborn and an elected magistrate, which explains his inclusion among men "manifestement trés honorés" (Andreau, *Jucundus* 172).

    50. Datable to A.D. 55 or 56: *Apochae* 12, 13, 14, 15, 17, 19, 25; datable to 55,
57, 58, or 60: *Apochae* 43; undatable: *Apochae* 67, 71, 73, 82, 88, 92, 99, 113. The
"A." Appuleius Severus of *Apochae* 49 and 106 (both undatable) is almost certainly Q. Appuleius Severus; the Appuleius of *Apochae* 10 must also be Q. Appuleius Severus. Andreau, (*Jucundus* 17, 161, 172) prefers to separate A. Appuleius Severus from Q. Appuleius Severus, thereby increasing his difficulties
over precedence among witnesses in the tablets of Caecilius Iucundus; he has
two men whose rank he cannot explain (172 n. 12). Instead, there was only one
Appuleius Severus, Q. Appuleius Severus, who was an elected magistrate and
appropriately respected.
    51. *CIL* IV.3526.
    52. For duovir: *CIL* IV.3421, 3506, 3526; for unspecified office: 3417.
    53. By the name of Cuspius Secundus in *Apochae* 12; Laelius Fuscus in 13
and 15; Caltilius Iustus in 19; Ti. Claudius Nedymus in 99; Aemilius Severus and

Q. Coelius Caltilius Iustus

Of the witnesses who signed before Appuleius on the wax tablets, only
two, L. Caltilius Iustus and L. Laelius Fuscus, are known from other
documentation as well. Caltilius Iustus, was in actuality Q. Coelius
Caltilius Iustus, who was duovir in A.D. 52–53.[54] He had apparently
been born L. Caltilius Iustus, son of L. Caltilius Pamphilus, a freedman
and new arrival in Pompeii, who is known only from the inscription of
the tomb of his wife, found in six fragments and apparently belonging
to the large tomb N34 outside the Porta di Ercolano.[55]

56:

L(ucius) Caltilius L(uci) l(ibertus)

Coll(ina tribu)

[P]amphilus

[---]ae uxori

[---]mo.[56]

[Lucius Caltilius Pamphilus, freedman of Lucius, tribe Collina [---] to
his wife [---].]

The large, well-located tomb and prominence of Pamphilus' name indicate considerable success—and appropriate pride—for this freedman,
who thanks to adoption was even able to see his son rise to the *ordo decurionum*. Although the son had been adopted by a Q. Coelius, the
adoption apparently took place after he had reached manhood and established himself, so that like M. Stlaborius Veius Fronto, discussed in
chapter 2, Caltilius Iustus continued to be known as well by his given
name, with which he signed before Appuleius on the tablet in A.D. 56.[57]

---

an unknown Saturninus in 113. In *Apochae* 10 the simple *Appuleius* is preceded
by *L[a]e[l]ius [Fuscus]*; in 49 and 106, signed by "A." Appuleius Severus, Postumius Primus and Vibius Macer, respectively, preceded Appuleius.

54. *Apochae* 138. On the Caltilii at Pompeii, see Castrén 147.

55. Mommsen at *CIL* X.1046: "litteris magnis saeculi Augustei." On the
tomb, see Kockel 162–65.

56. Kockel N34 = *CIL* X.1046.

57. *Apochae* 19. Nothing more is known (pace Della Corte 456–57) of Q.
Coelius, who may have lived at VIII.3.7–9; on the Coelii at Pompeii, see Castrén
155–56.

He was again referred to as Caltilius Iustus in the second reference to him, in tablet 138 (belonging to A.D. 53), where his full name, Q. Coelius Caltilius Iustus, appeared in the formal date that began the document, and to which as sitting magistrate he signed yet a third variation of his name, Coelius Iustus.[58] Caltilius Iustus, Coelius Iustus, and Q. Coelius Caltilius Iustus, one and the same, served as duovir in A.D. 52–53, obviously having begun his career some time earlier. For the second time in the history of Pompeii, we can therefore trace the son of a freedman rising to elected office, again that of duovir. In this case, however, the bloodline is not important, since it was effectively erased when Caltilius Iustus was adopted by Q. Coelius, a man presumably free of the taint of freedman.

L. Laelius Fuscus

The L. Laelius Fuscus whose name twice preceded that of Appuleius in the wax tablets is also known to have played a role in local politics. He was supported by three programmata—one with no office specified, one for aedile, and the last for duovir.[59]

57:

Laelium Fuscum
d(uo) v(irum) i(ure) d(icundo) Fabi(i) rog(ant).[60]

[The Fabii ask Laelius Fuscus as duovir *iure dicundo.*]

His signature on the wax tablets links him to these same years, as does this programma. It was one of a pair painted to either side of the doorway at VIII.5.37, the house of otherwise unknown Fabii.[61] Its mate supported a Iunianus.

---

58. Despite the evidence of *Apochae* 138, Andreau (*Jucundus* 203) prefers to distinguish L. Caltilius Iustus as father and Q. Coelius Caltilius Iustus as his son. As in the case of M. Stlaborius Veius Fronto (see chap. 2), the variations of the name underscore, rather, the adoption of Caltilius at an adult age.

59. For aedile: *CIL* IV.102; for unspecified office: *CIL* IV.7128. On the Laelii, see Castrén 180–81.

60. *CIL* IV.3592.

61. At *CIL* IV.3591: *ad d. n. 37 in tabella ansata;* at 3592: *ad sin. n. 37 in tabella ansata.* On the house and the Fabii, see Della Corte 507.

58:

Iunianum IIvir(um)
d(ignum) r(ei) p(ublicae) Fabi(i) rog(ant).[62]

[The Fabii ask Iunianus, a man worthy of the state, as duovir.]

C. Memmius Iunianus

Only C. Memmius Iunianus carried this cognomen at Pompeii, and he is known to have been aedile in A.D. 56–57, when three new *ministri Fortunae Augustae* were named.[63]

59:

Martialis C(aii) Ol⟨l⟩i Primi
M(anlius) Salarius Crocus
Primigenius C(aii) Ol⟨l⟩i Primi
min(istri) Fortunae Aug(ustae)
iussu
Q(uinti) Postumi Modesti C(aii) Vibi Secundi
d(uo) v(irorum) i(ure) d(icundo)
C(aii) Memmi Iuniani Q(uinti) Brutti Balbi aedil(ium)
(L[ucio] D)uvio P(ublio) Clodio co(n)s(ulibus).[64]

[Martialis (slave) of Gaius Olius Primus, Manlius Salarius Crocus, and Primigenius (slave) of Gaius Olius Primus (are named) attendants of Fortuna Augusta by order of Quintus Postumius Modestus and Gaius Vibius Secundus, duovirs *iure dicundo,* and of Gaius Memmius Iunianus and Quintus Bruttius Balbus, aediles, Lucius Duvius and Publius Clodius (being) consuls (at Rome).]

Memmius Iunianus was just beginning his career when this stone was carved, but the duovirs of the year, Q. Postumius Modestus and C. Vibius Secundus, had obviously started their careers some time ear-

---

62. *CIL* IV.3591.
63. On the Memmii, see Castrén 190–91.
64. *CIL* X.826.

lier, again in the forties A.C. I have already discussed Vibius Secundus; of Postumius Modestus, considerable will be said in our second section.

Q. Bruttius Balbus

Q. Bruttius Balbus, the aedilician colleague of Memmius Iunianus in A.D. 56–57, is known to have stood also for duovir and to have been alive and politically active into the final years of Pompeii's existence.[65] Only four programmata remain from his candidacies,[66] one of which, emphasizing his fiscal reliability (*hic aerarium conservabit* [this one will conserve the treasury]), securely attests his stand for duovir.

60:

IIvir(um)
Bruttium Balbum Genialis.
Hic aerarium conservabit r(ogat).[67]

[Genialis asks Bruttius Balbus as duovir. He will preserve the treasury.]

Bruttius' house, which he seems to have shared with T. Dentatius Panthera, has been identified at IX.2.15–16 (fig. 4), where he posted programmata supporting several of the candidates of Pompeii's final years.[68] Bruttius also signed two of the wax tablets of Caecilius Iucundus.[69] However, with Bruttius and Memmius Iunianus we have reached men that may well be better seen as early risers of the next era, the

---

65. On the Bruttii (or Brittii), see Castrén 143–44.

66. *CIL* IV.935g, 3607, 3702, 3773. Programma 935g seems, as recorded in the *CIL,* to be mingled lines of two programmata (but cf. Mouritsen, *Elections* 127; Mouritsen prefers to alter the offices sought: "The disposition of offices between the candidates . . . is not convincing"); 3773 seems also to attest Balbus' stand for duovir but is highly fragmentary.

67. *CIL* IV.3702. The Genialis of this notice was a worker in the *pistrinum* at IX.3.19–20 and is known also from *CIL* IV.3680 (Della Corte 373).

68. On the house, see Della Corte 428–29. *CIL* IV.935b, 935e, and 935i support A. Vettius Caprasius Felix (A.D. 71); 935h, A. Vettius Caprasius Felix and P. Paquius Proculus (A.D. 71); 935d, Cn. Helvius Sabinus (A.D. 79).

69. *Apochae* 56 and 74. In 56 his name is preceded by the otherwise unknown A. Saenius Aper (on whom see Castrén 215).

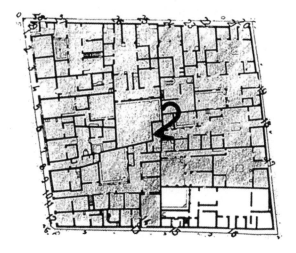

Fig. 4. Block IX.2 and the house of Bruttius Balbus

Neronian, than true actors in the Claudian, although they certainly must have begun to be noticed in Claudian days.

Claudians I

Although all were members of the *ordo decurionum,* the men discussed thus far in this chapter are notable for their lack of renown and for the rapidity of the rise and fall of the families they represent. With the exceptions of Vibius Severus and Gavius Proculus—apparent sons of Secundus and Pastor, respectively—no candidate for or holder of political office is known from any of their gentes. They presumably represent the lower rank of the *ordo,* successful men who were unable to establish more than their own successes. Even Q. Coelius Caltilius Iustus, son of a prominent freedman adopted by a second family, was unable to secure the prominence of his adopted line. Nor was the only one of these men to stand twice for duovir, L. Rusticelius Celer, any more successful for his part.

L. Terentius Felix is known to have fathered a son, and one can assume that several others of the group did so as well. Physically, at least some of their bloodlines must have continued; lack of descendants is not the sole explanation for their families' disappearance. Rather, the main factor in their decline is likely to have been the insubstantial fortunes on which their prominence was based. Most signed as witnesses on tablets of Caecilius Iucundus, an indication of moderate fortune only.[70]

Only two of the houses of these families have been identified. Pupius Rufus lived at VI.15.4,5,24,25; Bruttius Balbus at IX.2.15–16.[71] While Pupius' house was spacious and comfortable, Bruttius' was apparently shared and decidedly modest. Indeed, if there is an odd man out in this group, it is Pupius Rufus himself. His house was large, and he was looked up to; his support was sought for other candidates, and the phrase *idem probat* added to a standard programma (*CIL* IV.3537 - inscription 47) seems to emphasize the significance of his influence. Yet it would be a mistake to overemphasize the limitations of these men, who were, after all, able to rise to membership in the *ordo*. This is simply our first glimpse of this lower level of the *ordo*, and the picture must be balanced with some highly successsful men who also got their start or continued their climb to power in these years. The foremost of these will have been D. Lucretius Valens, whom we met in chapter 2 and who was raised to equestrian rank now by Claudius. Unfortunately, we cannot trace his activities at Pompeii in these years, so our beginnings must lie with Postumius Modestus, who served as duovir with Vibius Secundus in A.D. 56–57, when the freedmen of Numisius Rarus were named *ministri Fortunae Augustae*. Obviously, his career had begun some years earlier.

II

Q. Postumius Modestus

The house of Q. Postumius Modestus and his son, Proculus, has been securely identified at VIII.4.4,2–6,49,50 (fig. 5),[72] although it early and incorrectly acquired the name Casa di Olconio. Standing across the Via

---

70. Andreau, "Remarques" 253–54 and, more succinctly, *Jucundus* 62: "Néanmoins Jucundus semble bien appartenit au niveau inférieur d'une seconde couche sociale de la colonie,—familles aisées, bien logées, qui possèdent suffisamment pour briguer les magistratures municipales, et parfois les briguent, mais qui ne font pas partie de la véritable oligarchie dominante de la cité."

71. According to Della Corte 428, a Coelius Caldus lived at VIII.3.7–9, but the house cannot be securely linked to Coelius Caltilius Iustus.

72. The house was identified at Della Corte 470–71. On the Postumii at Pompeii, see Castrén 210.

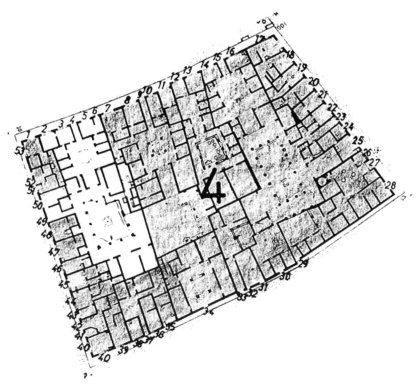

Fig. 5. Block VIII.4 and the house of Q. Postumius Modestus and
Q. Postumius Proculus

dell' Abbondanza from the regularly frequented Terme Stabiane, it will
have been one of the city's most conspicuous properties. Behind an elegant atrium complex, it featured a peristyle heavily piped for fountains
and, at its far (south) end, an exedra paved with expensive *opus sectile,*
an inset basin, and, within the basin, a statue base piped for water (although the statue the base supported was lost)—sure signs of the wealth
and importance of a family easily able to draw off the city's aqueduct
lines. Near the tablinum but several feet above ancient ground level was
the skeleton of a woman; beside her lay her combined jewelry-and-cos-
metics box, which she was carrying with her as she too late tried to
escape the eruption and found herself struggling through the vol-
canic pellets. The box contained, among other items, a gold necklace
with multiple magic pendants and two tesserae deeply inscribed with

numbers—one in the shape of an oversized ring, the second in that of a plucked chicken—apparently tickets to the theater or amphitheater.[73] Perhaps even more interesting, a small collection of gold jewelry and seven pieces of the house's silver collection, which someone seems to have been carrying while fleeing the eruption and to have jettisoned at the house of Epidius Primus at I.8.14,[74] were recovered there in 1941.[75] The larger silver pieces were carefully labeled with their weights, and all carried not only the name Blaesia Prima, apparently the wife of Modestus,[76] but also the initials Q.P.M., which fit only Quintus Postumius Modestus. With the Postumii, therefore, we catch far more vivid glimpses of the last minutes of the city than is usually the case.

Two graffiti found in the house also captured vivid images of its inhabitants. The first discouraged idleness, while the second, a fragmentary elegiac couplet, praised masturbation, if its most recent restoration is indeed correct.

61:

moram si quaeres
sparge muliu(m) *[sic]* et col
lige.[77]

[If you want to waste time, scatter millet and pick it up.]

62:

[Moles] multa mihi curae [pr]esserit artus
has ego mancinas stagna refusa dabo.[78]

[When many a weight, trouble for me, will have pressed my limbs, I will give these hands abundant floods.]

---

73. *Giornale* (1861) 17–18; both the necklace and the tesserae are illustrated in plate 5.

74. Identified at Della Corte 680.

75. Details at *NSc* (1946), 111–12.

76. So Della Corte at 472 and 681–82.

77. *CIL* IV.2069. On *mulium* for *milium* (*u* for *i*) in Pompeian inscriptions, see Väänänen 25–26.

78. Varone, *Erotica* 92 = *CIL* IV.2066. On the history of study and restorations

Finally, there was reference to some rather unappetizing groceries laid in on 15 July of an unspecified year.

63:

IIX id(us) iulias axungia p(ondera) CC
aliu(m) manuplos *[sic]* CCL.[79]

[On the eighth day before the ides of July: animal fat, two hundred weights; garlic, two hundred fifty handfuls.]

Just up the street from the house of the Postumii, a notice posted by his neighbors supported Modestus for quinquennial, and elsewhere along this side of the block, both father and son posted a notice in support of Epidius Sabinus.

64:

Q(uintum) Postumium
Modestum quinqu(ennalem)
vicini [---].[80]

[His neighbors [---] Quintus Postumius Modestus for quinquennial.]

65:

[E]pidium Sabinum
IIvir(um) [P]o[st]umi faciunt.[81]

[The Postumii are electing Epidius Sabinus duovir.]

These notices remain from later times, when Modestus stood for quinquennial and Proculus himself had grown to manhood and could participate in his father's recommendation; indeed, Epidus Sabinus, whom

---

of this difficult graffito, see Varone, *Erotica* 92 n. 149. *Mancina*, "hand," is unparalleled.

79. *CIL* IV.2070. On *manuplos* for *maniplos* ("u" for "i"), see Väännen 26.
80. *CIL* IV.778.
81. *CIL* IV.738; restored by Zangemeister at the *CIL* entry.

they supported, was a candidate of Flavian days, so Modestus clearly lived into that era, when he stood for quinquennial duovir.[82] Of his earlier struggle for aedile in these Claudian days, one sole notice remained outside the rear door to the house of P. Vedius Siricus, to whom we shall turn shortly.

66:

[---] Siricum [---]
II (virum).
[Post]umium Modestum aed(ilem)
Sirice fac facias.[83]

[[---] Siricum [---] for duovir. Siricus, see to it that you elect Postumius Modestus aedile.]

Long-lived and prosperous, Modestus must have proved a local favorite; he at least is the first of our notables to have merited the salute that, as we shall see, was frequent for Pompeii's most popular magistrates.

67:

Q(uinto) Postumio Modesto fil(i)c(iter) *[sic].*[84]

[Happily to Quintus Postumius Modestus.]

To achieve such prominence, Modestus, like our earlier men of less spectacular achievements, had begun his climb to power in Claudian days.

---

82. Postumius Modestus probably stood for quinquennial in A.D. 75 (see Franklin, *Electoral* 67, where, however, the large number of notices attesting his candidacy, which probably make it one of Pompeii's last, go unmentioned). Supporting Modestus for quinquennial were *CIL* IV.195, 279, 736, 756, 778, 786, 1156, 1160, 3679, 7244, 7466, 7486, 7502, 7580, 7598, 7609, 7629, 7705, 7732, 7741, 7970, and perhaps 3017.

83. *CIL* IV.805.

84. *CIL* IV.10167. On *filiciter* for *feliciter* (*i* for *e*), see Väänänen 20.

P. Vedius Siricus

As we saw in inscription 66, Postumius Modestus sought the support of
P. Vedius Siricus when he stood for aedile. Vedius Siricus himself must
have begun his career at about the same time, although he seems to be
addressed as a junior in the notice soliciting his support and may in fact
have been a few years younger. Siricus rose to duovir in A.D. 60, and,
like Modestus, he later stood for quinquennial duovir.[85] Indeed, we will
spot Vedius Siricus, his son Nummianus, and their retainers throughout
the following chapters.

On the basis of a breadstamp naming Siricus and a painted salute to
Nummianus, the house of Vedius Siricus has been securely identified at
VII.1.25,46,47 (fig. 6).[86]

68:

Nummiano
feliciter.[87]

[Happily to Nummianus.]

Interestingly, on the north wall in the room at the southwest corner of
its peristyle, an admittedly low-grade painting showing a magistrate
rendering judgment between two litigants seemed to capture Siricus at
work—one of the few representations of daily life in the corpus of Pompeian wall painting.[88] The house stood north of the Terme Stabiane, and
its rear door, where Postumius' request for support was recovered,
opened just across the Via dell' Abbondanza and halfway up the block

---

85. Siricus is attested as duovir in *Apochae* 144; *CIL* IV.214, 596, 824, 7134b,
7138, 7332, and 7937 support him for quinquennial duovir. On the Vedii, see Castrén 234–35.

86. Della Corte, pp. 9–11. The breadstamp is *CIL* X.8058.81.

87. *CIL* IV.917.

88. So E. Brizio at *Giornale* (1868), 37–38. To Schefold (166) this was perhaps
a painting of Paris and Helen ("Paris mit Begleiter vor Helena?"). For such personalized paintings, compare the three panels depicting a wreck of a cart in the
northernmost cubiculum on the east side of the atrium of the Casa del Marinaio
(J.L. Franklin, Jr., *Pompeii: The "Casa del Marinaio" and Its History*, MonSAP 3
[Rome 1990] 25–26).

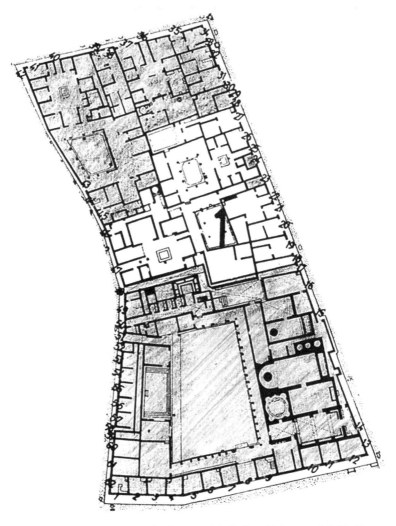

Fig. 6. Block VII.1 and the house of P. Vedius Siricus and P. Vedius
Nummianus

from Postumius' own house. Directly across from the front entrance of the house of the Vedii on the Via Stabiana was another programma confirming their ownership.

69:

[---]
[---]
rog(ant) Siricus et Nummi[anus] .[89]

[Siricus and Nummianus ask [---].]

Unfortunately, the name of the candidate they supported is lacking from the poster, so we cannot trace their political enthusiasms further. The involvement of Siricus in the early campaign of Modestus, however, is certain, and on that basis we can date the early rise of Siricus also to late Claudian days.

A. Trebius Valens I

Although we have no direct evidence connecting him to these Claudian days, the elder A. Trebius Valens,[90] who rose to stand later for quinquennial with Cn. Audius Bassus, must also have begun his career about now.

70:

A(ulum) Trebium Valentem
et Cn(aeum) Audium Bassum
d(uo) v(iros) i(ure) d(icundo) quinq(uennales) o(ro) v(os) f(aciatis).[91]

[I ask that you elect Aulus Trebius Valens and Cnaeus Audius Bassus quinquennial duovirs *iure dicundo*.]

Only this one notice attests Trebius' stand for quinquennial, while one additional poster attests that of Audius,[92] suggesting that their cam-

89. *CIL* IV.916.
90. On the Trebii at Pompeii, see Castrén 230–31.
91. *CIL* IV.7488.
92. *CIL* IV.7943.

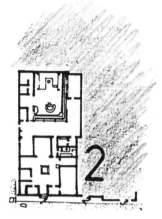

Fig. 7. Block III.2.1 and the house of the AA. Trebii Valentes

paign was waged some time before Pompeii's destruction, probably in the sixties A.C. To have reached such prominence then, Trebius and Bassus both will have begun their careers in Claudian days.

The house of Trebius Valens was recovered across town from the houses of Postumius and Vedius, at III.2.1 (fig. 7).[93] Although elegant, it is decidedly more modest, and it seems to reflect the personality of Trebius' homonymous son rather than that of the quinquennial candidate. Its frequently passed facade attracted many campaign posters in Flavian times, and since no poster painted there mentioned both Trebii (as we saw in the cases of the Postumii and Vedii), it is likely that the elder Trebius was by then deceased and consequently spared the horrors of Pompeii's last days. All, therefore, points to a floruit of Claudian and Neronian days for Trebius Valens the elder.

L. Veranius Hypsaeus, Cn. Audius Bassus, C. Cuspius Pansa

To Postumius, Vedius, and Trebius, we must add four of Pompeii's most successful men, who also began their careers in Claudian times, but whose houses remain unidentified: L. Veranius Hypsaeus, Cn. Audius Bassus, the eldest C. Cuspius Pansa, and Cn. Alleius Nigidius Maius. Like Trebius Valens, the first two of these men were to rise to stand for quinquennial duovir probably in the sixties A.C., since programmata supporting each for that office were very few and some were noticeably

---

93. Identified at Della Corte 739*a–p*.

old *(antiquiora.)*[94] In addition, we know that Veranius Hypsaeus was duovir, probably for the second time, in A.D. 58–59;[95] more posters remain from his stand for quinquennial than from that of Trebius or that of Audius, and he appears to have been the youngest—at least the last to stand for quinquennial—of the three. As we saw, Trebius seems to have been deceased by Flavian times, when his homonymous son was active, but of Audius, nothing more is known. To achieve such success in the sixties, these men must have begun their careers by the mid-forties to mid-fifties A.C., although only two notices supporting Audius Bassus for aedile remain to attest any of their earlier activities.[96] Of the highly distinguished Cuspius Pansa, who will reappear in A.D. 62 as *praefectus iure dicundo ex decreto decurionum lege Petronia* after having served as duovir on four earlier occasions, little need now be said, save that he obviously had served Pompeii through Claudian times.[97] Of Alleius Nigidius Maius, considerably more is known.

Cn. Alleius Nigidius Maius

A very distinguished man, Cn. Alleius Nigidius Maius vied with Cuspius Pansa as the most important Pompeian of his day.[98] He had been born a Nigidius, a gens about which little is known, and adopted an Alleius, a powerful Campanian family, earlier members of which we met in chapter 2.[99]

---

94. Supporting Veranius Hypsaeus: *CIL* IV.170, 187a, 191, 200, 270, 3670 (*antiquior*), 7160, 7193, and probably 193; Trebius Valens: *CIL* IV.7488 (*antiquior*), 7633; Audius Bassus: *CIL* IV.7488 (*antiquior*), 7943. On the Veranii, see Castrén 236–37; on the Trebii, 230–31; on the Audii, 140.

95. Dating Hypsaeus' duovirate: *Apochae* 142, 147, 150.

96. *CIL* IV.7613: *Audium Bassum aed(ilem) o(ro) v(os) f(aciatis); CIL* IV.7808: *Cn(aeum) Audium / aed(ilem) clientes rogant.*

97. So also Mouritsen, *Elections* 101.

98. For a detailed study of his career, see Franklin, "Maius." For the interesting but epigraphically unsubstantiated suggestion that the statues of a male (Ruesch 997 = *MusNazNap* 6044) and female (Ruesch 998 = *MusNazNap* 6041) found in the Macellum represent its donors, Maius and his daughter, the public priestess of Venus and Ceres, see S. Adamo Muscettola, "I Nigidi Mai di Pompei: Far politica tra l'età neroniana e l'età flavia," *RivIstArch,* 3d ser., 14–15 (1991–92) 193–218; however, the simple fact that Maius would have been portrayed as younger than his daughter would seem to invalidate the argument.

99. On the Nigidii, see Castrén 195; on the Alleii, 133. To Andreau ("Remar-

Only two direct relatives of Maius are known. First, his adoptive mother, Pomponia Decharcis, was buried outside the Porta di Nocera in the tomb of the famous Eumachia, to whom the gens Alleia, which had gained control of the property, was somehow related.[100]

71:

Pomponia Dech
arcis Allei Nobilis
Allei Mai mater.[101]

[Pomponia Decharcis (wife) of Alleius Nobilis, mother of Alleius Maius.]

Second, Alleia, *sacerdos Veneris et Cereris* and daughter of Maius, is also attested, again from an inscription probably indicating that her tomb too was built at public expense.[102]

72:

[---]
[A]llei[a Ma]i f(ilia)
[s]acerd(os) V[eneri]s
et Cerer[is si]bi
ex dec(urionum) decr(eto) pe[cunia publica?].[103]

---

ques" 224), Alleius Nobilis, adoptive father of Maius, represented a servile branch of the family.

100. So also Andreau, "Remarques" 221. The gens Alleia continued to use the tomb; Eros the freedman of Maius was also buried there: *Cn(aeo) Alleo Mai lib(erto) Eroti augustali / gratis creato cui / augustales et pagani / in funeris honor(ibus) / HS singula milia / decreverunt vixit / annis XXII* (D'Ambrosio and De Caro 11OS.10).

101. D'Ambrosio and De Caro 11OS.13.

102. The inscription was found in four fragments at VIII.2.21, a part of the Sarno bath complex, but seems to have escaped the notice of A.O. Koloski-Ostrow (*The Sarno Bath Complex,* Monografie della Soprintendenza Archeologica di Pompei, 4 [Rome 1990]. It is uncertain how the stone came to be here; it was found with several other broken inscriptions in rubble fallen from upper stories to lower.

103. *NSc* (1890) 333.

[[---] Alleia, daughter of Maius, priestess of Venus and Ceres, for herself in accordance with a decree of the decurions with public money.]

Of Maius himself, the first secure record is one of the wax tablets of Caecilius Iucundus, which dates his quinquennial duovirate to A.D. 55–56.[104] Previous to this, in Claudian or even earlier times, he will have served as aedile and duovir, but the exact dates he held those offices are unknown.[105] During his quinquennial year, he presented gladiatorial games, of which two announcements were recovered.

73:

Cn(aei) Allei Nigidii

Mai quinq(uennalis) sine impensa publica glad(iatorum) par(ia)
XX et eorum supp(ositicii) pugn(abunt) Pompeis.[106]

[Twenty pairs of gladiators of Gnaeus Alleius Nigidius Maius, quinquennial, and their replacements will fight at Pompeii without public expense.]

74:

(C)n(aei) Allei Nigidii

Mai quinq(uennalis) par(ia) XXX et eor(um) supp(ositicii)
pugn(abunt) Pompeis VIII, VII, VI k(alendas) dec(embres).
Ellios *[sic]* [et]
ven(atio) erit[107]

[Thirty pairs of gladiators of Gnaeus Alleius Nigidius Maius, quinquennial, and their replacements will fight at Pompeii the eighth, seventh, and sixth days before the calends of December. There will be Ellius and a hunt.]

---

104. *Apochae* 148.

105. Seemingly attesting Maius' candidacy for aedile is *CIL* IV.512, although it includes only the cognomen *Maius;* attesting his candidacy for duovir is the fragmentary *CIL* IV.499: [. . .]*ium Maium d(uo) v(irum) i(ure) d(icundo) / Aurelius civem bonum fac.*

106. Sabbatini Tumolesi N. 9 = *CIL* IV.7991.

107. Sabbatini Tumolesi N. 10 = *CIL* IV.1179.

Although differing in number of gladiators, the notices seem to refer to the same performances on 24, 25, and 26 November (8, 7, and 6 days before the calends of December) and must both refer to Maius' quinquennial year, since he is termed quinquennial on both.[108] In the first notice, the sparing of the public coffers *(sine impensa publica)* is emphasized; in the second, the name of an apparent star *venator*, Ellius, is prominently displayed.[109] In both notices, the *supposticii* appear to have been additional gladiators destined to take the place of the defeated, so that the winner of a single bout then defended his position in a second round.[110] Clearly Maius was a wealthy and munificent man and deserved the salutes attached to the second of these notices and also elsewhere, where he is further called *princeps munerariorum,* "prince of games givers."[111]

75:

Maio quinq(uennali) feliciter Paris.[112]

[Paris happily to Maius, quinquennial.]

76:

Marti[alis M]aio [feliciter].[113]

[Martialis happily to Maius.]

---

108. So Sabbatini Tumolesi 36, postulating a lettering error or change in details between the posting of the two notices; there is no evidence for a second quinquennial duovirate held by Alleius, as argued by W.O. Moeller ("Maius" 518–19).

109. For the corrected *Ellius* (or *[-]llius*), see Sabatini Tumolesi 36–37.

110. Sabbatini Tumolesi 35; M.G. Mosci Sassi, *Il linguaggio gladiatorio* (Bologna 1992) 176–77.

111. There is, however, no indication that Maius himself owned a *familia gladiatorum,* as assumed by Della Corte (169–70) and followed by Moeller ("Maius" 519–20). So Sabbatini Tumolesi (52), writes "i *paria gladiatorum,* esprimerebbero i semplici gladiatori presi in appalto dall' *editor* e momentaneamente considerati di sua proprietà."

112. *CIL* IV.1179b. Sabbatini Tumolesi N. 10 restores somewhat differently and more cumbrously: *Maio quinq(uennali) feliciter. Paris [scr(ipsit?)].*

113. *CIL* IV.1179c. Sabbatini Tumoesli N. 10 restores somewhat differently: *Marti[alis M]aio [salutem?].*

77:

Cn(aeo) Alleio Maio
principi munerarior(um)
feliciter.[114]

[Happily to Gnaeus Alleius Maius, prince of games givers.]

Having culminated his elected career as quinquennial, Maius likely focused on his private affairs while nevertheless retaining his position of prominence in the *ordo decurionum,* in what has now been identified as a typical life pattern.[115] A wealthy man, he was a major landowner, and perhaps as late as A.D. 79,[116] he advertised for rent various spaces in one of his properties, the *insula Arriana Polliana,* with availability to begin the first of July. The rental notice for the property—advertised in detail as shops and their upper floors *(tabernae cum pergulis suis),* quality apartments *(cenacula equestria),* and a house *(domus)*—was recovered at VI.6.18–19.[117] The business was to be handled by Primus, the slave of Maius.

---

114. *CIL* IV.7990.

115. Dyson, *Community* 212: "Most civic responsibilities had ended by the time he reached fifty-five, although men as old as seventy could be called upon for special public service."

116. Presumably the notice would have been erased had it belonged to an earlier year (see Van Buren, "Maius" 388), but Maius may in fact have died shortly before the eruption (see below, chap. 6).

117. *CIL* IV.138. B.W. Frier, "The Rental Market in Early Imperial Rome," *JRS* 66 (1977) 28: "The *cenaculum* (along with its synonym *aediculae*) is a general description of any multiple room apartment within an *insula,* apartment building; but the word is usually confined to the better class of apartments." Zangemeister (at *CIL* IV.138) first deduced the location of the notice at VI.3.18; later (*Add.* p. 193), however, he corrected the location to somewhere near the southwest corner of VI.6 (followed by Mau, *Pompeii* 489–90). G. Fiorelli (*Descrizione di Pompei* [Naples 1875] 105) located it more exactly at VI.6.18–19: "Ivi di fatti parmi intravederne le vestigia nelle nere lettere, che scorgonsi sul pilastro di mattoni un tempo coverto da tettoia, e dove sulla sommità stanno i due fore per gli assicelli posti a sostenerla: il qual modo di preservazione affato insolito, non sarebbesi d'altronde adottato, che solo per un' epigrafe giudicata di assai grande importanza."

78:

Insula Arriana
Polliana [C]n Al[le]i Nigidi Mai
locantur ex [k(alendis)] iulis primis tabernae
cum pergulis suis et c[e]nacula
equestria et domus. Conductor
convenito Primum [C]n Al[le]i
Nigidi Mai ser(vum).[118]

[The *insula Arriana Polliana* of Gnaeus Alleius Nigidius Maius is for rent from the calends of next July. Shops with their own upper storys, quality dining areas, and a house. Renter see Primus, the slave of Gnaeus Allieus Nigidius Maius.]

Mau observed that given its placement in a prominent location along a major street, the notice could describe nearly any block in town, which would have been known to the ancient reader by its name, *insula Arriana Polliana*.[119] But block VI.6, or the Casa di Pansa, on which the notice had been painted, so perfectly fits the description that it can unhesitatingly be identified as the rental property of Maius.[120] Curiously, the *domus* here seems still to have been occupied,[121] yet the rest of the property had been remodeled just prior to the eruption and even perhaps left undecorated so that it could be painted to meet its renters' tastes.[122]

While he had withdrawn from the electoral fray, Maius, as we shall see, was destined again to return to public service of a major sort under the emperor Vespasian.

Claudius Augustus

Finally, we must note two references to the emperor himself, found on a column of the peristyle at V.1.23,25,26,27,10, the house of Caecilius Iucundus.

---

118. *CIL* IV.138.

119. Mau, *Pompeii* 489–90.

120. So the most recent mention of the property, in A. Wallace-Hadrill, *Houses and Society in Pompeii and Herculaneum* (Princeton 1994) 106.

121. So Della Corte 171, following the report of G. Vinci, *Descrizione delle ruine di Pompei* (Naples 1839) 70–71. On this the house of Ol(l)ius Primus, see further below, in chap. 4.

122. The suggestion is that of Richardson (*Architectural* 123).

79:

Ti(berii) Claudi Caesaris[123]

80:

Ti(berii) Cla[u]di[124]

Isolated as they are, their significance is uncertain, but in the shop of Erastus at VI.16.10,[125] there appears to be evidence of an imperial visit, which, if accurately recorded, must have been made by Claudius on Sunday, 24 May A.D. 50; the day and date, although not the year, are scratched into the wall.[126]

81:

IX k(alendas) Iunias imperator.
Dies fuit Solis.[127]

[The emperor (was here) on the ninth day before the calends of June. The day was Sunday.]

Claudians II

With the addition of the preceding seven powerful Pompeians, most of whom continued their roles in politics for years to come, our picture of the Claudian years has become far clearer—in fact, the most detailed we have so far been able to paint. Yet we paradoxically began with what promised to be lean pickings, so much so that it had even mistakenly been argued that local government was superseded. What has

---

123. *CIL* IV.4089.

124. *CIL* IV.4090.

125. On Erastus, see Della Corte 122.

126. Della Corte (103) suggested that the graffito referred to a visit of Nero, but see Magaldi, "Echi II" 203, following A. Sogliano, "Di una salutazione imperatoria in una epigrafe graffita pompeiana," *Miscellanea Ceriana* (Milan 1910) 251; Sogliano calculated that the only possible years for the visit were A.D. 22, 50, or 78. Had an imperial visit taken place in A.D. 78, we would surely have more record of it, and it is difficult to believe that the graffito remained from A.D. 22. Therefore, A.D. 50 must be the date.

127. *CIL* IV.6838.

changed from earlier eras is the nature of the evidence. For these years we have turned to the chance preservation of old electoral programmata, not careful inscriptional presentations of careers intended for generations to come. There was no "Claudian crisis" as has been argued from the lack of stone-cut inscriptions. Indeed, with the exceptions of Memmius Iunianus and Bruttius Balbus, who represent the coming generation, all these men began to come to the front precisely in the Claudian years. By the early fifties, with a solid ten years behind them, they were being elected duovirs and were signing as responsible witnesses or being cited as eponymous magistrates in the *apochae* of Caecilius Iucundus.

Why the Claudian years are so dismally attested in the stone-cut record remains a problem. Perhaps the city's earlier devotion to Caligula, whom it twice elected honorary duovir, hung heavy over it under Claudius. This could explain the lack of record, both on stone and in the programmata, for the more substantial families who, like the Holconii and Lucretii, had been strong supporters of Caligula, serving as prefects in his stead. Probably more important, however, is the simple explanation that many of these men—Postumius Modestus, Vedius Siricus, and Alleius Nigidius Maius, for example—remained alive until the very end. In fact, we lack not just the stone-cut record from Claudian times but rather the record of those and all subsequent times. These tombs and the inscriptions that would have labeled them were not lost; rather, they were never built or carved.

Partially to compensate for those nonexistent stones, we have the houses of several of these men to turn to for a more lively, if ultimately less detailed, record. Following such scraps of evidence as names in political posters and even graffiti, we have been able to study the enthusiasms of these men and their families, often to bring them to even greater life than those for whom we have stone-cut lists of offices held. In chapter 4, graffiti found in their houses will serve to identify Pompeii's great supporters of Nero. The houses that we have been able to identify underscore for the most part the substance of Pompeii's major figures in this era, while our inability to identify the houses of most of the figures discussed in the first part of this chapter probably also can be used to distinguish their markedly more insubstantial positions—like that of Bruttius Balbus, the only one of these men whose modest house can be identified. Even within the *ordo decurionum,* there was wide variation of fortunes.

Fortunately as we proceed to more recent eras, the properties of increasingly more men can be identified, and we will be able to use the evidence they preserve even more directly. Besides, we have the abundant, more recent parietal inscriptions and even the city's graffiti, to which I now turn almost exclusively, to fill in these later years.

Middle to Late Julio-Claudians—Claudians

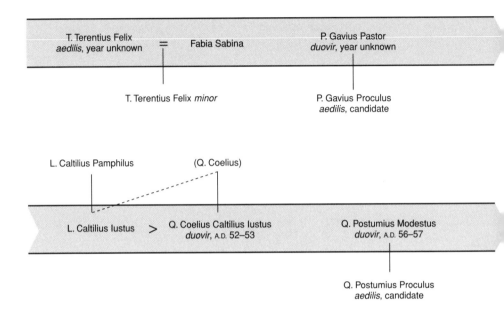

T. Terentius Felix
aedilis, year unknown = Fabia Sabina

P. Gavius Pastor
duovir, year unknown

T. Terentius Felix *minor*

P. Gavius Proculus
aedilis, candidate

L. Caltilius Pamphilus   (Q. Coelius)

L. Caltilius Iustus > Q. Coelius Caltilius Iustus
duovir, A.D. 52–53

Q. Postumius Modestus
duovir, A.D. 56–57

Q. Postumius Proculus
aedilis, candidate

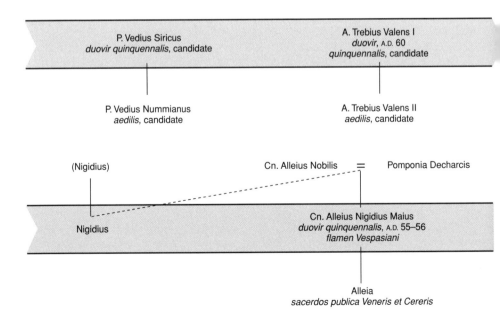

P. Vedius Siricus
duovir quinquennalis, candidate

A. Trebius Valens I
duovir, A.D. 60
quinquennalis, candidate

P. Vedius Nummianus
aedilis, candidate

A. Trebius Valens II
aedilis, candidate

(Nigidius)   Cn. Alleius Nobilis = Pomponia Decharcis

Nigidius

Cn. Alleius Nigidius Maius
duovir quinquennalis, A.D. 55–56
flamen Vespasiani

Alleia
sacerdos publica Veneris et Cereris

Chapter 4

Middle to Late
Julio-Claudians—Neropoppaeenses

D. Lucretius Satrius Valens is one of the few Pompeians of whose life extensive details are known.[1] Born M. Satrius Valens *filius,* he was married and fathered three children—a daughter and two sons. By A.D. 50–54, when Nero had been adopted by Claudius, he was named lifelong priest of the heir apparent, *flamen Neronis Caesaris Augusti filii perpetuus,* and had been adopted by D. Lucretius Valens, whom we first met in early Julio-Claudian days and whose daughter and homonymous son had unfortunately perished early. D. Lucretius Satrius Valens' own son Iustus also had perished early, and so together with his wife, Iusta, his daughter, Valentina, and his son D. Lucretius Valens *filius,* he lived at II.3.3 (fig. 8), the Casa della Venere in Conchiglia, apparently across the street from his ancestral home at III.6.2.[2] He four times mounted gladiatorial shows, and he and his children were saluted for his munificence.[3]

1. See Franklin, "Valens." On the Lucretii and Satrii in general, see Castrén 185–86, 216–17. On the recently recovered tomb of the Lucretii, see De' Spagnolis Conticello and, correcting her analysis of the finds, above, chap. 2, n. 42.

2. Valentina and D. Lucretius Valens *filius* were identified at Franklin, "Valens" 411–12. The burial of D. Lucretius Iustus, the third child, who died at age thirteen and had been named after his mother, Iusta, was recently discovered in the family tomb found under modern Scafati (De' Spagnolis Conticello 156–59). Further on the burials in this tomb, see above, chap. 2, n. 42. On the unexcavated *insula Satriorum* (III.6) and the Casa della Venere in Conchiglia, see Della Corte 810–13f.

3. On the *edicta* announcing the games (*CIL* IV.1185, 3884, 7992, 7995), see Sabbatini Tumolesi 24–32. Mouritsen and Gradel (Mouritsen, *Elections* 35; Mouritsen and Gradel 154–55) would date the shows to A.D. 68–69 and have them mounted to support the candidacy of Valens *filius* for aedile. But it seems financially impossible for them all to have been mounted in one year, and the three dates preserved are 28 March, 4 April, and 8–13 April, the last two of which would immediately follow the elections. Rather, the clustering of dates suggests

82:

Satrio Lucretio Valenti munifico
IV sibi liberis feliciter. Pro Valente ex rog[---][4]

[Happily to Satrius Lucretius Valens, generous on four occasions on
his own part and that of his children. On behalf of Valens in accordance with rog[---].]

The political connections of this flamen, the distinguished scion of
two prominent families, were obviously powerful but have not previously been traced.[5] In fact, Lucretius stood at the center of what must
have been the major faction of the early Neronian era at Pompeii, one
that had begun to be encouraged even before Nero's accession to rule,
by the establishment of the flaminate of "the son of Caesar Augustus,"
Caesaris Augusti filius.

D. Lucretius Satrius Valens

Graffiti and painted notices found both in his own house and on nearby
properties demonstrate not only Lucretius' local prominence but also
connections with Rome. Across the street, to the east, at III.7.1, the house
of Metellicus, for example, was a painted salute to the flamen, while to
the west, at III.6.2, was one of the announcements of games he provided,

---

annual shows roughly timed to commemorate an unknown event. Moreover,
Valens *filius* would not have required such an introduction to electoral politics.
Besides, given the regular references (*CIL* IV.7454, 9889) to Valens and Valentina
as *liberi* even after the mounting of the games (*CIL* IV.1084 = inscription 83),
there is no need to move the games to later dates. Mouritsen and Gradel were
ultimately disturbed by the preservation of the *edicta* from Claudian times, but
as should be clear from earlier chapters, a number of programmata and *edicta
munerum* survived, including those of M. Tullius (*CIL* IV.9979, 9980) from Augustan days.

    4. *CIL* IV.1084. The meaning of the last four words of this notice is uncer-
tain. Della Corte (763–67) believed that the preposition *ex* was misread for the
number *lx,* in which he saw reference to the Pompeian Iuventus.

    5. Castrén (108 n. 8, 186, and 273), however, misconstruing a reference to
his adoptive father, D. Lucretius Valens, for a reference to D. Lucretius Satrius
Valens, in error assigned the flamen a prefecture between A.D. 53 and 55. See,
rather, Andreau, *Jucundus* 57; Andreau assigns Lucretius Valens' magistracy (as
duovir, not prefect) to A.D. 60.

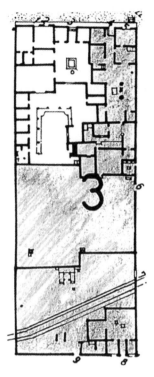

Fig. 8. Block II.3 and the house of D. Lucretius Satrius Valens

this set scheduled for the fifth day before the calends of April, or 28 March. After *damnatio memoriae,* the name of Nero was erased from the notice of games, but the details—twenty pairs of gladiators provided by Lucretius Satrius Valens the flamen, ten more pairs in the name of his son D. Lucretius Valens, a hunt *(venatio),* and the provision for awnings *(vela)*—were left as evidence of the family's munificence.

83:

flamini
Neronis Ca[esaris Aug(usti) feliciter].[6]

[Happily to the flamen of Nero Caesar Augustus.]

---

6. *CIL* IV.7996, where the second line is restored simply as *Neronis Ca[esaris feliciter].*

84:

D(ecimi) Lucreti Satri

Valentis flaminis [[Neronis]] Caesaris Aug(usti) f(ili) perpetui
glad(iatorum) par(ia) XX et

D(ecimi) Lucreti Valentis fili [glad(iatorum)] paria X

ex a(nte) d(iem) V k(alendas) april(es). Venatio et vela er[unt][7]

[Twenty pairs of gladiators of Decimus Lucretius Satrius Valens, per-
petual flamen of Nero, son of Caesar Augustus, and ten pairs of gladiators of Decimus Lucretius Valens, his son, from the fifth day before
the calends of April. There will be a hunt and awnings.]

The house at III.6.2, on the facade of which the notice of games was
posted, appears to have been that of M. Satrius Valens, natural father of
our flamen and himself a powerful politician, and its location across the
street from the Casa delle Venere in Conchiglia as well as family ties will
have meant steady interchange between the two. In the fauces of this
house was recovered a salute to the most sacred colony and populace of
Pompeii by Poliaeus Marsus, bedroom attendant of the emperor *(cu-
bicularius Augusti)* and apparent visitor from Rome.

85:

Poliaeus Aug(usti) cubic⟨u⟩larius Marsus hic et ubique sa(lutem)

[sa]n[cti]ssimae coloniae et populo Pompeieno *[sic]*
ubique sal(utem).[8]

[Poliaeus Marsus, bedroom attendant of the Augustus, here and
everywhere health to the most holy colony, and to the Pompeian people everywhere health.]

With this were three fragmentary lines apparently referring to the Augusta Poppaea Sabina, while on the opposite wall seemed to be a mention of her father's gens, the Ollia.[9] Coupled with Lucretius' office of

7. Sabbatini Tumolesi N. 6 = *CIL* IV.7995.

8. *CIL* IV.7755.

9. Poppaea Sabina, probable owner of the magnificent villa at Oplontis, had
strong local connections and has been thought to belong to a Pompeian family,
on which see Della Corte 97; Van Buren, "Poppaea"; and A. Maiuri, *La Casa del*

flamen Neronis, this accumulation of references confirms that Marsus functioned in the Neronian court.[10]

86:

> a: [Pan]ormus
> b: [Au]gutsa *[sic]* pret[---]
> c: Popp(aea)
> d: Ol⟨l⟩io[11]

These are not the only traceable links between the Satrii and Rome. In the small house at I.19.3, of which only the entranceway has yet been excavated, the only nameplate identifying a house's inhabitant ever found at Pompeii was recovered. The plate, in the shape of a *tabula ansata* measuring 49 millimeters by 118 millimeters, identified L. Satrius Rufus, an imperial secretary (*evocatus Augusti a commentariis*), apparently retired to Pompeii.[12]

87:

> L(uci) Satri Rufi
> evocati Aug(usti)
> a commentar(iis).[13]

[Of Lucius Satrius Rufus, keeper of notebooks of the Augustus.]

Menandro e il suo tesoro di argenteria (Rome 1932) 21. Rather than local origins, however, De Caro ("Sculptures" 131) more convincingly argues for a "connection . . . between the city of Pompeii and the Roman Poppaei." For a similar argument, see A. Łoś, "Interesy Poppaei w Pompejach," *Eos* 79 (191) 63–70. On the gens Poppaea at Pompeii, see Castrén 209, Maiuri, op. cit., 20–22; P. Miniero, "Indagini, rinvenimenti, e ricerche nell' ager Stabianus," *RStPomp* 1 (1987) 185; Giordano and Casale 72. On the gens Ol(l)ia, see Castrén 199, to which should now be added an amphora found "in una casa contigua a quella di Fabio Rufo" (Giordano, "Polibio" 23), with the inscription *C Olio Sec(undo)* (also at Giordano and Casale 338).

10. Della Corte (812) thought Marsus Vespasianic but does not consider the graffiti or the office of Lucretius.

11. *CIL* IV.7756.

12. So Della Corte 627 bis.

13. *NSc* (1933) 322–23 and Della Corte 627 *bis*. The inscription has not yet been included in the *CIL*.

Here the argument for yet another connection to Neronian Rome is strong; the time required to retire and resettle in Pompeii is more likely to have passed if Satrius served under Nero rather than under Vespasian. Unfortunately, the exact connection of this Lucius Satrius to the Marci Satrii is uncertain, although a connection must exist.[14] The access to Rome, nevertheless, remains patent.

References to Nero, Poppaea Sabina, imperial attendants, imperial officials, and Rome were recovered similarly clustered around other select Pompeian notables. This clustering contrasts with other random references scattered around the city and allows the identification of these Pompeians as imperial proponents. Between them, their families, and Lucretius, moreover, further interconnections can be traced to produce a detailed picture of powerful alliances.

P. Paquius Proculus

Of actual references to the emperor, perhaps the best recorded were found at I.7.1 (fig. 9), the house of Paquius Proculus.[15] Over seventy-five graffiti were recovered on this property, and of these, several refer to Nero in one fashion or another.[16] His name appears to have been intended three times in *CIL* IV.8064 and may have been written in the genitive in tiny letters beneath the figure of a bird in *CIL* IV.8095. *CIL* IV.8119 included a crudely drawn head of a male, perhaps intended to be the emperor, and the legend *Roma felix*.

Two dates employed the name *Neroneus* for the month of April, and if Della Corte is correct in his reading of the second, *Olympia* refers to the famous Neapolitan games, Ἰταλικὰ Ῥωμαῖα Σεβαστὰ Ἰσολύμπια founded by the emperor Augustus.[17]

---

14. So also Castrén 216–17.

15. On P. Paquius Proculus, see Della Corte 638 and Della Corte, "Publius Paquius Proculus," *JRS* 16 (1926) 145–54; on the *gens Paquia,* Castrén 202–3.

16. *CIL* IV.8059–135; see Della Corte 638–41 and Della Corte at *NSc* (1929) 438–54. On these graffiti, see also Magaldi, "Echi II" 129–32; Magaldi concludes (132), with Della Corte (443), "la famiglia *Paquia* annoverava non pochi ammiratori entusiasici di Nerone."

17. On *Neroneus* for "April," see Suet. *Ner.* 55. The games are not to be confused (pace Della Corte at *CIL* IV.8092) with Nero's performance in Naples in A.D. 64 (Suet. *Ner.* 20; Tac. *Ann.* 15.33), in which year the games did not fall (see R.M. Geer, "The Greek Games at Naples," *TAPA* 66 [1935] 215).

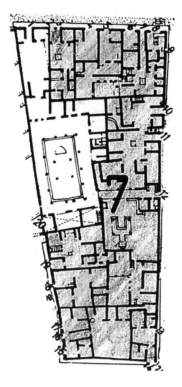

Fig. 9. Block I.7 and the house of P. Paquius Proculus

88:

Nonis Neron⟨e⟩is sal(utem).[18]

[Health to the nones of Neroneus.]

89:

Ol[ympia] III k(alendas) Ner(oneas).[19]

[Olympics the third day before the calends of Neroneus.]

---

18. *CIL* IV.8078a.
19. *CIL* IV.8092.

Most important, however, are three graffiti naming a Cucula or Cicuta, another official of the imperial household, this time an accountant *(ab rationibus)*.[20]

90:

Cucuta[21]

91:

Cu
Cucuta Ner(onis)[22]

92:

Cucuta ab ra[t]ioni[b]us
Neronis Augusti.[23]

[Cucuta, (keeper of) account books of Nero Augustus.]

If another graffito that was found in the house can be connected with him, however, this Roman seems to have been less taken with the delights of Pompeii than was Poliaeus Marsus. Although highly fragmentary and not properly aligned, this was in fact a couplet that can be reconstructed from numerous recurrences both around Pompeii and at Herculaneum.[24]

93:

[Venimus huc] cupidi, multo magis [ire] cupimus,
[ut liceat nostros visere, Roma, Lares].[25]

---

20. On *Cucuta* for *Cicuta*, see E. Diehl, *Pompeianische Wandinschriften und Verwandtes,* 2d ed. (Berlin 1930) 862b, followed by Della Corte 638; for linguistic analysis of the variation, see Väänänen 26.

21. *CIL* IV.8065.

22. *CIL* IV.8066.

23. *CIL* IV.8075.

24. See M. Gigante, *Civiltà delle forme letterarie nell' antica Pompei* (Naples 1979) 228; Magaldi, "Echi" 40–41. At Pompeii were *CIL* IV.2995, 6697, 8114, 8231, 9849, 10065a, and possibly also 9095 and 9122; the first line was recovered at Herculaneum in *CIL* IV.10640.

25. *CIL* IV.8114.

[Though eager we came here, we are far more eager to go, so that it be allowed us to see Rome and our own Lares.]

Finally, there was a Romanus who left his name just below Cucuta's graffito on the exterior of the house (*CIL* IV.8066 = inscription 91).

94:
Rom Roma Romanus[26]

Just as around D. Lucretius Satrius Valens, so around P. Paquius Proculus, references to Rome and the imperial household indicate strong Neronian interests. Yet the most direct references to Nero and Poppaea Sabina were clustered around the two famous Pompeian properties identified as possessions of the gens Poppaea, the Casa del Menandro and the Casa degli Amorini Dorati.

Q. Poppaeus Sabinus

Over seventy-five graffiti were also recovered on the interior and exterior walls of the Casa del Menandro (I.10.4,15; fig. 10), which was owned by Q. Poppaeus Sabinus, who began his career as aedile in Claudian times, as mentioned in chapter 3.[27] To the right of the main doorway of the house was a graffito probably left by a dawdler dreaming of better places; in it the words *Roma,* its reverse *amor,* and *olim* and its reverse were worked into a magic square, a trick now attested also at Ostia in Hadrianic times.[28]

---

26. *CIL* IV.8067–68.

27. *CIL* IV.8285–357; the count is inexact since several *CIL* entries contain more than one graffito. On the graffiti, see Della Corte's introductory note at *CIL* IV.8310–357; on Poppaeus Sabinus, Della Corte 97B and 592–95. On the house, see Maiuri, op. cit. (above, n. 9).

28. M. Guarducci, "Il misterioso 'quadrato magico': L'interpretazione di Jerome Carcopino, e documenti nuovi," *ArchCl* 17 (1965) 262–66. See A. Varone, *Presenze giudaiche e christiane a Pompei,* Quaderni della Società per lo Studio e la Divulgazione dell' Archeologia Biblica, 1 (Naples 1979) 68, for the extensive bibliography on this square.

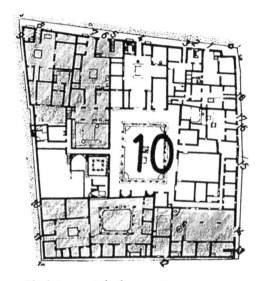

Fig. 10. Block I.10 and the house of Q. Poppaeus Sabinus

95:

R   O   M   A
O   L   I   M
M   I   L   O
A   M   O   R[29]

Within the house the Roman allusions continued, with several graffiti
seemingly relating to Roman luminaries.

On columns of the peristyle were apparently another reference to the
Neapolitan games—this time echoing their official title in Greek—as
well as mentions of the infamous Tigellinus and the emperor Tiberius.

96:

ευϛεβαϛτα [sic][30]

---

29. *CIL* IV.8297.

30. *CIL* IV.8325. Della Corte notes at the *CIL* entry, "Huiusmodi verbis ac-
clamatur, ut putaverim, ludi isolympici Neapolitani, Grece Ἰταλικὰ Ῥωμαῖα
Σεβαστὰ Ἰσολύμπια." Magaldi ("Echi II" 208–9) equates Σεβαστά with Σεβαστή
and sees this as a salute to Poppaea Sabina.

97:

N Tigil⟨l⟩i

ni[31]

98:

Tib(erius) Aug(ustus)[32]

In a cubiculum opening off the peristyle, Della Corte also saw reference to an Antistius Vetus, perhaps the consul of A.D. 55, although he actually recorded the cognomen as *Veius*.[33]

99:

Antistius Veius[34]

Nearby, just outside the doorway to the small shop and attached *caupona* (I.10.2) tucked in beside the Casa del Menandro and almost certainly one of its dependencies, was an apparent salute to Nero and Poppaea, the Pompeian Augusti.[35]

100:

Pomp(eianis) Aug(ustis)

[feliciter].[36]

[Happily to the Pompeian Augusti.]

---

31. *CIL* IV.8330a. The praenomen of Tigellinus is uncertain; on other problems of the name, see *RE*, s.v. "Ofonius Tigellinus."

32. *CIL* IV.8320g.

33. Della Corte 595d and Della Corte at *CIL* IV.8342. In *CIL* IV.8324, *Neratius / Pansa / Cleopatra*, Della Corte also saw reference to M. Hirrius Fronto Neratius Pansa, consul suffectus under Vespasian, and to the Cleopatra who was the wife of Gessius Florus, procurator of Judea, and who was a friend of Poppaea.

34. *CIL* IV.8342.

35. On these properties as dependencies of the Casa del Menandro, see Della Corte 589. Studying its building history, R. Ling ("The Insula of the Menander at Pompeii: An Interim Report," *AntJ* 63 [1983] 34–57) wonders (55) whether the gens Poppaea owned the entire insula.

36. *CIL* IV.8253.

The *vestibulum* here contained a small semicircular Lararium labeled *Lares Augustosi* (*sic; CIL* IV.8282), while the exterior wall even held a prayer for the deposed Octavia (her name misspelled), wishing her good health.[37]

101:
    Oc{c}tavia Augusti [vale. H]abias *[sic]* [pr]opit[---] sa(lutem)[38]

[Octavia (wife) of the Augustus, farewell. May you have fitting health.]

Finally, inside the small, contiguous house at I.10.1 was another recurrence of the homesick Roman's couplet, this time more complete.

102:
    venimus h *[sic]* huc cupidi multo magis ire cu[pi]mus,
    [ut liceat nostros visere, Roma, Lares].[39]

[Though eager we came here, we are far more eager to go, so, that it be allowed us to see Rome and our own Lares.]

Spreading from the Casa del Menandro to its dependencies and to neighboring homes and businesses, graffiti again record Roman sympathies and Roman visitors, and although the visitors' names are lacking, specific references date many of the graffiti to the Neronian era. Moreover, although it cannot now be explained with exactitude, there is also evidence of local interconnections; on the exterior of the house were greetings for another member of Lucretius' natural family, the gens Satria.

103:
    Satria[e] sal(utem).[40]

[Health to Satria.]

---

37. On the *Lares Augusti,* see I.S. Ryberg, *Rites of the State Religion in Roman Art,* MAAR 22 (Rome 1955) 53–63; K. Hopkins, *Conquerors and Slaves,* Sociological Studies in Roman History, 1 (Cambridge 1978) 211–12.
38. *CIL* IV.8277.
39. *CIL* IV.8231.
40. *CIL* IV.8294.

Cn. Poppaeus Habitus

The Casa degli Amorini Dorati at VI.16,1,2,6,7,38 (fig. 11) was owned by another member of the gens Poppaea, Cn. Poppaeus Habitus, and like the Casa del Menandro, it was the center of a cluster of graffiti referring to Rome, Nero, and Poppaea Sabina.[41] Moreover, in the small house at VI.16.35, probably a dependency of the Casa degli Amorini Dorati,[42] was another instance of the word *Roma* followed by a sketch, apparently of the emperor's head.

In the fauces of the Casa degli Amorini Dorati itself, a salute from a Campylus to a Poppaea, perhaps Poppaea Sabina, was recovered, and in the peristyle of the house was a Greek graffito of a *servus publicus* Primogenes remembering a Caesar.

104:

Campylus Poppaeae sal(utem).[43]

[Campylus (sends) health to Poppaea.]

105:

[ἐ]μνήσθη Πρειμ[ογ]ένς πύπλεικος Καίσαρος.[44]

[Primogenes, public (slave), remembered Caesar.]

In addition, just opposite the rear entrance, further imperial greetings, to which I will return in discussion of the *iudicia Augusti,* were found painted in large red letters to the north of doorway VI.15.1.

---

41. On the house and Cn. Poppaeus Habitus, see Della Corte 98–106; F. Seiler, *Casa degli Amorini Dorati,* Deutsches Archäologisches Institut: Häuser im Pompeji 5 (Munich 1992), especially 136–38.

42. *CIL* IV.6856. On the relationship of the properties, see Della Corte 107 and Eschebach 135.

43. *CIL* IV.6817.

44. *CIL* IV.6828. Mau there translates, "i.e. Prim(og)enes (servus) publicus meminit Caesaris."

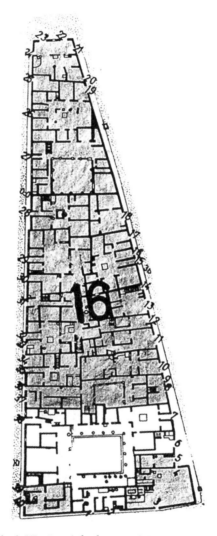

Fig. 11. Block VI.16 and the house of Cn. Poppaeus Habitus

106:

iudici⟨i⟩s Aug(usti) felic(iter). Puteolos Antium Tegeano Pompeios
hae sunt verae
coloniae[45]

[Happily to the judgments of the Augustus. Puteoli, Antium, Tegeanum, Pompeii: these are the true colonies.]

Like Lucretius Satrius Valens and especially his kinsman Poppaeus
Sabinus, Poppaeus Habitus not only harbored strong Neronian sympathies but also saw them reflected by his less powerful neighbor.

So far, then, the flamen Lucretius, the Poppaei, and with them
Paquius Proculus can be shown through fairly standard references to
have had Neronian leanings. Perhaps more interesting, they will have
been joined by others whose connections are less readily apparent but
far more flamboyant.

L. Popidius Secundus

According to Tacitus, Suetonius, and Dio Cassius, Nero was supported
in his artistic performances by a trained, rhythmic claque of young men,
the Augustiani.[46] At Pompeii, L. Popidius Secundus, the owner with his
fellow freedman Ampliatus of the huge Casa del Citarista at I.4.5,25,28
(chapter 6, fig. 21), was three times termed Augustianus, twice with such
references to Caesar ("may you have a supportive Caesar")—parallel to
those of Octavia that we saw earlier—as to leave little doubt that he was
one of the troupe.[47]

45. CIL IV.3525. This is the only reference to Pompeii as a Neronian colony.
On this and the identification of Tegeanum, see A. Sogliano, "Colonie Neroni-
ane," RendNap, 5th ser., 6 (1897) 389–95.

46. Tac. Ann. 14.15; Suet. Ner. 20, 25; Dio Cass. 61.20, 63.8, 63.18; RE, s.v. "Augustianus"; K.R. Bradley, Suetonius' Life of Nero, Collection Latomus 157 (Brus-
sels 1978) 127–28.

47. On L. Popidius Secundus, his fellow freedman and possible relation Ampliatus, and the Casa del Citarista, see Della Corte 497–98; on the gens Popidia,
Castrén 207–9. On the Casa del Citarista, see O. Elia, "La casa di un Augustiano
a Pompei," in Atti del III Congresso Nazionale di Studi Romani (Bologna 1934)
215–26. On Secundus as Augustianus, see Magaldi, "Echi II" 133; and Łoś, "Remarques" 287. Perhaps also tying the Popidii to this political circle was CIL

107:

Luci Augustiane
[h]ab[eas] prop(itium) Caes(arem).[48]

[Lucius, Augustianus, may you have a supportive Caesar.]

108:

Luci Augustiane
[h]ab[eas] prop(itium) [Caesarem].[49]

[Lucius, Augustianus, may you have a supportive Caesar.]

109:

L(ucio) Popidio Secundo
Augustiano feliciter
[---].[50]

[Happily to Lucius Popidius Secundus, Augustianus.[---]]

Callistus

The same is true of a Callistus, an Augustianus who left greetings for Ceratus, a slave of Vedius Siricus, whom we met in chapter 3.[51] The salute was recovered just one block from the house of the Vedii, and in its second line there even seems to be a garbled reference to Nero and Poppaea.

IV.8076, found at the house of Paquius Proculus: *Olbliato feliciter.* Della Corte suggested at the *CIL* entry that *Olbliato* stood for *Ampliato;* it would then refer to Popidius Ampliatus.

    48. *CIL* IV.2380.

    49. *CIL* IV.2381.

    50. *CIL* IV.2383.

    51. On the house of the Vedii and its inhabitants, see Della Corte pp. 9–11 and entries 406–8. Ceratus is known also from the records of Caecilius Iucundus (*Apochae* 40 of A.D. 57) as P. Vedius Ceratus, where his praenomen was incorrectly read as *L(ucius)* (on which see Mau at *CIL* IV.5914). He supported Vedius Nummianus, the son of his patron Vedius Siricus, in a programma (*CIL* IV.910); was apparently the wine producer named on one amphora (*CIL* IV.5914); and was the addressee of three other amphora inscriptions (*CIL* IV.5915

110:

Callistus Augustianus
Vedi Nepoppaesis [sic] Cerato.[52]

[Callistus, Augustianus, to Ceratus (slave) of Vedius, Neroppaesis [sic].]

As members of the famous claque, Popidius and Callistus will have been standout Neronians at Pompeii. Popidius' prominence and the reference to Nero and Poppaea in the graffito of Callistus certify their identification.

Elsewhere, however, care must be exercised. A few blocks up the Via Stabiana, where *augustianus* can mean little more than "classy," it recurs five times (*CIL* IV.1379, 1380, 1382, 1384, 1385), characterizing Iucunda, Aphrodite, and Ias, three of the staff of the lupanar at VI.11.14–15.[53]

111:

Iucunde [sic]
et Ias aucustiani [sic] s(alutem).[54]

[Health to Iucunda and Ias, *augustianae*.]

112:

Ap(h)rodite
aucustia(na) [sic]

———

et Ias aucustiana [sic].[55]

[Aphrodite, *augustiana*, and Ias, *augustiana*.]

= 2638–40)—but see Andreau, *Jucundus* 245–46 and, in general, 241–43, on the difficulties of interpreting these amphora inscriptions.

52. *CIL* IV.2413*i* (cf. *Add.* p. 222).

53. On the lupanar and its inmates, see Della Corte 63–71.

54. *CIL* IV.1379. That these are all women despite the masculine adjective *augustiani* and the *e* for *a* in *Iucunda* is clear from the next graffito (*CIL* IV. 1384), in which both Aphrodite and Ias are clearly feminine, and from the nearby 1388 (*Timele felatris*) and 1389 (*Nymphe felatrix*).

55. *CIL* IV.1384.

Likewise, at III.4.c, a property that is yet to be excavated although the street has been cleared, the term similarly recurred four times.[56] And, as if to confirm this understanding of the word, inside the famous brothel at VII.12.18 was apparently its negation, although exactly who was being insulted was not recorded.

113:

non aug(ustiana)[57]

[not an *augustiana*]

Finally, the word occurs again beside a street Lararium at I.21.3, where a Plocamus called *augustianus* apparently met often with friends; exactly how the term was there intended, however, is uncertain.

114:

Plocame
augus
tiane
va(le).[58]

[Farewell Plocamus, *augustianus*.]

115:

Plocam
us cum
Aulo hic sae
pe[---].[59]

[Plocamus with Aulus here often [---]]

---

56. Giordano and Casale 105: *Nereu augustiani;* 119: *[---]augustiana;* 120: *Cornelia / Fortunata / a(u)gustiana;* 121: *sph augustian[---].* The term is apparently likewise applied to an otherwise unknown Gastus in *CIL* IV.7077 at V.7.2. It is probably also used similarly at *CIL* IV.4754a at VII.7.5: *Successa / augustiana.*

57. *CIL* IV.2229.
58. Giordano and Casale 41.
59. Giordano and Casale 42.

116:

Firmus [---]omu[---]

saepe

va(le).[60]

[Firmus [---] often, farewell.]

We must, however, return to our obvious Neronian connections.

D. Caprasius Felix

On two columns in the peristyle of the house of D. Caprasius Felix at IX.7.20 (fig. 12), graffiti named both Satrius Valens and Nero.[61]

117:

Satrius

Vale⟨n⟩s[62]

118:

Nero[63]

It is unusual to find mention of a prominent man among the graffiti in another's house, and these otherwise incongruous references appear to identify Caprasius as another Pompeian linked to the Neronian faction. Caprasius' main interest for us, however, will lie in his adoption in the Flavian years, when he became A. Vettius Caprasius Felix.[64]

Iudicia Augusti

As has been often observed, Nero and Poppaea were especially popular at Pompeii, Poppaea herself having very strong local connections, especially through her probable ownership of the magnificent villa nearby

---

60. Giordano and Casale 43.
61. On the house, see Della Corte 426–27; on the gens Caprasia, Castrén 149.
62. *CIL* IV.5364. Mau writes at the *CIL* entry, "Agitur haud dubie de D. Lucretio Satrio Valente."
63. *CIL* IV.5376.
64. See chap. 6.

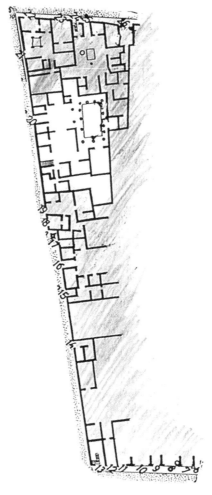

Fig. 12. Block IX.7 and the house of D. Caprasius Felix

at Oplontis.[65] And as we have seen, the imperial couple was saluted as
the Pompeian Augusti in a graffito outside the Casa del Menandro (*CIL*
IV.8253 = inscription 100), a greeting repeated outside doorway V.4.c
(*CIL* IV.6764), while Poppaea herself was singled out as Augusta outside the little house at I.11.17.

---

65. On the popularity of Nero and Poppaea, see Magaldi, "Echi" 70–82; on

119:

f(eliciter) Pop⟨p⟩a[e(ae)] August⟨a⟩e feliciter.[66]

[Happily to Poppaea the Augusta, happily.]

Including *CIL* IV.3525 (= inscription 106), there were eight enthusiastic references to *iudicia Augusti, iudicia Augusti et Augustae*, or *iudicia Augusti patri patriae et Poppaeae Augustae*, obviously of great importance, but nowhere specifically explained.[67] The fifth announced, "With you safe, we are happy forever."

120:

iudiciīs Aug(usti) felic(iter).[68]

[Happily to the judgments of the Augustus.]

121:

L(ucium) Aelium Magnu[m].
Iudici⟨i⟩s Aug(usti)[69]

[Lucius Aelius Magnus. To the judgments of the Augustus.]

Poppaea's ownership of the villa at Oplontis, De Caro, "Sculptures" 131–33, and n. 9 above.

66. *CIL* IV.10049.

67. Early inconclusive work on the *iudicia Augusti* (see at *CIL* IV.1074 [cf. *Add.* p. 199] and *CIL* IV.3525) is surveyed by Magaldi at "Echi" 75–82. His own magisterial discussion of the evidence follows at "Echi" 82–100.

68. *CIL* IV.528.

69. *CIL* IV.670. Assuming that this is a programma, Castrén (117) argues for Neronian interference in Pompeian elections. It is, however, the only potential instance in all the programmata (pace Castrén, "[f]ollowing the names of some candidates of the Neronian period," but who can produce only *CIL* IV.820a, 1074, 1612, none of which is a programma or follows a candidate's name), and Mouritsen (*Elections* 126) more plausibly concludes, "The inscription therefore probably has no particular connection with the election." In fact, this is also the only piece of evidence seeming to attest that Aelius Magnus stood for office, but it is merely his name in the accusative and quite possibly not even a programma. Mouritsen mistakenly lists also *CIL* IV.1991, 7243, 7247, 10039, but none of these is a programma. There is no evidence that Aelius Magnus stood for office, and certainly none that Nero recommended him. Zangemeister writes at *CIL* IV.670,

122:
Neronis iud(iciis).[70]

[To the judgments of Nero.]

123:
[iudici⟨i⟩s Cae]saris Augusti felicit(er).[71]

[Happily to the judgments of Caesar Augustus.]

124:
iudiciis Augusti Augustae felicit(er).
Vobis salvis felices sumus
p[e]rpetuo.[72]

[Happily to the judgments of the Augustus and the Augusta. With you safe, we are happy forever.]

125:
iudici⟨i⟩s Aug(usti) felic(iter).[73]

[Happily to the judgments of the Augustus.]

126:
iudici⟨i⟩s Augusti p(atris) p(atriae) et Poppaeae Aug(ustae)
feliciter.[74]

[Happily to the judgments of the Augustus, father of the country, and to Poppaea, the Augusta.]

Two of these eight graffiti were found on the south exterior wall of the basilica; the remainder were scattered around town, for example, op-

---

"671a et 671b cum ab eadem manu atque 670 scriptas esse videantur, illa quoque *iudicia Augusti* ad *Neronem* referenda esse probabile est." When examined as a group, there is no question that all these references are to Nero and Poppaea.

70. *CIL* IV.671a–b.
71. *CIL* IV.820a. Restoration by Zangemeister at the *CIL* entry.
72. *CIL* IV.1074.
73. *CIL* IV.1612.
74. *CIL* IV.3726.

posite the rear entrance to the Casa degli Amorini Dorati (inscription 106). Whatever the judgments, they therefore must have affected the entire city, not just specific individuals. Scholars have long been intrigued by the references, and the most enticing explanation given is that under Poppaea's influence Nero revoked the ban on gladiatorial games that the Roman Senate passed in A.D. 59 after the infamous riot in the amphitheater, recorded by Tacitus.[75] Indeed, a credible scenario for this argument can finally be written, thanks to new documents now at hand.

As we have seen, in A.D. 55, when he served as quinquennial duovir, Cn. Alleius Nigidius Maius provided amphitheater games—in fact, the last known to have featured gladiators previous to the riot of A.D. 59. After the riot, gladiator shows were forbidden for a ten-year span, during which the games of Claudius Verus, duovir in A.D. 61–62 and a central figure of chapter 5, were mounted with only "athletes" standing in for actual gladiators. On 28 February A.D. 62 the earthquake struck, and after repairs to the amphitheater or in a general remodeling at this time, Cn. Alleius Nigidius Maius provided for decoration of the wall surrounding the arena with an unusual series of paintings *(opus tabularum)* of gladiators and hunt scenes, in compensation for not being able to provide gladiators themselves.[76] This project was dedicated with an amphitheater show on 13 June of an uncertain year. Again the show featured only "athletes," since the ban persisted; but this time it was supplemented with a parade, a hunt, and awnings to protect the spectators. Indeed, such nondescript "athletes" as Claudius Verus and now Alleius Nigidius Maius were forced to provide were a feature only of games mounted during the ban.[77]

127:

Dedicatione
operis tabularum Cn(aei) Allei Nigidi Mai Pompeis idibus iunis
pompa venatio athletae vela erunt.[78]

---

75. Concluding that the senatorial ban was lifted by Nero are Magaldi ("Echi" 99), Della Corte (97B and at *NSc* [1939] 307), and Van Buren ("Poppaea" 970–71).

76. Franklin, "Maius" 442–44.

77. Sabbatini Tumolesi 45 and 140.

78. Sabbatini Tumolesi N. 12 = *CIL* IV.7993. Advertising the same event, but more fragmentary, are *CIL* IV.1177, 1178, 3883.

[For the dedication of the work of tablets of Gnaeus Alleius Nigidius Maius there will be a parade, a hunt, athletes, and awnings at Pompeii on the ides of June.]

By A.D. 64, Nero—yet to endure Rome's own natural disaster, the Great Fire—was in Naples performing at the theater,[79] and as has been recently learned from excavations in the house of Iulius Polybius, he made a visit to Pompeii.[80] Tacitus records a visit to Beneventum as Nero prepared for a trip to Greece that was shortly abandoned for Rome.[81] It was presumably on his way to Beneventum from Naples that Nero stopped at Pompeii, a stop unrecorded by Tacitus, since it was unnecessary—in fact, damaging—to his portrait of corrupt tyrant: at Beneventum Nero had endulged Vatinius, one of the foulest examples of his court, by attending gladiator shows that Vatinius had mounted during the same days that saw Torquatus Silanus forced to open his veins in Rome. In sharp contrast, two graffiti from the house of Iulius Polybius record a benevolent princeps and a very rewarding visit.

128:
Munera Poppaea misit Veneri sanctissimae berullum helencumque [*sic*]; unio mixtus erat.[82]

[Poppaea sent as gifts to most holy Venus a beryl and a drop-shaped pearl; a large display pearl was included.]

129:
Caesar ut ad Venerem venet [*sic*] sanctissimam ut tui te vexere pedes caelestes Auguste [*sic*] millia milliorum ponderis auri fuit.[83]

[When Caesar came to most holy Venus, when, Augustus, your heavenly feet carried you, there were thousands of thousand weights of gold.]

---

79. Tac. *Ann.* 15.33; Suet. *Ner.* 20.2.
80. Giordano, "Polibio" 24–25.
81. Tac. *Ann.* 15.34–36.
82. Giordano, "Polibio" N. 4.
83. Giordano, "Polibio" N. 5.

Perhaps the very point of Nero's visit was to pay homage to Venus Pompeiana, on both his own and Poppaea Sabina's behalf, as a gesture to help rally the city in mounting repairs necessary after the earthquake. As *misit*, "sent," in the first of these graffiti indicates, Poppaea did not visit Pompeii on this occasion.[84] Nero's offering was gold; Poppaea's was jewelry. The two graffiti recording the visit were scratched onto a wall replastered after the earthquake in which the temple building was destroyed (providing a *terminus post quem*), so that Nero must perforce have visited the cult statue of Venus and little else.[85] Hence the offerings were particularly appropriate—the jewelry for the statue, the gold to finance building repairs.

It will have been at this time that Nero relaxed the ban on gladiators, assuring himself a rapturous welcome and eliciting the notices heralding his decision *(iudicium)* that can now be seen also to attest his visit to the city. Local enthusiasms will have directed the inclusion of Poppaea in several of the salutes; even though she herself was not present, she was amply represented by her offering to the cult.

The Neronian faction will of course have gathered its share of the glory of both this actual visit of the emperor and the repeal of the ban on gladiators and will have become wildly popular. In fact, in honor of the Pompeian Augusti, the faction seems also to have become known as either the Neropoppaee(n)ses or the Nepopaee(n)ses, both terms being obvious compounds of *Poppaeenses* and *Neronenses*.[86] The former term is attested in a fragmentary graffito found in the small house at VI.16.35–36, immediately next door to the house of Poppaeus Sabinus (Casa degli Amorini Dorati); the latter, in a graffito found up the street at VI.16.15–17 (the Casa dell' Ara Massima).

130:

Poppaeenses
facimus
suntu[---]fre[---].[87]

[We the Poppaeenses make [---]]

---

84. Giordano, "Polibio" 24.

85. The postearthquake rebuilding of the temple was in only early stages when Pompeii was destroyed (see Richardson, *Architectural* 278).

86. On the compound, see Magaldi, "Echi" 74–75; on *-esis* for *-ensis*, see Väänänen 97–98.

87. *CIL* IV.6682. Mau writes at the *CIL* entry (found at VI.16.35–36, an ap-

131.

IIXX k(alendas) Ianuarias
se C k k Nerone⟨n⟩se[s].[88]

[Eighteen days before the calends of January [*se C k k*] the Neronenses.]

Neither graffito is thoroughly intelligible. The first records an action of
the Poppaeenses;[89] the second, the presence of the Neronenses in a December. A variation of the combined term, *Nepoppae⟨en⟩sis,* however,
is in fact exactly what Vedius Siricus—yet another member of the faction, and the patron of the Ceratus saluted by Callistus—was called in
inscription 111, found just outside his house, and the graffito (inscription 110) can now be so restored.

Callistus Augustianus
Vedi Nepoppae⟨en⟩sis Cerato.[90]

[Callistus, Augustianus, to Ceratus (slave) of Vedius, Neropoppaeensis.]

As a member of Nero's claque, Callistus will have had certain knowledge of other Neronians of whatever social status, and thanks to this
graffito, we can begin to see how Neronian enthusiasms of different
sorts permeated and united society on different levels.

Although as only an isolated reference, the term appears also outside
the *textrina* of Terentius Eudoxus at VI.13.6.[91]

132:

Nero poppaee⟨n⟩ses *[sic]*[92]

---

parent dependency of the Casa degli Amorini Dorati), "Titulus antiquior est et
latebat sub dealbatione posteriore, qua delapsa comparuit, sed non totus."

88. *CIL* IV.6841. The significance of the beginning of line 2 is unclear.

89. The Poppaeenses are not to be confused with the gens Poppaea, which
as a family supported Helvius Sabinus with a poster (*CIL* IV.357) signed by the
correct "Poppaei": *Helvium Sabinum / Poppaei aed(ilem) fieri rog(ant).* Cf. the
similar poster of the Postumii at *CIL* IV.738 (= inscription 65.)

90. *CIL* IV.2413i (cf. *Add.* p. 222).

91. On the *textrina* and its workers, see Della Corte 185–86r.

92. *CIL* IV.1499 (cf. *Add.* p. 704).

C. Ol(l)ius Primus

A final recurrence of the term *Neropoppaee(n)ses* was recovered in a fragmentary graffito found across the street from the *insula Arriana Polliana* of Cn. Alleius Nigidius Maius, the Casa di Pansa.

133:

Nero poppaee⟨n⟩ses factum[93]

As we saw earlier, the entire insula had been remodeled and was being let for rent at the time of the eruption, but the actual townhouse *(domus)* that was the center of the property was inhabited not by its owner Cn. Alleius Nigidius Maius but by another close relation of Poppaea Sabina likely to have been associated with the Pompeian Neronians, C. Ol(l)ius Primus.[94] Two slaves of Ollius had been named *ministri Augusti* in A.D. 56,[95] and he supported a candidate for office, a Suettius, well into Flavian days.[96] Related to Poppaea, who had taken her maternal grandfather's name in preference to that of her father, T. Ollius,[97] he must have been a major Neropoppaeensis.

134:

Suettium	Ol⟨l⟩ius Primus
aed(ilem) (dignum) r(ei) p(ublicae)	rog(at).[98]

[Ol⟨l⟩ius Primus asks Suettius, a man worthy of the state, as aedile.]

Neropoppaeenses

All this support for and alignment with Nero is remarkable, even if partly explained by the city's connections with Poppaea Sabina. Pompeii's enthusiam for Nero, however, long preceded Poppaea's rise to

---

93. *CIL* IV.259 (cf. *Add.* p. 696).
94. On the house and its inhabitants, see Della Corte 167–73; on the gens Ollia, see above, n. 9.
95. See chap. 3, under "C. Memmius Iunianus."
96. On the Suettii, see chap. 6.
97. Tac. *Ann.* 13.45.1.
98. *CIL* IV.250.

empress; in fact, it preceded even Nero's rise to emperor, with the early appointment of D. Lucretius Satrius Valens as *flamen Neronis Caesaris Augusti filii perpetuus*. As we have seen earlier, the Pompeians were burned by too close contact with the Julio-Claudian family only in the case of Caligula, and only the gentes Holconia and Lucretia, rather than the city itself, seem truly to have been scorched by being so closely associated with that emperor.

Thus when Nero's adoption became known, it took the Pompeians no long time to realize its significance; alignment was to begin at once. Given the youth of the boy, election as duovir, the method used for earlier heirs apparent, was probably impossible, but another approach could be taken. The post of flamen was created and filled, perhaps as an act of political reassertion, with a Lucretius, although a Lucretius of a different line than had become associated with Caligula earlier. To this reassertion we may ultimately owe the exceptional title *flamen perpetuus,* bestowed to emphasize the rehabilitation.[99] Likewise, the very unusual emphasis on Lucretius' children—both son and daughter—in graffiti, salutes, and announcements of games may be seen as an attempt to underscore the family's stability and staying power. Admittedly, the adjective *perpetuus* may more simply be meant to indicate that the flaminate was to continue when Nero eventually rose to the position of emperor, but even so, its force is patent; there was meant to be no challenge to the family's control of this office.

Apart from the flaminate of Lucretius Satrius Valens, however, nearly all this evidence is in one way or another linked with Poppaea Sabina, and so it nearly all also must be dated to the years preceding her tragic death in A.D. 65. Certainly the popularity of Nero survived that episode; indeed, he remained so popular at Pompeii that following *damnatio memoriae* his name was deleted from only one of the four notices of games mounted by Lucretius Satrius Valens;[100] moreover, the many graffiti I have surveyed in this chapter remained untouched on their

---

99. The significance of the adjective *perpetuus* in relation to flaminates continues to bedevil scholars. See the survey of previous scholarship and the conclusion that it is somehow an honorary title "parcimonieusement distribuée par l' *ordo*" in the most recent encounter with the problem at R. Étienne, *Le culte impérial dans la péninsule ibérique d' Auguste a Dioclétien, BEFAR,* 191 (Paris 1958) 237.

100. *CIL* IV.7995 (= inscription 84).

walls. But his special attraction for the city must have diminished beginning with the death of Poppaea.

Overall, the fourteen years of Nero's reign are a period of which relatively little is attested of municipal life and politics at Pompeii. Only the magistrates of A.D. 55 to A.D. 61 are known, and of the Neropoppaeenses, only P. Vedius Siricus appears in the lists. His appearance is highly significant, however, for he was one of the two duovirs called on to replace the government of the Pompeii Grosphi after the riot in the amphitheater in A.D. 59, and he therefore must have been considered especially reliable.[101] The suggestion has also been made that he was followed in office, in A.D. 60, by a regularly elected duovir, D. Lucretius Valens, adoptive father of D. Lucretius Satrius Valens, but this remains very uncertain.[102]

Beginning with the early seventies A.C., however, the slates of candidates for Pompeii's annual magistracies have been reconstructed, and the roles of several of the Neropoppaeenses and their descendants can be discerned.[103] Although the group's connection with Nero was doubtless sharply de-emphasized following *damnatio memoriae,* the men themselves continued to participate in local politics. These were, after all, local grandees, and they were needed for the successful functioning of the city. Besides, the years of their highest visibility had doubtless ceased with the death of Poppaea, and while connections with Rome and the emperor were necessary, they likely lost much of their strength after A.D. 65.

But even while the Neropoppaeenses were active, a second group of men was working its way into the local political scene. We have already met one of the most successful, Ti. Claudius Verus, giver of games featuring "athletes," and in chapter 5 I turn to him and his circle.

---

101. See Castrén 110, 235.
102. Andreau, *Jucundus* 57.
103. Franklin, *Electoral.*

Middle to Late Julio-Claudians—
Neropoppaeenses

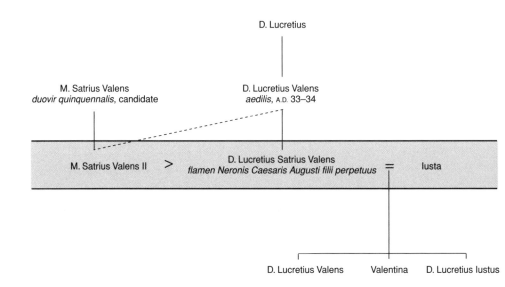

D. Lucretius

M. Satrius Valens
duovir quinquennalis, candidate

D. Lucretius Valens
aedilis, A.D. 33–34

M. Satrius Valens II >   D. Lucretius Satrius Valens
flamen Neronis Caesaris Augusti filii perpetuus = Iusta

D. Lucretius Valens   Valentina   D. Lucretius Iustus

Chapter 5

Middle to Late
Julio-Claudians— Newcomers

When rioting erupted in the amphitheater in A.D. 59, two men who would even otherwise draw our attention, Cn. Pompeius Grosphus and Cn. Pompeius Grosphus Gavianus, were serving as duovirs.[1] While there had been Pompeii active in the city for several years, they had nearly all carried the praenomen Quintus or Sextus,[2] and indeed Cn. Pompeius Grosphus was a newcomer, a Sicilian, who had adopted a local Gavius as his son.[3] The Gavii had earlier begun their climb up the political and social ladder and were a good choice for cementing local relations.[4] Two lines are known: P. Gavius Pastor and P. Gavius Proculus were active previous and up to roughly this period;[5] C. Gavius Rufus, in Flavian times. It therefore seems likely that Cn. Pompeius Grosphus Gavianus began life as a P. Gavius, probably son of Proculus, and

---

1. *Apochae* 143.

2. Q. Pompeius Macula had been aedile in A.D. 25–26 (*CIL* X.896), and Sex. Pompeius Proculus had served as duovir in A.D. 57–58 (*Apochae* 141). Except for an N. Pompeius Nepos, all the other known Pompeii (see Castrén 205–6) appear to have been related to these former magistrates.

3. See Castrén 205, following A. Stein, *Der römische Ritterstand, Münch-Beitr,* 10 (Munich 1927) 382.

4. On the Gavii, see Castrén 170–71, but on the duovirate of P. Gavius Pastor, see above, chap. 2, n. 1, and below, n. 5. Andreau ("Remarques" 224) believes that Pompeius Grosphus could not have been admitted to the *ordo* without this adoption, but access seems always to have been open to distinguished outsiders, such as, apparently, Cicero himself.

5. P. Gavius Pastor was duovir sometime in Claudian days (*CIL* X.827, on which see above, chap. 2, n. 1); P. Gavius Proculus was supported by four campaign posters (*CIL* IV.825, 895, 3564, 6686)—three of which were conspicuously old (825: *antiquior,* 3564: *programma antiquior,* 6686: *apparuit delapso tectorio posteriore*)—signed *Apochae* 96 with Postumius Modestus and Helvius Proculus, and belongs to the late fifties and early sixties A.C.

that while his adoption spelled the end of his natural line, the riot ended his adopted. Thereafter, the CC. Gavii came to the forefront.[6]

Cn. Pompeius Grosphus

Pompeius Grosphus must have been exceptionally eager to establish his family at Pompeii, and to distinguish it he seems to have decided on incorporating his cognomen as a permanent identifier of his line, so that his adopted son became Cn. Pompeius Grosphus Gavianus, not merely Cn. Pompeius Gavianus.[7] A Pompeius Grosphus was, of course, known to and mentioned by Horace;[8] if our Pompeius was in fact the son of Horace's friend, his decision to keep the family cognomen to memorialize its appearance in literature will make even further sense, but we must remain wary of excessive conjecture. In a very unusual arrangement, both father and son were elected duovir for the same year, another sign of a flashy start to the new line. Then the Pompeii Grosphi for some reason turned to or simply allowed a Livineius Regulus, a man who had been expelled from the Senate in Rome,[9] to mount the gladiator games that soon led to rioting and death. For the Pompeii Grosphi, too, the result was disastrous; they were replaced in office, and neither man nor any descendant of either again appears in the record.[10]

There must have been some coordination of Grosphus' efforts with the local gens Pompeia, and perhaps this is reflected by the appointment of Sex. Pompeius Proculus as prefect; intended to bear a solid measure of the burden of cleaning up the mess, he was a relative of Grosphus Gavianus, had very recently finished a term as duovir in A.D. 57–58, and could reliably be expected to handle the job. Replacing the Pompeii Grosphi as duovirs were N. Sandelius Messius Balbus, to us a cipher, and P. Vedius Siricus the Neropoppaeensis, by now a mature and reli-

---

6. On the CC. Gavii, see chap. 6.

7. Eventually at Rome, similar developments led to a consul of A.D. 169 with thirty-eight cognomina: see J.P.V.D. Balsdon, *Romans and Aliens* (Chapel Hill 1979) 147–48.

8. Hor. *Car.* 2.16; *Epist.* 1.12.22.

9. Tac. *Ann.* 14.17. Unfortunately, Tacitus' discussion of the reason for the expulsion, merely referred to here, has disappeared in the lost books of the *Annales*.

10. They were replaced before 8 May, the date of *Apochae* 144, which names the new magistrates.

able man, verging on the distinguished elderly quinquennial he was to become in Flavian days.

Disgrace, perhaps even exile—Tacitus reports such punishment for Livineius and others responsible[11]—thus brought to an end this attempt of a newcomer to establish a career and line in the city. Other such new men worked just as hard—albeit not so boldly—to build their careers, and we can trace just such a group of allies in place during the city's next appearance in the historical record.

Ti. Claudius Verus

The latest dated wax tablet of Caecilius Iucundus records the payment of a sales tax to the city of Pompeii through its agent, the public slave Privatus.[12] The date was 11 (?) January A.D. 62, and the first witness to the transaction whose signature survives was a duovir of the year, Ti. Claudius Verus.[13] Verus' magistracy soon proved one of the most demanding in the history of Pompeii, for within a month—on 5 February—the city was devastated by the earthquake from which its residents were still struggling to recover when Vesuvius erupted seventeen years later. In the city's distress, Verus must have turned especially to his friends and allies for support, and in fact, analysis of a number of electoral programmata supports the identification of those allies.

Claudius Verus lived near a short stretch of the Via di Nola in block IX.8, IX.9, V.3, or V.4, as programmata posted in his support by his neighbors *(vicini)* along the street and in the immediate neighborhood indicate.[14]

---

11. Tac. *Ann.* 14.17: "Livineius et qui alii seditionem conciverant exilio multati sunt."

12. *Apochae* 151.

13. On the Claudii, see Castrén 154. The second duovir of the year is unknown; his name is fragmentary (*L, C,* or *G.....us*) on this only secure record of the year. In the list of witnesses that closes the tablet, the name of C. Numitorius Audius Bassus is signed third, and that of an M. Antonius Tertius is fourth. Castrén has hesitatingly assigned Numitorius a magistracy for the year and suggested that Antonius may have been aedile. There is evidence for neither surmise. No Antonius achieved distinction at Pompeii (and the cognomen *Tertius* indicates lowly status), and as Andreau (*Jucundus* 215) observed, "Bassus . . . a été magistrat (non pas l'année où a été rédigée la tabl. 151, mais peut-être l'année précédente. . . .)."

14. Mau (at *CIL* IV.5229) suggested that Claudius Verus inhabited the Casa

135:

Ti(berium) Claudium Verum II vir(um)

vicini rogant[15]

[His neighbors ask Tiberius Claudius Verus as duovir.]

136:

Ti(berium) Claudium Verum

vicini rogant.[16]

[His neighbors ask Tiberius Claudius Verus.]

137:

Ti(berium) Claudium Verum

[duo virum] i(ure) d(icundo) o(rant) v(os) f(aciatis) vicini.[17]

[His neighbors ask that you elect Tiberius Claudius Verus duovir *iure dicundo*.]

Not all his neighbors were automatic in their support, however, and the MM. Obellii Firmi, father and son who lived in the grand house at IX.(14).2,4,b (fig. 13), had to be specifically solicited.[18]

---

del Centenario at IX.8.3,6,a, but Della Corte (216–17) argued that its owner was A. Rustius Verus, on whom see the discussion that follows in text; to Claudius Verus, Della Corte (215) assigned an unidentified property in block V.3. Eschebach (150) followed Della Corte and, further, assigned the house at V.3.7 to Claudius Verus. However, its small size alone makes V.3.7 an unlikely house for this city magistrate; the house of Claudius Verus remains unidentified.

15. *CIL* IV.367.

16. *CIL* IV.440.

17. *CIL* IV.3820. Extraneous elements also cluttered this notice. In small letters ending line 1 and between lines 1 and 2 was *scr(ipsit) Aemilius Celer.* Added to the end of line 2 in smaller letters was the partially indistinct *Himer[——].*

18. The house was identified by Della Corte (13–15). On the Obellii, see Castrén 198, now to be updated in light of the discovery of the tomb of Obellius Firmus (on which discussion follows in text), as by Jongman 362–63. On programmata soliciting specific individuals, see Franklin, *Electoral* 23.

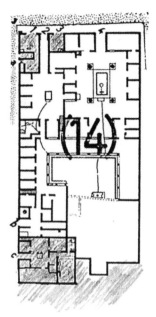

Fig. 13. Block IX.(14) and the house of the MM. Obellii Firmi

138:

(T)i(berium) Claudium Verum
II vir(um) Obelli cum patre fave. Scis Vero favere.[19]

[Obellius, with your father support Claudius Verus as duovir. You
know that you support Verus.]

Of Obellius *pater* little is known, although he seems to have been
specified as a witness in the wax tablets of Caecilius Iucundus, where
he may also be identified as a *vinarius*.[20] One or the other of the Obellii
also witnessed a transaction in A.D. 54.[21] The younger Obellius to whom
the poster was addressed, however, was a man of substance, having

---

19. *CIL* IV.3828. The grammar of this programma has been distorted between the formulaic accusative form of a candidate's name and the dative normally controlled by *favere*.

20. *Apochae* 81. On the Obellii in the tablets, see Andreau, *Jucundus* 200.

21. *Apochae* 8.

served as both aedile and duovir before his death sometime prior to the eruption of Vesuvius.[22] His tomb was recently unearthed outside the Porta di Nola, and some idea of his importance can be gained from the funerary inscription. The *ordo decurionum* had voted the land for his tomb in a conspicuous position near the pomerium and offered five thousand sesterces toward the cost of a sumptuous funeral; to it members of an unspecified suburb contributed thirty pounds of incense and a shield *(clupeum)*—probably a portrait embossed on a shield *(imago clipeata)*—while the officials of the same suburb contributed one thousand sesterces for scents and offered a second *clupeum*.

139:

M(arco) Obellio M(arci) f(ilio) Firmo aedili
IIvir(o) i(ure) d(icundo). Huic decuriones loc(um) sepulturae
et in funer(ibus) HS IƆƆ censuer(unt) pagani
thuris p(ondo) XXX et clupeum, ministr(i) eor(um) in
odorib(us) HS CIƆ et clupeum.[23]

[To Marcus Obellius Firmus, son of Marcus, aedile, duovir *iure dicundo*. To this man the decurions voted a place of burial and for his funeral five thousand sesterces; inhabitants of the settlement, thirty pounds of incense and a shield; their magistrates, one thousand sesterces for scents and a shield.]

Obellius Firmus was a distinguished Pompeian whose support for Claudius Verus would have proved highly valuable, and it is easy to understand why Verus petitioned this close neighbor.

No surviving programma indicates whether Claudius Verus won the support of Obellius, but Claudius was elected, and presumably a notice of games he announced dates to his term as duovir. Scheduled for 25 and 26 February in honor of the emperor Nero, the games were to feature a hunt, athletes, and sprinklings of scented water to refresh the

22. Programmata attesting his campaigns are *CIL* IV.6621, 7806; 3829 seems to attest him as *rogator* rather than candidate.

23. On the tomb and the funerary inscription, see A. de Franciscis, "Sepolcro di M. Obellius Firmus," *CPomp* 2 (1976) 246–48. On the correct reading *eorum* (for de Franciscis' *Fortuna*) in the middle of the last line, see De Caro, "Scavi," 68–70, followed also by W. Jongman, "M. Obellius M. f. Firmus, Pompeian Duovir," *Talanta* 10–11 (1978–79) 63.

crowd.[24] The meaning of the number 373 that seems to end the announcement remains unexplained, and it may not even belong to the notice.[25]

140:

Pro salute

Neronis Claudi Caesaris Aug(usti) Germanici, Pompeis Ti(beri) Claudi Veri venatio

athletae et sparsiones erint [*sic*] V, IIII k(alendas) mar(tias). CCCLXXIII.[26]

[In honor of the health of Nero Claudius Caesar Augustus Germanicus, at Pompeii on the fifth and fourth days before the calends of March, there will be a hunt, athletes, and sprinklings of Tiberius Claudius Verus. 373.]

If in fact planned for A.D. 62, the proposed date would have followed the earthquake by only twenty days, so that the games were likely cancelled, although they may have been mounted in whatever fashion possible for the sake of morale.[27] Whether they were staged or not, Verus, as we have already seen, was constrained by the ban imposed following the riot in the amphitheater in A.D. 59; no gladiators were advertised.

---

24. Sabbatini Tumolesi (47) notes that *pro salute Neronis* equals simply *ob honorem Neronis* and that the titulature accords with that used by Nero after his accession to the throne.

25. Sabbatini Tumolesi (47–48, and 141–43) argues that 373 sesterces, rather than sprinklings of water, were to be distributed to the crowd. The number, however, was written at the end of the notice, with considerable space left between the two elements, and, as Sabbatini Tumolesi herself observes (47), may have nothing to do with the notice itself.

26. Sabbatini Tumolesi N. 18 = *CIL* IV.7989a. Sabbatini Tumolesi observes that *erint* is likely simply a misreading for *erunt*. The very fragmentary *CIL* IV.1181 seems to refer to the same games (text of Sabbatini Tumolesi N. 19): *[Pro salute Ner(onis) Claudi Caes(aris) Aug(usti) Ger]man[ici Ti(beri)] Claudi V(e)ri / [V, IIII k(alendas) ma]rt(ias) Pompeis ven[atio, athle]tae, sparsiones qua dies patientur erunt.* As observed by Sabbatini Tumolesi (45–46), nothing securely connects with Claudius Verus either the games apparently announced in *CIL* IV.7988b or those mentioned in the highly fragmentary *CIL* IV.3822.

27. Sabbatini Tumolesi (47–48) notes that the entertainment could have been staged in the "Palestra Grande" if the amphitheater was too damaged for use.

A. Rustius Verus

In contrast to the Obellii Firmi, a second neighbor of Claudius Verus, A. Rustius Verus, who inhabited the huge Casa del Centenario at IX.8.3,6,a (fig. 14), recommended Claudius warmly as an upright young man *(iuvenem integrum)* and then claimed a due debt when he himself later stood for duovir.[28]

141:
Claudium Verum
II v(irum) i(ure) d(icundo) o(ro) v(os) f(aciatis) iuvenem integr[um].[29]

[I ask that you elect Claudius Verus, an upright young man, duovir *iure dicundo.*]

142:
Rustium Verum d(uovirum) i(ure) d(icundo): Vere
fac qui te fe[cit].[30]

[Verus, elect who elected you: Rustius Verus as duovir *iure dicundo.*]

As is shown by another, albeit fragmentary, programma, Rustius Verus teamed with a Claudianus in this campaign.

143:
Claudianum Rustium IIvir(os) i(ure) d(icundo) [d]ignos
r(ei) p(ublicae)
[---]it[---]iua[---].[31]

[Claudianus and Rustius, men worthy of the state, duovirs *iure dicundo* [---].]

---

28. On Rustius Verus and the assignment of the house to him, see Della Corte 216–17 and n. 14 above. On the Rustii, see Castrén 214; on the history of the Casa del Centenario, Richardson, *Architectural* 126–27.

29. *CIL* IV.3741.

30. *CIL* IV.3760. This notice was recorded near IX.8.7 and may have been posted by the resident of that shop, Urbanus *sa[comarius?]*, identified at Della Corte 226; regardless of who posted it, the information it conveys remains the same.

31. *CIL* IV.2947.

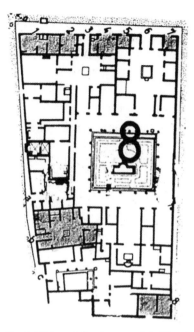

Fig. 14. Block IX.8 and the house of A. Rustius Verus

Only one Claudianus, Ti. Claudius Claudianus, was active in Pompeian politics; he was apparently a close connection of Claudius Verus, and this second connection makes it especially unlikely that Verus hesitated long in supporting Rustius. Besides, the closeness of the relationship between these men is further proved by a graffito found scratched into a column of the peristyle of the house of Rustius and presumably left by his idling neighbor.

144:

Ti(berius) Claudius Ver(us)[32]

Rustius' other enthusiasms, attested by programmata to which his name was signed, were for apparently younger men of new lines active in the last years of Pompeian politics: Popidius Secundus, candidate for aedile in 79 (CIL IV. 3738); Calventius Sittius Magnus, candidate for duovir in 78 (CIL IV. 3751); and Licinius Faustinus, candidate for aedile

32. CIL IV.5229.

sometime after 76 (*CIL* IV.3750).[33] Although the exact date of the candidacy of this last man is unknown, he proves the most interesting, for he leads also to other men of the generation of Claudius and Rustius.

145:

M(arcum) Licinium Faustinu(m)

aed(ilem) v(iis) a(edibus) s(acris) p(ublicisque) p(rocurandis)

v(irum) b(onum) d(ignum) r(ei) [p(ublicae) orat] v(os)

f(aciatis) Rustius rog(at).[34]

[Rustius asks that you elect Marcus Licinius Faustinus, a good man, worthy of the state, aedile *viis aedibus sacris publicisque procurandis*.]

M. Licinius Romanus

M. Licinius Faustinus appears to have been the son of M. Licinius Romanus, who is known from the wax tablets of Caecilius Iucundus and was himself once candidate for aedile.[35]

---

33. On the dates of these various candidacies except for the last, see Franklin, *Electoral* 61–68. In this case, the exact years are not so important as the simple fact that the candidacies belonged to the last few years of the city's existence. The case for dating the candidacy of Licinius Faustinus has been expanded by Varone ("Tituli" p. 100), who reports a poster supporting him and painted on a layer of plastering that can be dated to A.D. 76.

34. *CIL* IV.3750. As restored, the wording of this notice is redundant; both *orat* and *rogat* must be taken as main verbs. There clearly is space in the second line for the abbreviation *o* for *orat,* and I so restore it here.

35. Attesting Romanus' stand for aedile are *CIL* IV.829a, 3594, 3614, 7456, 7519, 7935. Castrén (182), followed hesitantly by Andreau *(Iucundus* 176 n. 5, 200), suggests that Faustinus and Romanus may be brothers, both candidates of Pompeii's last years, and sons of the Licinius Romanus known from *Apochae* 87 and 152. Nearly all the programmata attesting the candidacy of Romanus, however, are specifically termed *antiquior* in the *CIL;* the one Romanus attested in the tablets and programmata belonged to the older generation of Claudius Verus and Rustius Verus, while Faustinus was his son (so also Łoś, "Remarques" 291 n. 165). On the basis of his signature in second place in *Apochae* 153, Mouritsen *(Elections* 110) assigned Romanus a term as duovir in the period A.D. 52–61 (210 n. 455). An earlier Lucius Licinius, whose cognomen is not preserved, had been elected aedile in A.D. 40 (*CIL* X.904); any connection with the Marci Licinii

146:

M(arcum) Licinium M(arci) f(ilium)
Romanum iuvenem aedi(lem)
v(iis) a(edibus) s(acris) p(ublicisque) p(rocurandis) d(ignum)
r(ei) [p(ublicae) o(ro) v(os)] f(aciatis).[36]

[I ask that you elect Marcus Licinius Romanus, son of Marcus, a young man worthy of the state, aedile *viis aedibus sacris publicisque procurandis*.]

It was Romanus, then termed a very respectable *(verecundissimum)* young man, who was supported by an older programma found at VI.13.16, the so-called house of P. Gavius Proculus.

147:

M(arcum) Licinium rog(o)
[iu]venem verecundissim[um]
d(ignum) r(ei) p(ublicae) o(ro) v(os) f(aciatis).[37]

[I ask that you elect Marcus Licinius, a most respectable young man, worthy of the state.]

When copying the programma, Mau observed that it not only was older but also was like another older notice found on the same stretch of wall, which dates it securely to this period, for the second notice supported Claudius Verus himself.[38]

148:

Ti(berium) Clau[d]ium Verum
(II) vir(um) [i(ure)] d(icundo) o(ro) v(os) f(aciatis).[39]

[I ask that you elect Tiberius Claudius Verus duovir *iure dicundo*.]

---

is uncertain. Łoś ("Remarques" 291) writes, "Il faut dire que M. Licinius Romanus était le représentant d'une famille faisant partie de l'*ordo* pompéien depuis des décennies"

36. *CIL* IV.7456.
37. *CIL* IV.3463.
38. At *CIL* IV.3461: *antiquior;* at 3463: *antiquior, similis titulo 3461.*
39. *CIL* IV.3461.

The house of the Licinii has so far gone unidentified, but the name of Romanus was signed to a programma on the side of the Building of Eumachia along the Via dell' Abbondanza, so that at least the name of Iulius Polybius, one of the candidates he supported for aedile, is known.

149:

C(aium) Iulium Polybium
aed(ilem) Licinius Romanus
rogat et facit.[40]

[Licinius Romanus asks and elects Gaius Iulius Polybius aedile.]

C. Iulius Polybius

C. Iulius Polybius also stood for duovir, and he lived in the recently excavated house at IX.13.1–3 (fig.15), where a programma on the facade reveals that he supported Licinius in turn.[41]

150:

Licinium Romanum (II virum)
v(iis) a(edibus) s(acris) p(ublicisque) p(rocurandis) d(ignum)
r(ei) p(ublicae) o(ro) v(os) f(aciatis).[42]

[I ask that you elect Licinius Romanus, a man worthy of the state, duovir *viis aedibus sacris publicisque procurandis*.]

Moreover, other programmata on the house facade show that Polybius was also a sought-after supporter of Rustius Verus.

---

40. *CIL* IV.699.

41. On Polybius and other residents of the house, see Della Corte 707–10; on the Iulii at Pompeii, Castrén 178–79. Contra Franklin, *Electoral* 68, where the duoviral candidacies of M. Lucretius Fronto and C. Iulius Polybius are dated to A.D. 73, the men must have stood far earlier, for Fronto later was a quinquennial candidate, probably in A.D. 70. On the house, see now de Franciscis; Richardson, *Architectural* 119–20. Łoś ("Affranchis" 866) speculates on the status and relationships of Polybius and Philippus.

42. *CIL* IV.7935. As noted by Mouritsen (*Elections* 140), the first line may as well be restored as the more regular abbreviation for this office, *aed*.

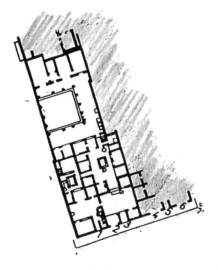

Fig. 15. Block IX.13 and the house of C. Iulius Polybius

151:

> A(ulum) Rustium Verum
> d(uovirum) i(ure) d(icundo) Polybi collega(m) fac.[43]

[Polybius, elect Aulus Rustius Verus duovir, your equal.]

152:

> Rustium V[erum]
> Polybiu[s rogat].[44]

[Polybius asks Rustius Verus.]

Inscription 151 suggests that Polybius was a political deal maker, and confirmation lies in a fragmentary third notice found directly across the street at I.9.1; addressed to a Iulius Philippus, perhaps a brother, it too proposed a deal for Polybius, although with whom is uncertain because the name in the first line is lost.

---

43. *CIL* IV.7942.

44. *CIL* IV.7954. Contra Mouritsen, *Elections* 150, the use of the accusative in the first line indicates that Rustius is the candidate here. As Mouritsen notes, there is no office specified, although one was restored by Della Corte in the *CIL*.

153:

[---]ium[---]
o(ro) v(os) f(aciatis) Iuli Philippe fac
et ille Polybium faciet.[45]

[I ask that you elect [---]. Iulius Phillipus, elect and he will elect Polybius.]

Interestingly, more has recently been learned about this Philippus, who, although less known to us, seems likely to have been more prominent than Polybius in antiquity. It was, after all, to Philippus that this last programma offering a political deal was addressed, and the bread-stamp recovered in one of four wooden strongboxes, or *arcae,* found in the peristyle of the house carried his name, not that of Polybius.

154:

C(ai)
Iuli
Philippi[46]

According to two graffiti recovered on the Lararium inside the house, Philippus had traveled and secured some form of victory.

155:

Pro salutem reditum et victoria(m)
C(ai) Iuli Philippi votum h[ic] fecit Laribus
P(ublius) Cornelius Felix et Vitalis Cuspi.[47]

[For the health, return, and victory of C. Iulius Phillipus, here, to his Lares, P. Cornelius Felix and Vitalis (slave of) Cuspius made a vow.]

---

45. *CIL* IV.7316. The formulaic Latin of the programma *(oro vos faciatis)* is redundant with the personalizing remainder of the notice. The heavy-handed restoration of line 1 by Della Corte in the *CIL* is *(A Rust)ium (Verum duovirum iure dicundo).* However, there is nothing to sustain the reading, and it was deduced *ex programma* 7942. In fact, the programma may have supported any candidate of the period (so also Mouritsen, *Elections* 159).

46. Giordano, "Polibio," N. 8. De Franciscis (30) also notes the importance of Philippus; he notes the findspot of the chests at 21.

47. Giordano, "Polibio" N. 6.

156:

Vicimus.[48]

[We have conquered.]

We can wonder at Philippus' travel and warmly saluted success, but whatever its nature, the trip was significant to this freedman and to this slave of two other well-known gentes, the Cornelia and the Cuspia.[49] If it could be connected to recovery efforts following the earthquake, in the form of a mission to Rome, the three gentes involved would prove highly suggestive—C. Iulius Philippus being the descendant of an imperial freedman; a Cornelius representing the original colonizer; and a Cuspius representing C. Cuspius Pansa, the man appointed prefect to deal with the emergency, as we shall see. Then, it might further follow that C. Cornelius Macer, who had previously served as duovir in A.D. 57–58 and was the only politically substantial member of this very numerous family,[50] was actually serving as colleague of Cuspius Pansa. Yet lacking secure evidence, this scenario can stand only as surmise.

M. Lucretius Fronto

Although not a member of this circle of friends, we can add to the lists of these years M. Lucretius Fronto, the first Marcus Lucretius to stand for office since the decline of M. Lucretius Epidius Flaccus following the assassination of Caligula. Lucretius Fronto lived in the elegantly decorated, small house at V.4.11,a (fig. 16), and in a very interesting coalition of recently freed and reascendant old blood, he and Iulius Polybius apparently stood together for duovir, although only one notice survived to attest the cooperation.

157:

C(aium) Iulium Polybium et M(arcum)
Lucretium Frontonem [---].[51]

[[---] Gaius Iulius Polybius and Marcus Lucretius Fronto.]

---

48. Giordano, "Polibio" N. 7.
49. Giordano ("Polibio" 26) suggests a military accomplishment.
50. On the Cornelii, see Castrén 157–58.
51. *CIL* IV.973. Although the office is not specified in this programma,

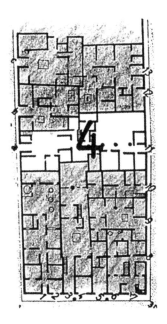

Fig. 16. Block V.4 and the house of M. Lucretius Fronto

Later Lucretius was candidate for quinquennial, perhaps for A.D. 70–71.

158:

Lucretium Fronto[nem]
quinq(uennalem) d(ignum) r(ei) p(ublicae).[52]

[Lucretius Fronto, worthy of the state, as quinquennial.]

M. Lucretius Fronto, however, is the last known of his gens to have stood for election, and indeed only M. Lucretius, *flamen Martis,* seems also to have belonged to late Pompeii.[53]

Mouritsen (*Elections* 139 and 141) also thinks that it applies to the candidates' stand for *duoviri.*
    52. *CIL* IV.7184.
    53. *CIL* IV.879, found in the late Casa di M. Lucrezio (IX.3.5), on which see E. Dwyer, *Pompeian Sculpture in Its Domestic Context: A Study of Five Pompeian Houses and Their Contents,* (Ann Arbor 1975) 11–96; Richardson, *Architectural* 285, 327, 398.

Newcomers

Ti. Claudius Verus, Ti. Claudius Claudianus, A. Rustius Verus, M. Licinius Romanus, and C. Iulius Polybius were all politically prominent in the sixties A.C. and, as this web of interconnections shows, actively supported one another in such ways as can be demonstrated for no other group of men. The evidence is relatively abundant and extant because they were active in years relatively near the eruption of A.D. 79; it had not yet all disappeared from the walls.

What held these men together is uncertain, if indeed there was any general principle around which their interests coalesced. However, none bore an old, established Pompeian name; rather, their lines all appear to have been more recent arrivals—which perhaps explains the emphasis on respectability that we saw in the posters supporting the "upright" Claudius Verus and "most respectable" Licinius Romanus, men of relatively unknown antecedents. All these candidates belonged to gentes attested also at Rome and either Puteoli or Delos,[54] so commercial interests seem likely for them elsewhere and also at Pompeii; and if we can use the houses of Rustius Verus (Casa del Centenario) and Iulius Polybius to judge, their wealth will have been substantial. Both houses are among the largest in the city, the Casa del Centenario featuring private baths and a nymphaeum,[55] the Casa di Iulio Polibio having an impressive *vestibulum* with a loggia unique at the site in addition to four strongboxes for storing valuables.[56]

Ti. Claudius Verus, Ti. Claudius Claudianus, C. Iulius Polybius, and

---

54. Della Corte (909–932d) attempted to distinguish Ti. Claudius Verus and Ti. Claudius Claudianus from imperial freedmen bearing the name Ti. Claudius, but his sole argument is that the men stood for elected office. Citing a supposed friendship with Cn. Alleius Nigidius Maius that has yet to be proved, Sabbatini Tumolesi (44) also argued that Verus and Claudianus were not descended from freedmen, but there are no known Ti. Claudii at Pompeii for them to have descended from, and there is no reason to think that Alleius Nigidius Maius would have scorned these successful men solely because of their lineage.

55. On the baths, see E. Fabbricotti, "I bagni nelle prime ville romane," *Cron-Pomp* 2 (1976) 73–74.

56. For a discussion of the *vestibulum*, see E.W. Leach, "The Entrance Room of the House of Iulius Polybius and the Nature of the Roman Vestibulum," in *Functional and Spatial Analysis of Wall Painting*, ed. E.R. Moormann (Leiden 1993) 23–28.

C. Iulius Philippus are names that little disguise ties to imperial house-holds. Indeed, these must have been descendants of imperial freedmen, Polybius and Philippus trumpeting their ancestor's imperial connec-tions with their striking Greek cognomina.[57] Thus Claudius Verus' re-quest for the support of the long-established Obellius Firmus may rep-resent a request for status and social recognition by older lines as well as for political help. Yet while the prominence of these men has sud-denly come into focus in these years, it should not be overly surprising; as we saw in chapter 3, in Claudian or early Neronian days, the local, freeborn duovir Q. Appuleius Severus was outranked in the wax tablets of Caecilius Iucundus by just such a descendant of an imperial freed-man, a Ti. Claudius, probably Verus.[58]

Their Roman—perhaps better, imperial—ties seem emphasized. The cognomen *Romanus* that the elder Licinius bore may have been chosen to emphasize his connections with the capital; his son's odd cognomen, *Faustinus,* the luck of the wealthy freeborn.[59] In this light, one last pro-gramma in support of Rustius Verus takes on added significance, for besides emphasizing his fitness to be an aedile, it contains also an inter-polated imperial salute, presumably recognizing his Roman connections as well.[60]

---

57. P.R.C. Weaver (*Familia Caesaris* [Cambridge 1972] 87) notes the high proportion of Greek cognomina in the *familia Caesaris* and, in general (84), ac-cepts B. Rawson's figures (in Rawson, review of *The Latin Cognomina,* by I. Ka-janto, *CP* 63 [1968] 157 n. 4) on exchange for Latin cognomina among descen-dants of freedmen at large: "When both parents had Greek names, 40% of their children were given Latin names. When the father had a Greek name and the mother a Latin one, 56% of their children had Latin names. When the father had a Latin name and the mother a Greek one, 72.5% of their children had Latin names. And when both parents had Latin names, 83.5% of their children had Latin names." The ancestors of Polybius and Philippus, therefore, must actively have insisted on retention of their Greek cognomina.

58. See chap. 3, under "Q. Appuleius Severus."

59. Apart from Licinius, the cognomen is known at Pompeii only in the case of Pomponius Faustinus, a *lanista* (see Castrén 252). On *CIL* IV.2476b *(familia gladiatoria Pomponi Faustini [---])* and Pomponius Faustinus, see Sabbatini Tu-molesi 74–75.

60. To Łoś ("Affranchis" 859) this is a Vespasianic salute; rather, like all the men of this chapter, Rustius Verus belongs to late Neronian times.

159:
    Rustium Verum a(edilem) v(iis) a(edibus) s(acris) p(ublicisque)
p(rocurandis).
    Augusto feliciter. Aediles sic decet[61]

[Rustius Verus for aedile. Hail to the Augustus! Thus it befits the aediles.]

Equally striking is the regionalism at once apparent when the houses of these men are pinpointed on the plan of the city.[62] The Claudii, Rustius, and the Iulii all lived on properties clustered in a small sector of the northeast corner of the city, at most a few minutes' walk from each other. All, too, were supported by campaign posters found almost exclusively in the same small area. Even Obellius Firmus, the one neighborhood grandee who cannot definitely be linked to the circle, was awarded a tomb as near as possible, just outside the Porta di Nola. Indeed, the pattern is so striking that we should expect to recover the house of the Licinii in this very neighborhood.

The careers of these men are also oddly compartmentalized. Without known antecedents, all these men flourished in the late Neronian years, lived into Flavian times, and, with the exception of Licinius Faustinus, left no identifiable descendants—hence there is a lean table of stemmata for this chapter. Is this due to circumstances following the earthquake of A.D. 62? It seems likely that Claudius Verus will have turned especially to these men, his political allies, for aid in helping the city weather the disaster. Unfortunately, we shall never know specifics. It is clear, however, that at the end of his term, the *ordo,* invoking the *lex Petronia,* preferred to fill the office with a man who seems to have stood above political categorization, one definitely not of this faction.

C. Cuspius Pansa

One of Pompeii's most distinguished politicians, C. Cuspius Pansa, whom we first met in Claudian times, was apparently able to trace his

---

61. CIL IV.427. I take *aediles sic decet* to mean "thus it (i.e., Rustius' election) befits the aediles (accusative of persons)," or loosely, "he would make a good aedile."

62. On regional support for candidates, see Franklin, *Electoral* 92–94.

lineage back to the early days of the Roman colony, when a Cuspius T. f. served as quattuorvir.[63] The CC. Cuspii Pansae lived in the house at IX.1.22,29 (fig. 17),[64] and Cuspius Pansa himself was honored with a statue and inscribed base in the forum as well as a detailed inscription under an unusual small shrine to the left of the north entrance to the amphitheater.[65] There termed *pater* to distinguish him from two homonymous descendants, he was described as four times duovir, once quinquennial, and a special prefect in accordance with the *lex Petronia*.

160:
> C(aius) Cuspius C(ai) f(ilius) Pansa pater d(uo) v(ir) i(ure)
> d(icundo)
> IIII quinq(uennalis) praef(ectus) i(ure) d(icundo) ex d(ecreto)
> d(ecurionum) lege Petron(ia).[66]

[Gaius Cuspius Pansa the father, son of Gaius, duovir *iure dicundo* four times, (once as) quinquennial, prefect by terms of the Petronian law in accordance with a decree of the decurions.]

The *lex Petronia* provided for the naming of extraordinary magistrates, *praefecti*, when regular elections were incapable of being mounted, and recently it has been observed that at Pompeii such circumstances could only have held following the earthquake.[67] It was to Cuspius, apparently the most trusted man of the day, that the decurions turned in March 62, a short month after the disaster. Cuspius can so far be connected with no faction, a factor that perhaps also recommended him to the decurions. At any rate, he certainly represents old, established blood.

---

63. *CIL* X.937, 938. On the Cuspii, see Castrén 161. For dating Pompeii's few attested *quattuorviri* to the early colony, see Castrén 51, following A. Degrassi, "Quattuorviri in colonie romane e in municipi retti da duoviri," *MemLinc*, 8th ser., 2 (1950) 281–345.
64. Della Corte 495–96.
65. In the forum: *CIL* X.790. On C. Cuspius Pansa, see Mouritsen, *Elections* 100–101.
66. *CIL* X.858.
67. Castrén 112.

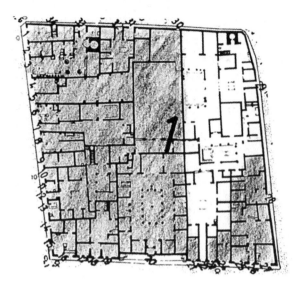

Fig. 17. Block IX.1 and the house of CC. Cuspii Pansae

A. Trebius Valens, Cn. Audius Bassus, and L. Veranius Hypsaeus

Cuspius was not alone in representing old families in these years. In A.D. 60 or 65, three men whose beginnings we have also traced in Claudian times rose to stand for quinquennial. A. Trebius Valens and Cn. Audius Bassus, from whose campaigns only three posters remain,[68] stood together (probably for office in A.D. 60–61), as a poster termed *antiquior* demonstrates.

161:

A(ulum) Trebium Valentem

et Cn(aeum) Audium Bassum

d(uo) v(iros) i(ure) d(icundo) quinq(uennales)

o(ro) v(os) f(aciatis).[69]

[I ask that you elect Aulus Trebius Valens and Gnaeus Audius Bassus quinquennial duovirs *iure dicundo*.]

---

68. Supporting both men: *CIL* IV.7488; supporting Trebius: *CIL* IV.7633; supporting Audius: *CIL* IV.7943.

69. *CIL* IV.7488.

Then, L. Veranius Hypsaeus sought to culminate his career with a third duovirate, this one quinquennial.[70]

162:

L(ucium) Veranium Hypsaeum
II vir(um) i(ure) d(icundo) tertio quinq(uennalem).[71]

[Lucius Veranius Hypsaeus duovir *iure dicundo* for the third time as quinquennial.]

Thus even in a chapter highlighting new bloodlines, we end with the old, in a mix that will characterize also my study of the Flavian years in chapter 6.

---

70. Also supporting Veranius' bid for quinquennial: *CIL* IV.170, 191, 200, 270, 3670 *(antiquior)*, 7160, 7193, and probably 193.
    71. *CIL* IV.187a.

Middle to Late Julio-Claudians—Newcomers

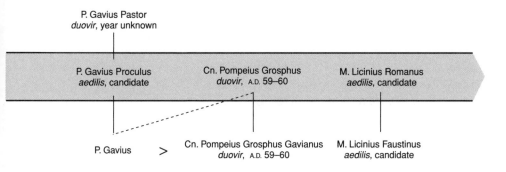

P. Gavius Pastor
duovir, year unknown

P. Gavius Proculus
aedilis, candidate

Cn. Pompeius Grosphus
duovir, A.D. 59–60

M. Licinius Romanus
aedilis, candidate

P. Gavius   >   Cn. Pompeius Grosphus Gavianus
duovir, A.D. 59–60

M. Licinius Faustinus
aedilis, candidate

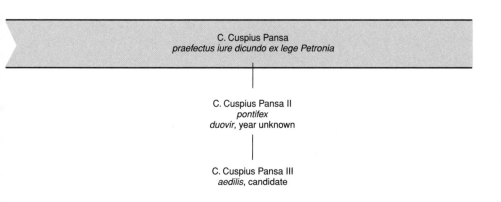

C. Cuspius Pansa
praefectus iure dicundo ex lege Petronia

C. Cuspius Pansa II
pontifex
duovir, year unknown

C. Cuspius Pansa III
aedilis, candidate

Chapter 6

Flavians

When Cn. Alleius Nigidius Maius completed his year as quinquennial duovir, Pompeii's highest elected magistrate, in A.D. 55–56, he will have intended to end his electoral campaigns and to focus his efforts on his own affairs. He did not, however, entirely withdraw from public life; he remained a powerful member of the *ordo decurionum,* and as we saw, he again demonstrated his munificence when he provided for the decoration of the wall surrounding the arena of the amphitheater while the ban on gladiators imposed following the riot was still in force. Nevertheless, he will have been perceived by the public eye as a man of earlier days, those preceding the accession of Nero. His return now to prominent visibility under Vespasian must therefore have served as a sharp statement of change.

Flamen Vespasiani

Given his distinction, age, and relative remove from Neronian politics, it was perhaps natural that Maius was turned to for help in establishing the Flavian dynasty at Pompeii. Indeed, this final stage of his career came when the elder statesman was named *flamen Vespasiani* and mounted yet another gladiatorial show, this time featuring not only a hunt, awnings, and refreshing sprinklings of scented waters but also again gladiators. Officially these games were to honor the new Flavian dynasty—here securely restored thanks to the reference to Titus and Domitian, Vespasian's children *(liberi),* in line 2—and to celebrate on 4 July a second dedication, that of an altar.[1]

---

1. The argument that the flaminate is that of Vespasian was first made by Van Buren ("Maius" 389–90) and is based on *CIL* VI.200 from the Roman Forum: *Paci aeternae / domus / imp(eratoris) Vespasiani / Caesaris Aug(usti) / liberorumq(ue) eius / sacrum.* . . . See also Sabbatini Tumolesi 42. Cf. Castrén 108; Castrén believes Alleius to have been the flamen of Claudius.

163:
Pro salute
[Imp(eratoris) Vespasiani] Caesaris Augu[sti] li[b]e[ror]umqu[e]
[eius ob] dedicationem arae [glad(iatorum) par(ia)---] Cn(aei)
[All]ei Mai
flami[nis] Caesaris Augusti pugn(abunt) Pompeis sine ulla dilatione
IIII non(as) iul(ias). Venatio [sparsiones] vela erunt.[2]

[In honor of the health of the emperor Vespasian Caesar Augustus and his children and on account of the dedication of his altar, [---] pairs of gladiators of Gnaeus Alleius Maius, flamen of Caesar Augustus, will fight at Pompeii without any delay four days before the nones of July. There will be a hunt, sprinklings, and awnings.]

The altar had long been thought to be the fine marble piece in the Temple of Vespasian on the forum, apparently the gift of Maius,[3] but recent analysis has firmly dated that altar to the original, Augustan phase of the temple.[4] Nevertheless, the altar, if not the entire building, must have been rededicated to subsequent emperors, in this case to Vespasian, and it was perhaps this rededication that Maius was celebrating.[5] Alternatively, it has recently been suggested that the nearby building traditionally termed the Santuario dei Lari Pubblici was the seat of imperial cult at Pompeii.[6] If so, Maius' altar will presumably have been located there and would now be lost. Yet whatever the specifics of the altar, the prominence given the new dynasty in the first two lines of the inscription and the insistence on haste in line 4 *(sine ulla dilatione)* seem to capture the exciting early days of Maius' flaminate and the new rulers at Rome.

For his new role as *flamen Vespasiani*, Alleius' obvious wealth and

---

2. Sabbatini Tumolesi N. 15 = *CIL* IV.1180.

3. Following Van Buren, "Maius" 390. On the building, see Richardson, *Architectural* 191–94.

4. J. Dobbins, "The Altar in the Sanctuary of the Genius of Augustus in the Forum at Pompeii," *RomMitt* 99 (1992) 251–63.

5. A. de Franciscis ("Ara sacrificale Pompeiana," *RendPontAcc*, 3rd ser., 23–24 [1947–1949] 186), who also dated the altar to the Augustan era, argued that it originally belonged to the Temple of Fortuna Augusta, which he believed was represented in the background of the sacrificial scene, and that it was moved, reused, and rededicated by Maius.

6. P. Zanker, *Pompeji* 28; and Dobbins, "Chronology" 687–88.

political distinction will have proved especially important. Establishing
the Flavian dynasty at Pompeii, while less difficult than had been the
establishment of Augustan connections, required a man of great skill
and authority. To replace D. Lucretius Satrius Valens as *flamen Neronis*
and make a break with the Julio-Claudian past, the Pompeians naturally
turned to the most distinguished man of the day. Distinction of this cal-
iber, however, came with age, and Alleius was by this time at least in his
mid-fifties and without an attested male heir. As a result, the last decade
of Pompeii's existence saw the rise of an additional, younger center of
Flavian activities.[7]

M. Epidius Sabinus

T. Suedius Clemens first appears in history at Rome as one of the leaders, a *primipilaris,* of the emperor Otho's expedition against the province
of Gallia Narbonensis in A.D. 69.[8] Described as a man who "used his
office to gain popularity, being as reckless toward maintaining discipline
as he was eager to fight,"[9] he in fact seems to have been responsible for
allowing his troops to loot Ventimiglia on their way to force the Maritime
Alps, then held by supporters of Vitellius.

Ten years later and a few months after the eruption of Vesuvius,
Suedius was in Egypt as an officer of Titus and, having heard the statue
of Memnon sound at dawn in November A.D. 79, celebrated his experience by having an inscription carved into its right foot.

164:

[Titus] Suedius Clemens
praef(ectus) castror(um).
Audi Memnone[m]
[---] II idus novembres
anno II T(iti) Imp(eratoris) N.[10]

---

7. Van Buren ("Maius" 388) thought Alleius to be about forty in A.D. 55,
when he held the quinquennial duovirate; Moeller ("Maius" 515–16) thought
him then perhaps as young as 32.
8. Tac. *Hist.* 1.87.
9. Tac. *Hist.* 2.12: *Suedius Clemens ambitioso imperio regebat, ut adversus
modestiam disciplinae corruptus, ita proeliorum avidus;* translated by C.H.
Moore in the Loeb series.
10. *CIL* III.33. The significance of the *N* concluding line 5 is uncertain.

[(Titus) Suedius Clemens, prefect of the camps. I heard Memnon
[---] on 12 November in year two of the emperor Titus [N].]

Although his lack of concern for the statue seems to parallel and even
underscore his lack of discipline in commanding troops, Suedius obviously had developed into a trusted imperial agent. Previous to this, he
had served for Vespasian at Pompeii, recovering public lands that had
been usurped by private developments.[11] Commemoration of this office
was recorded in three identical inscriptions, of which the first was recovered just outside the Porta di Ercolano in 1763.[12]

165:

ex auctoritate
Imp(eratoris) Caesaris
Vespasiani Aug(usti)
loca publica a privatis
possessa T(itus) Suedius Clemens
tribunus causis cognitis et
mensuris factis rei
publicae Pompeianorum
restituit.[13]

[In accordance with the authority of the emperor Vespasian Caesar
Augustus, Titus Suedius Clemens, his tribune, restored to the government of the Pompeians public lands taken over by private individuals, their cases having been heard and measurements taken.]

---

11. This appears to have been a not unusual service of the emperor. See
e.g., CIL VI.933: Imp(erator) Caesar / Vespasianus Aug(ustus) / pontif(ex)
max(imus) tribuni(cia) / potest(ate) VI Imp(erator) XIIII p(ater) p(atriae) /
co(n)s(ul) VI desig(natus) VII censor / locum viniae publicae / occupatum a privatis / per collegium pontificum / restituit; CIL X.3828: Imp(erator) Caesar /
Vespasianus / aug(ur) co(n)s(ul) VIII / fines agrorum / dicatorum / Dianae
Tifat(inae) a / Cornelio Sulla / ex forma divi / Aug(usti) restituit; Magaldi,
"Echi III"; F. Castagnoli, "Cippi di restituto agrorum presso Canne," RFIC 76
(1948) 280–86.
12. The first copy was found outside the Porta di Vesuvio (NSc [1910]
399–401), and a second was found outside the Porta di Nocera (P. Bruneau,
"Deliaca III," BCH 102 [1978] 124, fig. 14). Line divisions vary among the inscriptions, but the texts are duplicates.
13. CIL X.1018.

While carrying out this commission, Suedius also somehow involved himself in local politics, at least allowing his name to be used in support of the candidacy of M. Epidius Sabinus for duovir.[14]

166:

M(arcum) Epidium
Sabinum
II vir(um) iur(e) dic(undo) o(rat) v(os) f(aciatis) dignum iuven(em)
Suedius Clemens sanctissimus
iudex facit vicinis rogantibus.[15]

[His neighbors urging him on, Suedius Clemens, most sacred judge, elects and asks that you elect Marcus Epidius Sabinus, a worthy young man, duovir *iure dicundo.*]

167:

M(arcum) Epidium Sabinum
ex sententia Suedi Clementis d(uo) v(irum) i(ure) d(icundo)
o(ro) v(os) f(aciatis).[16]

[In accordance with the opinion of Suedius Clemens, I ask that you elect Marcus Epidius Sabinus duovir *iure dicundo.*]

Indeed, his support confirms the prominence of Epidius Sabinus in these final years of Pompeii's existence, while the unparalleled connivance of the *ordo* also to secure this election seems to identify M. Epidius Sabinus as the imperial choice—at least as that of the imperial agent. Six posters have survived to attest this awkward interference; here two can serve for illustration.[17]

---

14. So *CIL* IV.7780, although fragmentary, seems likely to support Epidius Sabinus, the only candidate with whom Suedius Clemens was associated: *[M(arcum) Epidium Sabinum] / II vir(um) [d(ignum)] r(ei) p(ublicae) o(ro) v(os) f(aciatis) S[uedio] / Clementi [fe]liciter.*

15. *CIL* IV.1059.

16. *CIL* IV.791.

17. See also *CIL* IV.7203: *M(arcum) Epidium / Sabinum d(uovirum) i(ure) d(icundo) o(rat) v(os) f(aciatis) sanctus ordo facit / Suedio Clementi sancto iudici / feliciter; CIL* IV.7576: *M(arcum) Epidium II vir(um) d(ignum) r(ei) p(ublicae) / Sabinum ordo sanctiss(imus) / facit / val(ete); CIL* IV.7584: *Sabinum /*

168:

M(arcum) Epidium Sabinum d(uovirum) i(ure) dic(undo)
o(rat) v(os) f(aciatis). Dig(nus) est.

defensorem coloniae ex sententia Suedi Clementis sancti iudicis

consensu ordinis obmerita [*sic*] eius et probitatem dignum
reipublicae [*sic*] faciat(is)

Sabinus dissignator cum plausu facit.[18]

[Sabinus the usher, with applause, in accordance with the opinion of
Suedius Clemens the sacred judge and with the agreement of the
ordo on account of his merits and probity, elects and asks that you
elect Marcus Epidius Sabinus, defender of the colony and worthy of
the state, duovir *iure dicundo*. He is worthy.]

169:

M(arcum) Epidium Sabinum

II vir(um) i(ure) d(icundo) o(rat) v(os) f(aciatis) dignissimum
iuvene[m]

sanctus ordo facit Clementi sancto iudici fel(iciter)[19]

[The holy *ordo* elects and asks that you elect Marcus Epidius Sabinus, most worthy young man, duovir *iure dicundo*. Greetings to
Clemens, the holy judge.]

The house of M. Epidius Sabinus and of his apparent father, Rufus,
has been identified as one of the city's most notable, that at IX.1.20,30,
along the Via dell' Abbondanza (fig. 18).[20] It was given great prominence
by being elevated on a podium above the level of the sidewalk, and it
centered on the handsomest Corinthian atrium yet recovered at Pompeii
(fig. 19). Sixteen Doric columns surrounded the impluvium; two Ionic

---

IIvir(um) i(ure) d(icundo) sanctus ordo / consensu populi facit; CIL IV.7605:
*Epidium Sabinum / II vir(um) iur(e) dic(undo) o(rat) v(os) f(aciatis) Trebius
cliens facit / consentiente sanctissimo / ordine.*

18. *CIL* IV.768. The combination of the formulaic language of the programmata and the fulsomeness of the praise makes parts of this notice redundant.

19. *CIL* IV.7579.

20. On the house, see Richardson, *Architectural* 111–14; on the identification
of its owners, Della Corte 489–94.

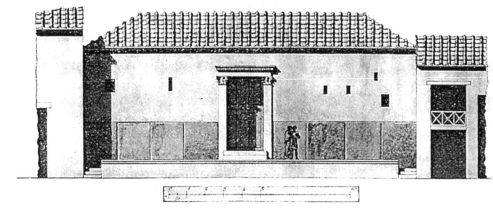

Fig. 18. Restored facade of the house of M. Epidius Sabinus

columns stood to the front of each ala, and pilasters with figured capitals framed their corners. To the rear was a large vegetable garden, and farther back at a higher level was a smaller flower garden. Decorated in Third and Fourth Pompeian styles, the house was not among the city's largest, although it was surely among its most impressive.

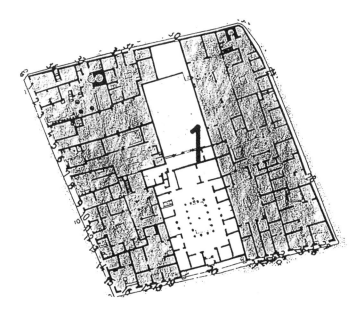

Fig. 19. Block IX.1 and the house of M. Epidius Sabinus

Little is known of M. Epidius Rufus the father, and he seems in fact to have died shortly before the eruption. The *signaculum,* or bread-stamp, of his freedman Italicus was found in the house and helped to identify its owners; and fixed on the Lararium in the ala to the right was a dedication by two of his freedmen named Diadumenus to the genius of a Marcus, the recently deceased Rufus.[21]

170:

Genio M(arci) n(ostri) et
Laribus
duo Diadumeni
liberti[22]

[The two freedmen Diadumenus to the genius of our Marcus and to the Lares.]

At the time of the eruption, this ala had been recently turned into a sacellum, and its Lararium had been built in the shape of an aedicula that held the marble figure of a Venus Pompeiana.[23] The sacellum is most interesting, however, for the paintings that were to the sides of the Lararium. On the left, three attendants led a bull to sacrifice, apparently to the altar painted on the right, where two togaed men, presumably Rufus and Sabinus, stood waiting.[24] A bull is regularly the animal sacrificed to a living emperor, and a similar sacrificial scene was carved on the front of the altar in the Temple of Vespasian on the forum.[25] It seems that these

---

21. Della Corte 492–493. Fröhlich (32) further takes this inscription as evidence of organization of a private cult of freedmen and slaves, a mistaken concept that further leads him to misinterpret the paintings in the sacellum into which the Lararium is built (see the discussion that follows in text).

22. *CIL* X.861.

23. G.K. Boyce, *Corpus of the Lararia of Pompeii,* MAAR 14 (Rome 1937) 79 n. 384 and pl. 29.2. On the figure of Venus, see *Giornale,* n.s., 1 (1868), 188 n. 2, and 229; Della Corte p. 245 n. 4.

24. The paintings are now lost. Della Corte (492–93) was alone in seeing a man and a woman to the right of the altar; cf. Fiorelli, *Descrizione* 372; Helbig 59b; Boyce, op. cit. (above, n. 23).

25. On the bull as imperial sacrifice, see L.R. Taylor, "The Worship of Augustus in Italy during His Lifetime," *TAPA* 51 (1920) 126. On the altar in the Temple of Vespasian, see Mau, *Pompeii* 106–9; Richardson, *Architectural* 193.

paintings intentionally recalled the relief on the altar and tied the Epidii firmly to imperial cult, that of the living emperor Vespasian.[26]

In the most extensive and laudatory of the programmata recommending him for duovir (*CIL IV.*768 = inscription 168) and in another fragmentary notice,[27] Epidius Sabinus was termed *defensor coloniae.* He seems to have been a *causidicus,* or case pleader, who worked with Suedius Clemens in his commission of recovering city property.[28] Such a position would have distinguished him once and for all in local eyes, and he may in fact have been positioning himself for replacing the elderly Cn. Alleius Nigidius Maius, *flamen Vespasiani,* or he may already have replaced Maius following the flamen's recent death. Such offices were referred to not in the electoral programmata but only in honorary inscriptions and notices of games, where they were relevant. No such document has been recovered in the case of Epidius, and therefore no explicit record confirms that he actually succeeded to the office, although the paintings that surrounded his Lararium and particularly the conversion of the ala to a sacellum that was centered on Venus Pompeiana seem clearly to signal the succession. Given the support of Suedius Clemens and the *ordo* when Epidius had stood for office, no one could have been a more obvious replacement for Maius.

Although an old Pompeian family, the gens Epidia had not been politically visible for several generations.[29] V(ibius) Popidius Ep(idii) f(ilius) had seen to the erection of the old colonnade around the forum sometime between 150 and 100 B.C.,[30] and in the early Julio-Claudian period successful Epidii had been adopted by the gentes Herennia and Lucretia.[31] Epidius Sabinus, however, is the only Epidius known to have

---

26. Fröhlich (181–82) prefers to read these paintings, unique at Pompeii, as mere inaccurate renditions of the domestic cult to Rufus, an example of a standard painting type misused in this context.

27. *CIL* IV.1032: *M(arcum) Epidium [---] / defensorem [---] / [---].*

28. For speculation on Sabinus' career, see the notes at Della Corte 493r and at *CIL* IV.7343. To G.O. Onorato (*Iscrizioni Pompeiane: La vita pubblica* [Florence 1957] 189–90), Sabinus was an agent of recovery following the earthquake; to the contrary, as we have seen, C. Cuspius Pansa, *praefectus iure dicundo ex decreto decurionum lege Petronia,* headed up those efforts (see above, chap. 5).

29. On the gens Epidia, see Castrén 164–65.

30. On V(ibius) Popidius Ep(idii) f(ilius), see *CIL* I².1627; on his colonnade, Mau, *Pompeii* 50.

31. On M. Herennius Epidianus, the Augustan, see *CIL* X.802, 831, 939; on

reached duoviral rank while still carrying his own gentilicial. His prominence and imperial support make his running mates also particularly interesting.

AA. Suettii, Certus et Verus

Standing in coalition with Epidius Sabinus were A. Suettius Certus and his son, A. Suettius Verus.[32] Certus was seeking the duovirate; Verus, the aedileship. They and the second candidate for aedile, Herennius Celsus, all shared the support of one programma, while numerous other programmata attest their various interrelationships as candidates.[33]

171:

Cer[t]um [et E]pidium
Sabinum II vir(os) Suettium Herennium aed(iles). Dign(i) sunt
[P]otitus [et]
Sabinus rogant[34]

[Potitus and Sabinus ask Certus and Epidius Sabinus as duovirs, Suettius and Herennius as aediles. They are worthy.]

Like Epidius, Suettius Certus was the first man carrying his nomen to appear in Pompeian politics. He had been elected aedile earlier in Neronian years and had delayed further political action until his coalition with Epidius could both ensure his election and start his son's career in impressive fashion. As aedile he had offered games from which

---

M. Lucretius Epidius Flaccus, *praefectus iure dicundo* in A.D. 33 and quinquennial in A.D. 40, *CIL* X.901–2, 904, and above, chap. 2.

32. On the Suettii, see Castrén 226; because he was unaware of the years between Certus' magistracies, he wrongly suggests that Verus could have been Certus' brother. There are in fact only two other Suettii known: an A. Suettius whose cognomen is uncertain *(. . . tenio)* and his freedman A. Suettius Niger. Both belonged instead to Puteoli, for that is where their games (their only attestation) were to take place, according to *CIL* IV.9970: *Glad(iatorum) par(ia) XX A(uli) Suetti / [Par]tenionis [e]t Nigri liberti pugna(bunt) / Puteol(is) XVI, XV, XIV, XIII kal(endas) ap(riles) venatio et / athletae [vela] erunt* (text of Sabbatini Tumolesi N. 75)

33. Franklin, *Electoral* tables 1, 2, 3.

34. *CIL* IV.359–60. On the reading of this poorly recorded programma, see the note at the *CIL* entry; Mouritsen (*Elections* 134) confirms *Potitus* in line 3.

four largely fragmentary notices survive, the most complete of which was found along the Via degli Augustali, where it was highly visible to passersby.[35]

172:

A(uli) Suetti Certi
aedilis familia gladiatoria pugnabit Pompeis
pri(die) k(alendas) iunias. Venatio et vela erunt.
Omnibus Nero[nianorum mun]eribus feliciter.[36]

[The family of gladiators of the aedile Aulus Suettius Certus will fight at Pompeii on the day before the calends of June. There will be a hunt and awnings. Happily to all the presentations of the Neronians!]

Unlike most of the Pompeian notices of games, this notice provides few details, substituting *familia gladiatoria* for specific numbers of gladiatorial bouts. The use of the term, however, seems to indicate that Suettius himself owned the troupe.[37] The notice advertises a show of only one day's duration, a fairly simple production. In the final line, there is reference to Neronian shows, probably in an attempt to tie the most famous gladiator school of the era, that of Nero at Capua, with this production of Certus; certainly enthusiasm for Nero's gladiators—in some places, for Nero—outlived the last of the Julio-Claudians himself.[38] The gens Suettia is well attested at Capua, and Certus and Verus are the first—in fact, the only—known members of the gens at Pompeii.[39] Cer-

35. On the location of the notice, see J.L. Franklin, Jr., "Games and a *Lupanar*: Prosopography of a Neighborhood in Ancient Pompeii," *CJ* 81 (1985–86) 319–21. Other notices are at *CIL* IV.1189, 1191, 7987.

36. Sabbatini Tumolesi N. 22 = *CIL* IV.1190.

37. Only the notices of Suettius and Popidius Rufus (on whom see the discussion that follows in text) used this term rather than *paria gladiatoria,* which would indicate rented performers. *Familia* here seems more likely to indicate straightforward ownership than, as Sabbatini Tumolesi 51–52 suggests, it "... potesse essere intesa come comprensiva, oltre che di gladiatori, di molte altre persone addette ai servizi dell'arena."

38. On the difficulties of interpreting the phrase *Neronianorum muneribus,* see Sabbatini Tumolesi 51–52. On Neronian pretenders, see Tac. *Hist.* 1.2; Suet. *Ner.* 57.

39. On the Suettii at Capua, see *CIL* I².677, 681; *CIL* X.3779, 3822, 4014,

tus may in fact himself have come from Capua and been presenting a small show of his own quality performers, trained in the best fashion.

N. Herennius Celsus II

As we have already seen, the Marci Herennii had long been prominent at Pompeii.[40] N. Herennius Celsus I had served twice as duovir in the Augustan era and is the first Numerius known.[41] His apparent son, N. Herennius Verus, served as aedile in A.D. 31, but nothing more is known of him.[42] N. Herennius Celsus II, apparent son of Verus, was now candidate with Epidius Sabinus and the Suettii.

By standing with Epidius Sabinus, Herennius and the Suettii allied themselves with the most promising man of the day. The Suettii were a new line in Pompeii, Herennius was a member of a line established in the Augustan Age, and Epidius was the first man of his line to stand for office, although his family had contributed several adopted men to the city's list of magistrates. It must have been an attractive coalition—and unbeatable, given the support for Epidius by Suedius Clemens and the *ordo decurionum*.

N. Popidius Rufus

As interesting as the members of Epidius' coalition, however, is a man with whom he did not stand for office, a former associate and presumably strong candidate, N. Popidius Rufus.[43] Indeed, apart from Epidius Sabinus, only Popidius Rufus was referred to as *defensor coloniae,* in a

---

4357–58; M.W. Frederiksen, "Republican Capua: A Social and Economic Study," *PBR,* n.s., 14 (1959) 116.

40. See chap. 2.

41. The career of Herennius Celsus I was recorded on the tomb of his wife, Aesquilla Pollia (*NSc* [1910] 390): *N(umerius) Herennius N(umerii) f(ilius) Men(enia tribu) / Celsus d(uo) v(ir) i(ure) d(icundo) iter(um) praef(ectus) / fabr(um) / Aesquilliae C(aii) f(iliae) Pollae / uxori vixit annos XXII / locus sepulturae publice datus / d(ecreto) d(ecurionum).*

42. *CIL* X.899–900; above, chap. 2.

43. On the Popidii, see Castrén 207–9, to which now add Varone, "Tituli" 2 (p. 92), a programma supporting Popidius Rufus for aedile. We have already met N. Popidius Moschus, *minister Augusti* and freedman of an ancestor of Augustan times; see above, chap. 1, under "*gens Mescinia.*"

salute paintcd at VIII.7.16, to the side of the entrance to the gladiator school located behind the Teatro Grande.

173:

> Popi[dio] Rufo invicto muneribus;
> defensoribus colonorum feliciter.[44]

[Happily to Popidius Rufus, unconquered in games; happily to the defenders of the colonists.]

Likewise, at I.10.4, the entrance to the Casa del Menandro, house of Poppaeus Sabinus, a cluster of notices suggests the title for Popidius.

174:

> defensoribus coloniae felic[iter].[45]
> [Happily to the defenders of the colony.]

175:

> [---dign]us est omnibus pompeianis feliciter scripsit Infantio.[46]

[[---] is worthy. Happily to all Pompeians. Infantio is writing.]

176:

> Popidio Rufo feliciter. Dignus est.[47]

[Happily to Popidius Rufus. He is worthy.]

Popidius must have also served as *causidicus* under Suedius Clemens in his commission to clear public lands, but, unlike Epidius, he apparently failed to impress—or to accommodate—Suedius Clemens, although the memory of his service remained worthy of notice locally.[48]

---

44. *CIL* IV.1094.
45. *CIL* IV.7342.
46. *CIL* IV.7343. On Infantio the *scriptor,* or letterer of signs, see Franklin, "*Scriptores*" 58–61.
47. *CIL* IV.7346.
48. *CIL* IV.7667 may also attest his service: *Popidium Rufum IIvir(um) / dignum coloniae Pompeianae.* The more usual phrase is *dignum rei publicae,* and the preference for *coloniae* here may depend on *defensor coloniae.*

Rufus will have lived with his father, N. Popidius Priscus, in the signoral Casa dei Marmi at VII.2.20,21,41 (fig. 20), where Priscus' *signaculum,* or breadstamp, was found.[49] The house was being redecorated at the time of the eruption, as walls prepared for the painters and stacks of marble for revetments and pavements attested. Famous among the survivors of the eruption, it was looted and even labeled—in Latin mistransliterated into Greek script—as entered and emptied by scavengers.

177:

δουμμος *[sic]*
περτουςα[50]

[House tunneled through.]

Fortunately, the scavengers were not interested in the limestone Oscan inscription proving the age and distinction of the family; it had been saved from an earlier monument and eventually reused for rebuilding.

178:

mr pú[p]idiis mr
pú.....an[51]

The last distinguished Popidius, N. Popidius Rufus stood for both aedile and duovir, and perhaps during one of his terms in office, he mounted a gladiatorial show for which an announcement has been recovered. Beginning 20 April, the show was to include a hunt, awnings, and, apparently, a distribution of apples *(mala).*[52] A salute to his manager, whose name is missing, concluded the notice.[53]

---

49. *CIL* X.8058.70. On the house and its inhabitants, see Della Corte 264–65; Della Corte argued on the basis of the pattern of oval shields with three thunderbolts in the tablinum pavement that Priscus had been a member of the praetorian guard.

50. *CIL* IV.2311.

51. Text of Conway n. 54 (= Vetter 22a).

52. So argues Sabbatini Tumolesi (55–56)—suggesting even a local apple jam, *mala cumana,* if fresh apples were not available—after rejecting two possible emendations of Zangemeister (at the *CIL* entry): *mali* (masts for the awnings) and *matutini,* for which Sabbatini Tumolesi's *matutina* (morning games) is better.

53. On the unlikely possibility that this procurator was a municipal official who oversaw the presentation of games, see Sabbatini Tumolesi 57.

Fig. 20. Block VII.2 and the house of N. Popidius Rufus

179:

N(umeri) Popidi
Rufi fam(ilia) glad(iatoria) [p]u[g]n(abit) Pompeis venati[o]
ex XII k(alendas) mai(as). Mala [e]t vela erunt. [---]o procurator[i]
felicitas.[54]

[The family of gladiators of Numerius Popidus Rufus will fight at
Pompeii beginning the twelfth day before the calends of May. There
will be a hunt, apples, and awnings. Happiness to [---] the agent.]

These games may not have been planned for one of the years of Popidius' magistracies, since in the salute that began this discussion (= inscription 173), he is termed "unconquered in games" *[invicto muner-
ibus]*, which suggests frequent entertainments, and since it seems from
this announcement of games that he owned his own troupe of gladia-

54. Sabbatini Tumolesi N. 25 = *CIL* IV.1186. An apparent second, highly fragmentary notice is *CIL* IV.1188: *N(umeri) Popidi [Rufi familia gladiatoria
pugnabit ?---]* (text of Sabbatini Tumolesi N. 26).

tors *(familia gladiatoria)*, which would have been easily available on a variety of occasions.[55]

Of Popidius Rufus himself no more is known, although a very wealthy freedman of his (or of his father), N. Popidius Ampliatus,[56] is famous to modern scholarship for rebuilding the Temple of Isis from the ground up *(a fundamento)* after the earthquake *(terrae motu conlapsam)*. This was done in the name of Ampliatus' six-year-old son, N. Popidius Celsinus, who was, according to the stone set to commemorate the project, in return named to the *ordo* gratis by the decurions.[57]

180:

N(umerius) Popidius N(umeri) f(ilius) Celsinus

aedem Isidis terrae motu conlapsam

a fundamento p(ecunia) s(ua) restituit. Hunc decuriones ob liberalitatem

cum esset annorum sexs ordini suo gratis adlegerunt.[58]

[Numerius Popidius Celsinus, son of Numerius, restored from its foundations the Temple of Isis, collapsed from the earthquake. On account of his generosity the decurions adlected him to their *ordo* gratis when he was six years old.]

L. Popidius Ampliatus II

Other Popidii, too, were highly visible in these years. We have already met L. Popidius Secundus, the freedman and member of Nero's famous claque. He shared with L. Popidius Ampliatus, a fellow freedman, the enormous Casa del Citarista at I.4.5,25,28 (fig. 21).[59] Little is known of Popidius Ampliatus, but he four times signed the *apochae* of Caecilius

---

55. See n. 37. So also Richardson, *Architectural* 86.

56. Ampliatus' status is clear from his inclusion in a list of obvious freedmen at *Apochae* 83, and as Andreau ("Remarques" 222) observes, the work in the name of his son is "signe manifeste qu'Ampliatus était lui-même un affranchi."

57. The relationship of Ampliatus and Celsinus is attested by the inscription (*CIL* X.847) on the plinth of the statue of Bacchus at the rear of the temple building: *N(umerius) Popidius Ampliatus / pater p(ecunia) s(ua)*.

58. *CIL* X.846.

59. On the LL. Popidii and the Casa del Citarista, see chap. 4, n. 47.

Fig. 21. Block I.4 and the house of the LL. Popidii Ampliatii and the
LL. Popidii Secundi

Iucundus as a witness along with other freedmen, so there can be no
doubt of his status. By A.D. 75,[60] his homonymous son was standing for
election as aedile,[61] in coalition with P. Vedius Nummianus, son of another man of the Neronian era, Vedius Siricus the Neropoppaeensis,
who since we last met him as duovir following the riot in the amphitheater had stood for and surely won election as quinquennial
duovir, gaining even more distinction for his family.[62]

---

60. A quinquennial year and so easily dated.

61. On the relationship, see also Andreau, *Jucundus* 200: "L. Popidius Ampliatus, témoin dans les tabl. 47, 71, 82, 94, 98, est le père du candidat à l'édilité
L. Popidius L. f. Ampliatus." So also Łoś, "Remarques" 287.

62. *CIL* IV.214, 7138. Łoś ("Remarques" 292) also comments on the interesting combination of candidates; to him Vedius Siricus was "un des plus influents
notables pompéiens."

181:

> L(ucium) Popidium Ampliatum et L(ucium) Vedium
> Nummianum aed(iles) o(ro) v(os) f(aciatis).[63]

[I ask that you elect Lucius Popidus Ampliatus and Lucius Vedius Nummianus aediles.]

Moreover, in a separate notice Nummianus was paired with the elderly quinquennial candidate of the year, M. Satrius Valens, the natural father of the *flamen Neronis Caesaris Augusti filii perpetuus* D. Lucretius Satrius Valens.[64]

182:

> Satr[iu]m quinq(uennalem) d(ignum) r(ei) p(ublicae)
> et Numm[ian]um.[65]

[Satrius, a man worthy of the state, quinquennial, and Nummianus.]

Apparently completing the slate of candidates this year was Q. Postumius Modestus, who had served as duovir in A.D. 56–57 and was supported for quinquennial duovir by more surviving posters than any other candidate.[66] As we have already seen, he and his son, Postumius Proculus, who was shortly to stand for aedile,[67] lived in the aristocratic house at VIII.4.2–6,49,50 (fig. 5), across the Via dell' Abbondanza from the Stabian Baths.[68] To have arranged cooperation with the Vedii, Satrii, and Postumii, the Popidii Ampliatii must have been as successful and wealthy as their (albeit shared) house, the Casa del Citarista, suggests.

---

63. *CIL* IV.3549.

64. M. Satrius Valens is the only Satrius known to have stood for quinquennial duovir, as attested at nearby *CIL* IV.7556: *M(arcum) Satrium / quinq(uennalem) o(ro) v(os) f(aciatis)*.

65. *CIL* IV.7564.

66. On the Postumii, see Castrén 210. Supporting Modestus for quinquennial are *CIL* IV.195, 279, 736, 756, 778, 786, 1156, 1160, 3017?, 3679, 7466, 7486, 7502, 7609.

67. E.g., *CIL* IV.7238: *Q(uintum) Postumium Proculum / aed(ilem) d(ignum) r(ei) p(ublicae) Masculus rog(at)*.

68. Della Corte 470–72.

L. Popidius Secundus II

The homonymous son of L. Popidius Secundus, too, stood for aedile in
the Flavian era—with his generation's Cuspius Pansa, an even more impressive running mate than Vedius Nummianus, with whom Popidius
Ampliatus stood.[69]

183:

C(aium) Cuspium̂ Pansam et

L(ucium) Popidium̂ L(ucii) f(ilium) Secundum aed̂(iles)

o(rat) v(os) f(aciatis)

Fabius Ululitremulus cûm Sula rog(at).[70]

[Fabius Ululitremulus, along with Sula, asks that you elect Gaius Cuspius Pansa and Lucius Popidius Secundus, son of Lucius, aediles.]

In both Claudian and Neronian times, we met the first well-known
C. Cuspius Pansa, who at the summit of a long career had been named
praefectus iure dicundo ex decreto decurionum lege Petronia in the aftermath of the earthquake. In addition to the shrine to the family in the
amphitheater, he was given a statue in the forum, and next to it stood a
statue of his son, an unspecified pontifex, who had also served as
duovir.[71] Now, the grandson had entered the political fray. Given the
distinction of the Cuspii Pansae and the wealth and success of the Popidii Secundi, the candidates must have stood at minimum age, which
would explain the references to their youth and claim of uprightness in
their campaign posters.[72]

---

69. Łoś ("Remarques" 292) also comments on the interesting combination
"Evidemment il augmentait ainsi ses chances pour le succès: son partenaire ap-
partenait à une des plus puissantes familles pompéiennes dans les trente
dernières années avant l'éruption du Vésuve."

70. *CIL* IV.7963. On the Fabii, Ululitremulus and Sula, see Della Corte
711–12.

71. *CIL* X.859: *C(aius) Cuspius C(aii) f(ilii) f(ilius) Pansa pontif(ex)* / *d(uo)
vir i(ure) d(icundo)*. The original Cuspius Pansa was the son of Caius, so this
man, his son, was "the son of the son of Caius."

72. Recommending Cuspius for his uprightness are *CIL* IV.317, 566, 702; so
recommending Popidius are *CIL* IV.720, 968, 1012, probably 1143 (= inscription
188), 3409, 7146, 7681; so recommending both are *CIL* IV.709, 785a, 1022.

184:

C(aium) Cusp[ium Pansam]
L(ucium) Popidium Secundum a[ed(iles)]
iuvenes probos dignos r(ei) p(ublicae) o(ro) v(os) f(aciatis).
S[c]r(ipsit) Infantio[73]

[I ask that you elect Gaius Cuspius Pansa and Lucius Popidius Secundus, upright young men worthy of the state, aediles. Infantio is
writing.]

From these posters of the second generation of the Lucii Popidii, we can
draw one final indication of the importance of the first generation. The
wealthy, freedmen fathers were so visible that the sons were forced to
underscore their own identities and freeborn status to avoid being confused with their fathers: they are the only candidates officially to have
specified filiation in their posters, and they specified it repeatedly.[74]

185:

L(ucium) Popidium L(ucii) f(ilium) Ampliatum aed(ilem)
o(ro) v(os) f(aciatis).[75]

[I ask that you elect Lucius Popidius Ampliatus, son of Lucius, aedile.]

186:

Popidium L(ucii) [filium]
Secundum
aed(ilem) o(ro) v(os) f(aciatis) veninosm.[76]

[I ask that you elect Popidius Secundus, son of Lucius, aedile [veni-
nosm].]

---

73. CIL IV.785a. On Infantio the letterer, see Franklin, "Scriptores" 58–61.

74. Also observed by Łoś ("Affranchis" 870). Programmata including filiation for Ampliatus are CIL IV.7168, 7175, 7474, 7510, 7618, 7632, 7665, 7702, 7706,
7851; for Secundus are CIL IV.1143, 7614; for one or the other are CIL IV.721, 749,
754, 779, 1076, 2966, 7161, 7321.

75. CIL IV.7168.

76. CIL IV.1143. The last word is obviously scrambled but seems to have
been iuvenem, at least in part. Zangemeister asks at the CIL entry, "Latetne vere-
cundum . . . (968) an iuven. innocuae aetatis (720)?" Castrén (115) restores the

Nevertheless, the Lucii Popidii also appear to have dug deep for their support. Of the 107 posters securely posted for them, 27 were signed by their supporters, only two of whom were even moderately prominent men: Paquius Proculus and Rustius Verus.[77] Otherwise, their attested supporters were of decidedly modest status, including Secundus' grandmother, Taedia Secunda.[78]

L. Ceius Secundus

Also digging deep for support was L. Ceius Secundus, whose family had some time before disappeared from the electoral scene.[79] Only one Ceius of earlier times is known; L. Ceius Labeo had belonged to the Augustan or early Julio-Claudian era, and his tomb inscription was recovered outside the Porta di Ercolano.[80]

187:

> L(ucio) Ceio L(ucii) f(ilio) Men(enia tribu) Labeoni
> iter(um) d(uo) v(iro) i(ure) d(icundo) quinq(uennali)
> Menomachus l(ibertus).[81]

[To Lucius Ceius Labeo, son of Lucius, tribe Menenia, twice duovir *iure dicundo,* (once as) quinquennial, (by) Menomachus, his freedman.]

---

word as *Veneriosus,* a term for a member of an association of the worshipers of Venus, as in *CIL* IV.7791: *Ceium Secundum IIv(irum) i(ure) d(icundo) / Veneriosi rog(ant) iuvenem.*

77. The count is that of Castrén 207–8, under "L. Popidius," "L. Popidius Ampliatus II," and "L. Popidius L. f. Secundus." Paquius supported Ampliatus (*CIL* IV.7210); Rustius supported Secundus (*CIL* IV.3750). Trebius Valens was solicited by both Ampliatus (*CIL* IV.7618, 7624, 7632) and Secundus (*CIL* IV.7614).

78. *CIL* IV.7469: *L(ucium) Popi[dium] S[ecun]d[u]m aed(ilem) o(ro) v(os) f(aciatis) / Taed[i]a Secunda cupiens avia rog(at) et fecit [sic].*

79. On the Ceii, see Castrén 151–52.

80. The inscription seems to have belonged to tomb N39: see Kockel 176–179; with the dating at 179. On Ceius Labeo, see Mouritsen, *Elections* 100. Castrén (118) thinks Ceius Labeo a descendant of Ceius Serapio, probably a late republican *argentarius.*

81. Kockel N39 = *CIL* X.1037. The final word of the inscription may as well be restored as *l(ocavit).* Menomachus, however, can only be a freedman, whichever restoration is preferred (so Castrén [151], on the strength of this inscription, identifies L. Ceius L. l. Menomachus). Labeo's apparent wife was buried in the same tomb (*CIL* X.1038: *Ceiae L(ucii) f(iliae) uxor[i]*).

After twice serving as duovir, he had reached the rank of quinquennial and was obviously a man of importance, but he was buried not at public expense but by his freedman, a sign that something serious—lack of progeny, loss of fortune—had gone wrong. Thus our Ceius Secundus, who stood for both aedile and duovir, was in fact probably the descendant of a freedman—although, unlike the Lucii Popidii, not one of enormous wealth—rather than of Ceius Labeo.[82]

188:

L(ucium) Ceium Secundum aed(ilem) o(rant) v(os) f(aciatis)
Proculus et Canthus r[o]g(ant)[83]

[Proculus and Canthus ask that you elect Lucius Ceius Secundus aedile.]

189:

L(ucium) Ceium Secundum II vir(um)
Passaratus nec sine Maeniano
rog(at).[84]

[Passaratus, not without Maenianus, asks Lucius Ceius Secundus as duovir.]

Secundus lived in the modest house at I.6.15 (fig. 22), across from the Casa del Menandro.[85] On the house facade were found campaign posters in favor of L. Sextilius, C. Cornelius, Postumius Proculus, Veranius Hypsaeus, and Cuspius Pansa, all powerful figures of slightly earlier times.[86] These, coupled with the posters in support of Ceius Secundus himself gathered from around town, appear to reveal the pattern of his climb to elected office. He and his household had for years supported men of prominence, even noting the thoughtfulness of

---

82. So also Łoś, "Affranchis" 867.
83. *CIL* IV.1140.
84. *CIL* IV.995.
85. Della Corte 540. On the house, see Michel, *Cei.*
86. *CIL* IV.7187 and 7192, 7190, 7194, 7193, 7188, respectively. Although signed by members of his household as well as himself, they may be taken as indications of Ceius' enthusiasms throughout; as owner of the house, he would presumably have approved of their posting. See also Michel, *Cei* 17–18.

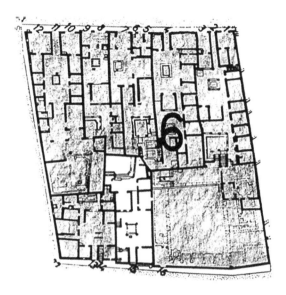

Fig. 22. Block I.6 and the house of L. Ceius Secundus

L. Sextilius (*multis fecit benigne* [he has dealt kindly with many]).[87] When he himself at length stood for office, he was supported by a wide collection of hoi polloi. In addition to Proculus and Canthus (inscription 188) and Passaratus and Maenianus (inscription 189), his *clientes* as a group, Amiullius *(sic)*, Cosmus, Euhode *perfusor* (bath attendant), Felicio *lupinarius* (lupine dealer), Primus *fullo* (cleaner), and Sutoria Primigenia *cum suis* (with her dependents), among others, posted notices in his favor.[88] In fact, Papilio the *scriptor*, or sign letterer, even signed his own name to five notices scattered around town.[89] Finally, Secundus seems to have tried to work out a deal of exchanged support with a Loreius.

---

87. *CIL* IV.7187.

88. *CIL* IV.7490, 737, 840, 3423, 3478, 7464, respectively. See others at Castrén 151–52, and add Giordano and Casale 4, 7, 11, 14, 16.

89. *CIL* IV.908, 1157, 3367, 7251, 7298. On Papilio, see Franklin, "*Scriptores*" 63–64, and add now to his corpus Giordano and Casale 7. Giordano and Casale 8, *Ceium IIvirum / Astylus rog(at)*, is perhaps owed to the letterer Astylus, on whom see Franklin, "*Scriptores*" 64–66.

190:

L(ucium) Ceium Secundum

II vir(um) o(rat) v(os) f(aciatis) Lorei et ille te faciet.[90]

[Loreius, (Secundus) asks that you elect Ceius Secundus duovir, and he will elect you.]

L. Caecilius Capella

Parallel to Ceius Secundus was Caecilius Capella. The Caecilii, however, appear to have stretched back further than the Ceii and to have gone into an even deeper decline before rising again in Pompeii's final years.[91] Q. Caecilius had early stood for an office best restored as quattuorvir in two programmata, and two more attest his campaign for an unspecified office.[92]

191:

Q(uintum) Caecil(ium) q[uattuor] v[irum] benific(um) [sic] o(ro) v(os) [faciatis].[93]

[I ask that you elect the kindly Quintus Caecilius quattuorvir.]

The quattuorvirate was an institution of the early colony,[94] and in fact all four notices are *antiquissima* and therefore belong to the early imperial era at the latest. Thereafter no politically active Caecilius is known

---

90. *CIL* IV.7539. The formulaic aspects of this personalized notice make it in fact ungrammatical; *Loreius,* the name of the person to whom the notice is addressed, is singular, but the formulaic subject and verb are plural. On the problem, see Mouritsen, *Elections* 131, on this notice.

91. On the Caecilii, see Castrén 144–45.

92. *CIL* IV.24, 29, 30, 36. Castrén also restored *quattuorvir.* Zangemeister in the *CIL,* however, restored *quaestor,* an office of the Samnite period, from which it is scarcely possible that a poster could remain. Another possible restoration, *quinquennalem* is regularly abbreviated as *quinq.*

93. *CIL* IV.29.

94. On *quattuorviri* as magistrates of the early colony, see Castrén 50, following H. Rudolph, *Stadt und Staat in römischen Italien* (Leipzig 1935) 88 n. 2, and G.O. Onorato, "Pompei *municipium* e colonia romana," *RendNap,* n.s., 26 (1951) 115–56.

until L. Caecilius Capella, who stood now in Flavian times, once sharing a poster with N. Popidius Rufus.

192:
> N(umerium) Popidium Ruf[um et] Caeciliu[m]
> Capellam II vir(os) i(ure) d(icundo).[95]

[Numerius Popidus Rufus and Caecilius Capella (as) duovirs *iure dicundo*.]

Given the disappearance of the family from the lists of elected offices for several generations, we are here again likely dealing with a descendant of a freedman line, probably a relation of L. Caecilius Iucundus, the *argentarius* and keeper of *apochae* himself.[96] Only the Caecilius under discussion here is known to have carried the cognomen *Capella* at Pompeii, and on the basis of its recurrence twice in campaign posters outside the door of VII.12.3–4 (fig. 23), the modest house there has been identified as that of Caecilius.[97] It is in fact parallel to that of Ceius Secundus in scale and could easily be that of a successful family descended from a freedman.

Cn. Helvius Sabinus

In contrast to Ceius Secundus and Caecilius Capella are the representatives of four families who had climbed steadily in the political scene and continued their rise in the Flavian years. The most traceable of these are the Helvii.[98] A Felix Helvi and Meleager Helvi were unspecified *ministri,* either earlier *Mercurii et Maiae* or later *Augusti.*[99] We then met two

---

95. *CIL* IV.3548.

96. So Łoś, at "Affranchis" 869: ". . . fils du banquier ou, au moins, son parent proche"; likewise at "Remarques" 287: "Tous les deux pouvaient être proches (frères?)." *CIL* IV.3433 names a Q. and S. of Caecilius Iucundus: *Ceium Secundum / IIvir(um) Q S Caecili Iucundi rogam(us);* these have been identified as his sons (Zangemeister at *CIL* IV, p. 277 n. 1; Della Corte 140–41; Castrén 145), but the use of the genitive of Caecilius Iucundus indicates, rather, his slaves.

97. Della Corte 345.

98. Castrén 173–74.

99. *CIL* X.906 and *NSc* (1899) 496, where A. Sogliano observed, "senza dubbio . . . dei *ministri Mercurii Maiae, postea Augusti.*" Both inscriptions are highly fragmentary, although the names seem secure.

Fig. 23. Block VII.12 and the house of L. Caecilius Capella

additional slaves, Nymphodotus Helvi and his slave Auctus Helvi Nymphodoti, in Tiberian days, when they were named *ministri Augusti*.[100] Twenty years later, in A.D. 52–53, the family produced a duovir in the adopted L. Helvius Blaesius Proculus, known from the *apochae* of Caecilius Iucundus.[101] Indeed, a number of the freedmen of Marcus, Lucius, Sextus, and Cnaeus Helvius served as witnesses to the transactions of Iucundus.[102] Now, Cn. Helvius Sabinus was standing for aedile and was widely advertised in the electoral programmata.

193:

Cn(aeum) Helvium Sabinum aed(ilem).[103]

[Gnaeus Helvius Sabinus (as) aedile.]

M. Cerrinius Vatia

Likewise with the Cerrinii, straightforward progress upward through the social ranks can be demonstrated.[104] The first Cerrinius attested is an M. Cerrinius who was a *magister pagi et compiti* in 47 B.C.[105] In the

---

100. Inscriptions 33 (= *CIL* X.895) and 37 (= *CIL* IV.899).

101. *Apochae* 138.

102. Andreau, *Jucundus* 155 n. 1.

103. *CIL* IV.3410. As Mouritsen (*Elections* 136) notes, the phrase *Primigenia rog(at)* belongs to this or to notice 3411 or 3412, but to which is uncertain.

104. On the Cerrinii, see Castrén 152–53.

105. *CIL* IV.60.

imperial period, a number of freedmen are attested in the *apochae* of
Caecilius Iucundus in the fifties A.C., and M. Cerrinius Restitutus, an *au-
gustalis,* was buried on land given by the decurions just outside the
Porta di Ercolano, probably in the sixties or seventies A.C.

194:

M(arcus) Cerrinius
Restitutus
augustalis loc(o) d(ecreto) d(ecurionum) d(ato).[106]

[Marcus Cerrinius Restitutus, augustalis. Place given by decree of the
decurions.]

Then finally the freeborn M. Cerrinius Vatia, probably the son of Restitutus, stood for aedile.[107]

195:

M(arcum) Cerrinium
Vatiam aed(ilem).[108]

[Marcus Cerrinius Vatia (as) aedile.]

L. Albucius Celsus II

The rise—more accurately, the consolidation—of the Albucii is less detailed, but we know of L. Albucius Celsus, who was aedile in A.D. 33–34,
apparently shortly after the family arrived in Pompeii and took posse-
sion of the huge Casa delle Nozze d'Argento at V.2.c,d,e,i (fig. 2).[109] His
son L. Albucius Iustus, next served as duovir in A.D. 58–59 with L. Veranius Hypsaeus.[110] The family now proposed L. Albucius Celsus II,
grandson of the original Celsus, for aedile.

---

106. Kockel S1 = *CIL* X.994. A similar inscription is *CIL* X.995; on the tomb
and its date, see Kockel 47–51.
107. To Łoś, ("Affranchis" 858), Cerrinius Vatia was "probablement fils d'un
affranchi," although not specifically Cerrinius Restitutus. To Castrén (119),
Vatia was "a probable descendant of the Augustalis, M. Cerrinius Restitutus."
108. *CIL* IV.115.
109. *CIL* X.901–2. See above, chap. 2, under "A.D. 33–34" and "Early Julio-
Claudians."
110. *Apochae* 70, 142, 147, 150.

196:

L(ucium) Albucium Celsu[m]
aed(ilem) o(ro) v(os) f(aciatis). Earinu s *[sic]* rogat d(ignum)
r(ei) p(ublicae).[111]

[I ask that you elect Lucius Albucius Celsus, a man worthy of the state,
aedile. Earinus asks.]

A. Vettius Caprasius Felix

In Augustan times, P. Vettius Celer had served as duovir, but the exact
date of his incumbency is unknown,[112] and although his possible son
P. Vettius Syrticus later stood for aedile,[113] the family thereafter flourished in another line.[114] Probably in Claudian days, but perhaps in
Neronian,[115] A. Vettius Firmus stood for aedile and was warmly supported by his neighbors *(vicini)* in general and specifically by Caprasia and Nymphius, who ran the *caupona* at VI.10.3–4, the location of
their house also, just down the street from Vettius' house at VI.9.3–5
(fig. 24).[116]

---

111. *CIL* IV.7387.

112. *CIL* X.907, 908. Both lack consular dating, but Celer's colleague as
duovir, D. Alfidius Hypsaeus, had been aedile in A.D. 2–3 (*EphEp* 8.316, for
which see above, chap. 1, under "Eumachia, *sacerdos publica*"), and their
duovirates should have followed within a few years.

113. *CIL* IV.568, 935g, and possibly 9936.

114. On the Vettii, see Castrén 239–40, to which now add Varone, "Tituli" 3
(pp. 94–95), a programma supporting Vettius Caprasius Felix with no office
specified. On A. Vettius Caprasius Felix, see now J.L. Franklin, Jr., "Aulus Vettius Caprasius Felix of Ancient Pompeii," in *Qui Miscuit Utile Dulci: Festschrift
Essays for Paul Lachlan MacKendrick,* ed. G. Schmeling and J.D. Mikalson
(Wauconda, Ill. 1998) 165–75.

115. Castrén thought Vettius Firmus a Flavian candidate, but several of the
programmata supporting him were clearly older (*CIL* IV.7143: *antiquior;* 7504:
antiquior; 7738: *antiquior;* 7911: *supersunt reliquiae delapso tectorio;* 7930: *antiquioris vestigia;* 7964: *superest antiquioris linea prima;* 7971: *antiquior*) and he
belongs to earlier days.

116. On Caprasia, Nymphius, and their *caupona,* see Della Corte 53; on the
identification of the house of A. Vettius Firmus, Della Corte 40–41.

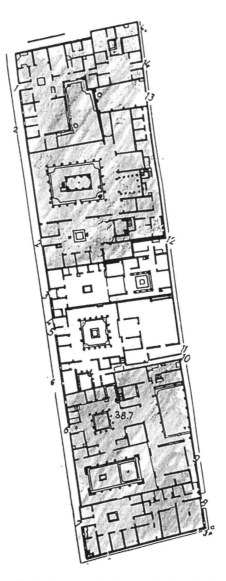

Fig. 24. Block VI.9 and the house of A. Vettius Firmus

197:

A(ulum) Vettium Firmum
aed(ilem) o(rat) v(os) f(aciatis). Dign(us) est.
Caprasia cum Nymphio rog(at)
una et vicini o(rant) v(os) f(aciatis).[117]

[Caprasia, along with Nymphio, asks that you elect Aulus Vettius Firmus aedile. He is worthy. Together with the neighbors, they ask that you elect.]

There is no indication that he sought higher office, but Firmus later adopted D. Caprasius Felix, whom we met in Neronian days and who must somehow be connected with Firmus' neighbor Caprasia. Caprasius became A. Vettius Caprasius Felix and rose to stand for duovir in Flavian times with another former Neronian and Neropopaeensis, P. Paquius Proculus. At the same time, Epidius Sabinus, whom we know later to have become *defensor coloniae,* began his elected career by standing for aedile.

198:

P(ublium) Paquium Proculum II vir(um) virum b(onum) d(ignum)
r(ei) [publicae] o(ro) v(os) f(aciatis).

A(ulum) Vettium [Caprasi]um Felicem II vir(um) v(irum) b(onum)
d(ignum) r(ei) p(ublicae) o(ro) v(os) f(aciatis). Digni sunt.

Q(uintum) Marium [Rufum] M(arcum) Epidium Sabinum
aediles v(iis) a(edibus) s(acris) p(ublicisque) p(rocurandis)
o(ro) v(os) f(aciatis). Digni sunt.

S[crip]sit [---]sius de albatore *[sic]* Onesimo.[118]

[I ask that you elect Publius Paquius Proculus, a good man worthy of the state, duovir. I ask that you elect Aulus Vettius Caprasius Felix, a good man worthy of the state, duovir. They are worthy. I ask that you elect Quintus Marius Rufus and Marcus Epidius Sabinus aediles *viis aedibus sacris publicisque procurandis.* They are worthy. [—]sius wrote with the whitewasher Onesimus.]

---

117. *CIL* IV.171.

118. *CIL* IV.222. The last line of this notice originally identified its letterer and whitewasher *(dealbator),* who prepared the space for the lettering. On Onesimus, the whitewasher here, see Franklin, *"Scriptores"* 56.

As we saw earlier, Caprasius Felix lived in the small but comfortable house at IX.7.20 (fig. 12), where even after his adoption, his neighbors posted a notice in support of his stand for aedile.

199:

A(ulum) Vettium Caprasium
Felicem aed(ilem) v(iis) a(edibus) sacr(is) p(ublicisque)
p(rocurandis) vicini rogant.[119]

[His neighbors ask Aulus Vettius Caprasius Felix as aedile *viis aedibus sacris publicisque procurandis.*]

Likewise, the neighbors of his adoptive father's grand, double-atrium house at VI.9.3–5 posted a similar programma in his support, for A. Vettius Caprasius Felix had in fact two sets of neighbors, although he would presumably eventually have disposed of one of the properties.

200:

A(ulum) Vettium C[ap]r[as]ium Felicem aed(ilem)
o(rant) v(os) f(aciatis)
vicini.[120]

[His neighbors ask that you elect Aulus Vettius Caprasius Felix aedile.]

This adoption confused Della Corte, who postulated close consanguinity to explain the first of these notices, posted at Caprasius Felix's house, where he thought Vettius Caprasius Felix could not have actual neighbors.[121] Rather, as in the case of like D. Lucretius Satrius Valens, *flamen Neronis,* this is an adoption of an adult already well known and well attested under his original name, so some confusion was certain to arise among far later scholars, if not among the candidate's own contemporaries. In fact, it is clear from a poster signed by the candidate's old friend Bruttius Balbus that in Balbus' eyes, at least, Caprasius was still his functional name, though Balbus admitted his new praenomen.[122]

---

119. *CIL* IV.3687.
120. *CIL* IV.204.
121. Della Corte 427.
122. Balbus lived near Caprasius' original house at IX.2.15–16 and supported Caprasius also with *CIL* IV.935*e* and 935*k;* 935*i* solicited his support for

201:

> A(ulum) Caprasium et Paquium Proculum II vir(os)
> i(ure) d(icundo) Balbus facit.[123]

[Balbus is electing Aulus Caprasius and Paquius Proculus duovirs *iure dicundo*.]

Finally, we can add two more figures to the gens, the freedmen A. Vettius Restitutus and A. Vettius Conviva, *augustalis*, who lived in the famous Casa dei Vettii at VI.15.1.[124] Apparently freedmen of Vettius Firmus, their responsibilities and obligations will have passed to Vettius Caprasius Felix on the death of his adoptive father.

C. Gavius Rufus

In chapter 5 we met the Publii Gavii, who saw the adoption of the the last of their line as Cn. Pompeius Grosphus Gavianus. Now, in Flavian times, C. Gavius Rufus, representing a different branch of the family, stood for both aedile and duovir.

202:

> C(aium) Gavium Rufum aed(ilem) o(rat) v(os) f(aciatis)
> Granius rog(at).[125]

[Granius asks that you elect Gaius Gavius Rufus aedile.]

203:

> C(aium) Gavium Rufum d(uovirum) i(ure) d(icundo)
> o(ro) v(os) f(aciatis).[126]

[I ask that you elect Gaius Gavius Rufus duovir *iure dicundo*.]

Caprasius. The names of Caprasius and Balbus are mingled in *CIL* IV.935g (but see above, chap. 3, n. 66, on the problems with this notice), and Balbus had supported A. Vettius Firmus (*CIL* IV.935b). Further on Balbus, see above, chap. 3.

123. *CIL* IV.935h.

124. On the house and its inhabitants, see Della Corte 89–93. Castrén listed Vettius Restitutus as a candidate for aedile, an impossibility for a freedman, and the evidence is nonexistent since the gentilicial is completely lacking from the only notice supposedly posted in his support: *CIL* IV.7947: [---]m Restitutum aed(ilem).

125. *CIL* IV.9883.

126. *CIL* IV.7468.

Somewhat earlier, C. Gavius Firmus had signed three of the wax tablets
of Caecilius Iucundus, once even before the important M. Obellius Firmus.[127] If we were correct in seeing the end of the Publii Gavii in the
adoption of Pompeius Grosphus Gavianus, C. Gavius Firmus may have
been the younger brother of the adoptee and may have attended to the
recovery following his brother's adoption and disgrace and then
launched his son C. Gavius Rufus into politics.

A. Trebius Valens II

Interesting, too, are the men with whom Gavius Rufus stood for office.
Twelve shared posters show that the Trebius Valens of this generation
paired with Gavius when they stood for aedile.

204:

[Ga]vium Rufum
[et] Trebium a[e]d(iles) o(ro) v(os) f(aciatis).[128]

[I ask that you elect Gavius Rufus and Trebius aediles.]

In chapter 5 we reencountered the senior Trebius Valens, who had begun his career in Claudian times and eventually stood for quinquennial,
probably in Neronian days. His son—and the father himself, if still
alive—lived in the house at III.2.1 (fig. 7), which, because of its useful
location along the Via dell' Abbondanza, attracted a number of programmata, both those posted by Trebius and others seeking his en-
dorsement.[129] Trebius Valens II, however, did not rise to the office of
duovir before the city's destruction.

M. Holconius Priscus

Gavius Rufus, in contrast, not only stood for duovir but also, with his
fellow candidate, M. Holconius Priscus, was in office when Pompeii was

---

127. *Apochae* 81, 89, 95; his signature precedes that of Obellius Firmus on
81, and he therefore cannot have been a freedman, whose lower rank would
have disallowed such precedence.
128. *CIL* IV.1135.
129. All those notices addressed to Trebius Valens are in the singular (*CIL*

destroyed. No programma supporting either candidate for the duovirate was overpainted anywhere in the city, so their campaigns must be the last waged, in the spring of A.D. 79.[130]

205:

M(arcum) Holconium Priscum
C(aium) Gavium Rufum II vir(os)
Phoebus cum emptoribus
suis rog(at).[131]

[Phoebus, with his customers, asks Marcus Holconius Priscus and Gaius Gavius Rufus as duovirs.]

M. Holconius Priscus is the first and only Holconius known to have played a role in politics since the difficulties of his ancestor M. Holconius Macer following the assassination of Caligula; with his person the family had at length returned.

M. Samellius Modestus

As in Neronian times, there were new families on the scene also. M. Samellius Modestus stood for aedile in these years, yet of him absolutely nothing else—even ancestors—is known.[132]

206:

M(arcum) Samellium
Modestum aed(ilem) o(ro) v(os) f(aciatis).[133]

[I ask that you elect Marcus Samellius Modestus aedile.]

IV.7429, 7614, 7618, 7619, 7624) or are addressed also to a Sotericus (*CIL* IV.7632 and probably 7627), suggesting that the elder Valens was now deceased. On the attractions of the location of the house of Trebius Valens for posting programmata, see Franklin, *Electoral* 88.

130. See Franklin, *Electoral* 61 and, on the general stratigraphical principle, 35.

131. *CIL* IV.103.

132. Castrén 216.

133. *CIL* IV.3501.

M. Casellius Marcellus

Likewise, apart from his candidacy for aedile, essentially nothing is known of M. Casellius Marcellus, although he was once termed a great giver of games *(munerarius magnus)*.[134]

207:

> M(arcum) Casellium
> Marcellum aed(ilem).[135]

[Marcus Casellius Marcellus (as) aedile.]

208:

> (Marcum) Casellium Marcellum aedilem bonum et munerarium
> magnum.[136]

[Marcus Casellius Marcellus, a good aedile and great games-giver.]

Disappearances

Finally, we must return to two of the candidates recommended by Ceius Secundus, for they clearly belong to earlier days.

Cornelii

The Cornelii are surprising for their limited role in Pompeian politics, especially given their wide attestation at lower ranks.[137] The Roman colony, after all, had been led by a *tresvir coloniae deducendae,* P. Sulla, probably nephew of the dictator P. Cornelius Sulla at Rome.[138] The colony took Sulla's gentilicial name as its own when it became the *colonia Cornelia Veneria Pompeianorum,* and as is certain from the dedicatory inscription labeling both sides of the altar in the Temple of Apollo in which two are named, Cornelii were prominent grandees of the early colony.[139]

---

134. Castrén 150.
135. *CIL* IV.7366.
136. *CIL* IV.4999.
137. See Castrén 157–58.
138. Cic. *Sul.* 62.
139. On *quattuorviri* as magistrates of the early colony, see n. 94.

209:

M(arcus) Porcius M(arci) f(ilius) L(ucius) Sextilius L(ucii) f(ilius)
Cn(aeus) Cornelius Cn(aei) f(ilius)

A(ulus) Cornelius A(uli) f(ilius) IIII vir(i) d(e) d(ecurionum)
s(ententia) f(aciundum) locar(unt).[140]

[Marcus Porcius son of Marcus, Lucius Sextilius son of Lucius, Cnaeus Cornelius son of Cnaeus, and Aulus Cornelius son of Aulus placed (this altar), having seen to its making in accordance with the opinion of the decurions.]

Yet no Cornelius is known to have again played a significant role in local politics until C. Cornelius Macer, whom we met as duovir in A.D. 57–58. Apparently one of the few extant posters attesting his career, preserved just to the right of the doorway of Ceius Secundus, belongs to his campaign for the aedileship.[141] Although many lower rank Cornelii are known, Macer is the last to have stood for election.

The house of the Cornelii has been identified at VII.4.14–16 (fig. 25), in the same block as that of the Postumii and directly across from the Stabian Baths.[142] But the epigraphical evidence found there pertains to an apparent freedmen Audiutor,[143] suggesting that the house had fallen into his keeping, perhaps because the family withdrew following the earthquake of A.D. 62, as did the next family in this discussion, the Sextilia.

Sextilii

The L. Sextilius also attested in the inscription from the altar of the Temple of Apollo is the first known member of his gens at Pompeii.[144] We know also of an A. Sextilius Gemellus who twice held an office, but that is all the stone records.[145] No other prominent Sextilii are known until L. Sextilius Restitutus, candidate for aedile, and L. Sextilius Syrticus,

---

140. *CIL* X.800.

141. *CIL* IV.7190.

142. Della Corte 478–81.

143. His breadstamp, *CIL* X.8058.22 (reading *C Corneli A⟨d⟩iutoris*), was found in the house:

144. See Castrén 221.

145. *CIL* X.959: *A(ulus) Sextilius A(uli) f(ilius) Gemellus iter(um)*. Mouritsen (102–3) dates the stone prior to A.D. 40.

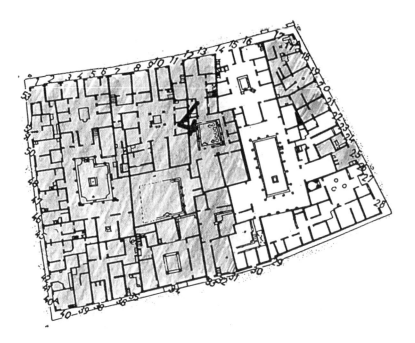

Fig. 25. Block VIII.4 and the house of the Cornelii

candidate for duovir, from whose candidacies, probably sometime during the Neronian years, a few programmata were recovered.[146] The
poster on the facade of the house of Ceius Secundus must refer to one
of these men, for no further Sextilii took part in elections. In fact, it
has recently been suggested that the house of the Sextilii was the Casa
del Labirinto (VI.11.8–10; fig. 26) and that it was left to the care of a
procurator when the Sextilii themselves left Pompeii following the
earthquake.[147]

There was, however, one additional Sextilius who reached quinquennial rank, and his tribe, the Falerna, was from nearby Nola, where

---

146. Della Corte identified a Vettius Restitutus at *CIL* IV.7826 and 7947,
where no evidence for the nomen Vettius existed. Following Della Corte, Castrén suggested that *CIL* IV.9858 was a conflated programma supporting a Sextilius and a Vettius Restitutus, but as Mouritsen (*Elections* 151) observes, the
name in every case is Sextilius Restitutus.

147. V.M. Strocka, *Casa del Labirinto,* Deutsches Archäologisches Institut:
Häuser im Pompeji 4 (Munich 1991) 134–36.

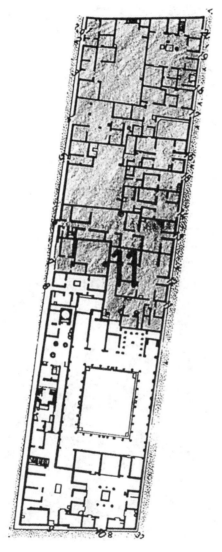

Fig. 26. Block VI.11 and the house of the Sextilii

he was adlected a decurion *ex veteribus,* apparently "from the original
inhabitants."[148] There the tomb he built for his mother, Aufidia Maxima,
and stepfather, L. Petronius Verus, himself a decurion of Nola, carried
the details.

> 210:
>
> P(ublius) Sextilius P(ublii) f(ilius) Fal(erna tribu)
> Rufus
> aid(ilis) *[sic]* iterum II vir quinq(uennalis) Pompeis
> decurio adlectus ex veterib(us) Nola(e)
> Aufidiae St(atiae) f(iliae) Maximae
> matri
> L(ucio) Petronio L(ucii) f(ilio) Fal(erna tribu) Vero vitrico
> decurioni Nola(e)
> ex testamenio *[sic]* HS CIƆ IƆƆ abitratu fidi *[sic]* l(ocavit).[149]

[Publius Sextilius Rufus, son of Publius, tribe Falerna, aedile, twice
duovir, (once as) quinquennial at Pompeii, adlected decurion from the
old inhabitants at Nola, in accordance with their will (spending) four
thousand sesterces in loyal adjudication, located (this tomb) to his
mother, Aufidia Maxima, daughter of Statia, and to his stepfather, the
decurion at Nola, Lucius Petronius Verus, son of Lucius, tribe Falerna.]

According to Castrén, Sextilius Rufus belonged to the Neronian era at
Pompeii as well and was therefore a contemporary of Sextilius Restitutus and Syrticus.[150] This, then, was a family that virtually disappeared
from the political scene between the time of the early colony and the
Neronian years—when, in fact, it may have returned to politics only
thanks to the impetus of Sextilius Rufus, émigré from Nola.

   Vibii. Also to be added to our list of disappearing families are the
Vibii.[151] A T. Vibius Varus was duovir in an unknown but early year;[152]

---

148. The explanation of *ex veteribus* as "from the original inhabitants," in
distinction from later colonists, is that of Castrén (221).
   149. *CIL* X.1273.
   150. Castrén 221. Mouritsen (*Elections* 103) thinks the stone Augustan.
   151. On the gens, see Castrén 240–41.
   152. *CIL* X.8148 (cf. p. 1006) = *EphEp* 8.314 = *CIL* I².1634. Castrén hesitatingly assigns him to the late Republic.

and a Vibius Coeianus, quattuorvir from Nuceria, even appears to have moved to Pompeii, where he was later buried.[153] The last member of this family to participate in politics, and the only one well known to us, was C. Vibius Severus, duovir in A.D. 56–57 with Postumius Modestus; several posters from Severus' campaign were recovered.[154] The family does not appear ever to have been all that prominent to us, but as a graffito recovered in the basilica shows, their former glory had become proverbial.

211:

[[Pum[pei]s]] fueere [*sic*] quondam Vibii opulentissumi *[sic]*
   non ideo tenuerunt in manu sceptrum pro mutunio
   itidem quod tu factitas cottidie in manu penem tene(n)s.[155]

[The Vibii were once most wealthy at Pompeii, but not for this did they hold in their hand a scepter instead of a cock, (doing) similarly what you repeatedly do daily holding a penis in your hand.]

Flavians

Thanks to the abundance of campaign posters that remain from these years, we can develop a more detailed picture of the political scene for the Flavian era at Pompeii than for others. Yet it is also more fragmentary, since we see individual pieces of evidence that time and additional accumulation had no chance to shape into discernible strands, and since we of course lack any highly informative funerary inscriptions.

Still, there was again a strong connection with Rome, first through Cn. Alleius Nigidius Maius, *flamen Vespasiani,* and then through M. Epidius Sabinus and, to a lesser degree, N. Popidius Rufus, *defensores coloniae.* Although all members of established families, none of these men had been politically powerful under Nero. It was a time for

---

153. *CIL* X.1075: [---] *Vibius M(arci) f(ilius)* / *Men(enia tribu) Coeianus* / *Nucerinus* / *IIIIvir* / *ex testamento* / *Vibiae M(arci) f(iliae) Tertiae.*

154. *CIL* IV.333, 730 (cf. *Add.* p. 196), 739, 888, 1033, 3831, 7291. C. Vibius, aedile in an uncertain year, must be the same man (see above, chap. 2, n. 1). Attesting Vibius Severus as duovir in A.D. 56–57 are *Apochae* 145 and 149 and *CIL* X.826.

155. Varone, *Erotica* 91 = *CIL* IV.1939 (cf. *Add.* pp. 465, 704). On the long history of this difficult graffito, see Varone at his entry.

new faces in such visible positions. None, however, seems to have become the center of a recognizable circle of allies, perhaps because alignment with the central powers at Rome had by now become automatic.
Tacitus' secret of empire had also been revealed at Pompeii.[156] The presence of imperial agent T. Suedius Clemens and his attention to the *res
publica Pompeianorum* will presumably have spurred uniform allegiance to the Flavian household, and Vespasian himself offered little of
the flamboyance and none of the personal connection that had nourished the Neropoppaeenses.

Perhaps most notable are the sons of freedmen who in these years began to play a role in politics.[157] In early Julio-Claudian days, we were
able to identify the very first such son of a freedman, M. Lucretius Manlianus. Behind his success lay a presumably very successful father and
the considerable power of the most powerful gens of the times, the Lucretia. Now, different patterns of approach to the *ordo* can be discerned.
First, Cerrinius Vatia, son of the distinguished *augustalis* Restitutus, belonged to a family that had long struggled upward, a pattern of success
that we might well anticipate. Second, L. Popidius Ampliatus II and
L. Popidius Secundus II mark a significant development, for their rise
seems to be owed simply to the stunning wealth and high visibility of
their fathers. In fact, compared with those of other candidates, the size
of their house alone indicates their domineering fortunes and explains
their resultant entrée into the *ordo*. Third, and in sharp contrast, the Ceii
and Caecilii—to judge from their houses, gentes descended from freedmen of more restricted resources—had taken more than one generation
to escape the stigma of slavery. Even now therefore, it would seem to
have been unusual for the son of a local freedman to move into politics;
a substantial fortune or at least a highly successful *augustalis* for a father was requisite. Yet, as we saw in chapter 5, for descendants of imperial freedmen, who flaunted their status, different rules applied.

Of families, the Helvii, Cerrinii, Albucii, and Gavii continued their
climb toward ever higher offices. The Ceii and Caecilii reappeared in
lines apparently descended from freedmen. And the Suetti, Samellii,

---

156. Tac. *Hist.* 1.4: . . . *evulgato imperii arcano posse principem alibi quam
Romae fieri.*

157. As in the case of Q. Coelius Caltilius Iustus (see chap. 3), adoption earlier allowed some sons of freedmen to enter politics, but the adoption also
moved the son into a new family, thus removing the taint of the *libertus.*

and Casellii now first appeared on the scene. Indeed, among the established families, we can discern a wide variety of patterns, from success and reappearance to failure and disappearance. But to discuss those and other overall developments adequately, it will be necessary in conclusion to look back over all the years studied in this book.

Flavians

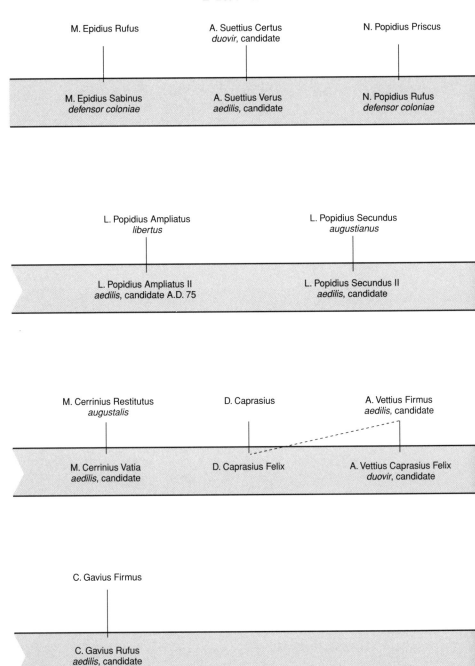

M. Epidius Rufus

A. Suettius Certus
duovir, candidate

N. Popidius Priscus

M. Epidius Sabinus
defensor coloniae

A. Suettius Verus
aedilis, candidate

N. Popidius Rufus
defensor coloniae

L. Popidius Ampliatus
libertus

L. Popidius Secundus
augustianus

L. Popidius Ampliatus II
aedilis, candidate A.D. 75

L. Popidius Secundus II
aedilis, candidate

M. Cerrinius Restitutus
augustalis

D. Caprasius

A. Vettius Firmus
aedilis, candidate

M. Cerrinius Vatia
aedilis, candidate

D. Caprasius Felix

A. Vettius Caprasius Felix
duovir, candidate

C. Gavius Firmus

C. Gavius Rufus
aedilis, candidate

Conclusion: *Pompeis Difficile Est*

When describing the aftermath of the riot in the amphitheater at Pompeii, Tacitus reported, in addition to the ten-year prohibition of gladiatorial games and the exile of the Pompeii Grosphi, the dissolution of groups, *collegia,* organized outside the law.[1] The loose associations and temporary alliances that I have been tracing were hardly organized well enough to qualify as such groups, nor were they outside the law. They do, however, abundantly testify to the tendency of the Pompeians to form loose alliances around all sorts of causes, those represented in this book supporting not only shared political interests but also even passing enthusiasms. Thus far, I have focused on these temporary associations and the individuals who composed them. To conclude this study, I must now move from the individuals to their families, which have in fact already become an increasing aspect of my discussions. In so doing, I can address those continuities—as well as the more visible discontinuities—of which the individual is only a part but of which social and political history are made.

Two earlier scholars, Paavo Castrén and Henrik Mouritsen, have examined their catalogues of the evidence and come to differing conclusions about the nature of political life at ancient Pompeii. As we have already seen, Castrén, whose focus was his lists of families, concluded that intrusions from Rome dominated early Julio-Claudian times—first, in the persons of the *tribuni militum a populo* I introduced in chapter 1, whom he wrongly thought to have been dispatched or at least directed from Rome; second, in the suspension of local government during his erroneously postulated "Claudian crisis." In later Julio-Claudian and Flavian times, he saw the rise of new, recently moneyed families as forming a plutocracy that was in the process of replacing the landed aristocracy of earlier days.[2] To Mouritsen, who attempted a statistical

---

1. Tac. *Ann.* 14.17: . . . *collegiaque quae contra leges instituerant dissoluta . . .*
2. Castrén 118–21.

analysis of his lists of magistrates and candidates, two types of families were represented in all periods: the well-established families dominated, while lesser gentes rose and fell with the times. In contrast to Castrén, he could discern no significant change in the sources of money that supported rising families of late Julio-Claudian and Flavian times as compared with those of earlier days.[3]

My studies show that Mouritsen's analysis was the more correct. We have seen certain families present in all eras, even dominating in some, and while I have traced the rise of several in late Julio-Claudian and Flavian days, there is no indication that their sources of wealth were in general different from those of their predecessors. Still, varying times allowed for some striking variations in the cases of imperial freedmen and even perhaps imperial toadies—the Augustiani—although much work needs to be done on sources of income before definite conclusions can be reached on economic matters. The different nature of my studies, however—the careful tracing of interconnections and development of pictures of individual eras—has allowed me to study the evidence in far greater detail, so that I can now add considerably to the discussion.

I begin with the family on the most basic level, that of survival, and pursue larger, more involved issues from that starting point. And I shall more closely look at what properties can be assigned to various families, seeking for further confirmation of my conclusions. Logically, we could expect five general patterns of survival or disappearance, and in fact those patterns can be traced among the families I have surveyed. They are general patterns, however, and we shall see significant illustrative variations within each.

Steady Prominence

For the city's few best-known gentes, political prominence can be demonstrated fairly steadily throughout the imperial years. Included among these families are the Holconii, Lucretii, and Alleii and the steady but less visible Herennii. The Cuspii Pansae too belong to this group, although we lose their traces in the Augustan years. Because of their continued successes, these families at first glance provide us with ironically the least interesting of patterns, although the temporary occlusion of the Holconii and Marci Lucretii that apparently occurred be-

---

3. Mouritsen, *Elections* 118.

cause of their too close association with Caligula is a fascinating down-side of success.

The need of the Lucretii and Alleii to rely on adoption, however, is notable and adds considerable interest to this pattern. The very first known men of these lines, M. Lucretius Decidianus Rufus and M. Alleius Luccius Libella, were themselves adopted, and their families were repeatedly forced into the practice over the years. This legal fiction demonstrates how frequently a family's bloodline could fail. Lack of progeny—probably more accurately, early mortality of carefully planned progeny due to a partible inheritance system—was not an un-usual occurrence.[4] Yet families as successful as the Lucretii and Alleii could look on this as an opportunity as well; in adopting, after all, they could incorporate genuine talent rather than suffer descendants of ques-tionable ability. And that certifiable talent was a concern is revealed by those adoptees who were adults of known qualities when adopted and whose names were thereafter confused by different levels of acquain-tances—and even by themselves. These, at least, were not emotional de-cisions, taken for the joy of watching boys spin tops in lofty atria.[5]

Adoption carried benefits for the adoptee and his natural gens, too. It permanently linked the two families involved and could provide an important leg up for the gens whose son had been chosen by his politi-cal and social superiors; he could look to the interests of his natural fam-ily while a member of his new, adopted gens. Interestingly, however, these advantages seem to have proved short-lived, for the adopted son's natural family was itself practicing the same system of progeny planned to protect assets, and adoption therefore normally meant the end of the adoptee's birth line.[6] So in the case of D. Lucretius Satrius Valens, one

---

4. So R. Saller, "Roman Heirship Strategies in Principle and in Practice," in *The Family in Roman Italy From Antiquity to the Present,* ed. D. Kertzer and R. Saller (New Haven and London 1991) 26: "Senatorial families disappeared and were replaced by new families at an astonishing rate of up to 75 percent per generation, because to avoid dividing their estates too many ways in a thor-oughly partible inheritance system (sons and daughters receiving full shares), they had quite small families. Given ancient mortality rates, the family bearing only two or three children was likely to avoid the risk of division, but also un-likely to produce a surviving male heir."

5. Verg. *Aen.* 7.378–80: *ceu quondam torto volitans sub verbere turbo / quem pueri magno in gyro vacua atria circum / intenti ludo exercent. . . .*

6. Contra Andreau ("Remarques" 224), who contended that the most good resulted to the adopted family. Rather, it resulted to the adopted *man* who be-

of our most visible adoptees, M. Satrius Valens, the natural father and a man of distinction himself, became the last Satrius at Pompeii, despite three attested grandchildren. Likewise, we know of no Nigidii following the adoption of Cn. Alleius Nigidius Maius. In the practice of adoption, then, lies one of the contributing factors for the rapid turnover of lesser families that I noted when beginning this study.

Finally, adoption demonstrates a family's economic viability. Indeed, economic concerns must have played a twofold role in adoption decisions. First, a family could scarcely adopt unless it was to the advantage of the adoptee, that is, unless there were financial resources to be passed along. Second, if the adoptee also brought financial strength to the union of the families, that was all the better.[7] Wealth, therefore, dispersed into more established and powerful gentes, as did the adoptees themselves.

Interestingly, we know the houses associated with only two of these families powerful over the entire course of this study, those of the Cuspii Pansae (fig. 17) and Lucretius Fronto (fig. 16). That of the Cuspii is large and elegantly decorated and may have been theirs for generations. That of Lucretius Fronto is decidedly modest, although quite elegantly decorated, and can hardly be the seat of his distinguished gens. The similar house of his obvious relative M. Lucretius (IX.3.5,24; fig. 27) is also not likely to have served for that purpose. Rather, the major property and source of wealth of the Lucretii and in fact of all these families will have lain outside the city proper. The Holconii are the one family about whose sources of wealth we have even hints, after all, and those hints are of decidedly rural nature: the *vitis Horconia*, or *vitis Holconia*, was named for them, and they also produced roof tiles.[8] Similarly, the family property of the Decimi Lucretii lay outside Pompeii proper, under modern Scafati. In her study of Roman property owners of the late Republic, Rawson noted the lack of identification of noble Romans with their properties.[9] At Pompeii, in contrast, properties over time took on the names of their owners—the *insula Arriana Polliana* of Alleius Nigid-

---

came a part of the adopting family. Moreover, Andreau is not accurate in saying, "C'est la famille adoptante qui, dans la plupart des cas, se révèle la moins connue. . . ."

7. Other scenarios are of course possible. The property of the adoptee's family, for example, could be split between brother and sister, where it would be vital to assure her marriage and status.

8. *CIL* X.8042, 57: *Holconiae M(arci) f(iliae).*

9. Rawson, "Properties" 88–89.

ius Maius and the *fundus Audianus* of the wax tablets,[10] for example—
apparently because of their long-term possession, again in contrast to
the short-term ownership Rawson traced among her Romans.[11] We
must remember, too, the Sextilii, who were able to leave the Casa del
Labirinto following the earthquake, presumably because they had precisely such property to retire to while their townhouse was being re-
paired. Indeed, levelheaded concentration on their property and
sources of wealth may explain their only intermittent participation in
Pompeian—and Nolan—politics.

Finally, we must observe the double strength of the Lucretii, who
throughout my studies are visible in two lines. The Augustan M. Lucretius Decidianus Rufus is the earliest Lucretius known to us, and he
may have known as a young contemporary the D. Lucretius who fathered the Claudian D. Lucretius Valens and managed to have him
adlected into the *ordo decurionum* at age eight. We cannot know at
what point the Decimi and Marci Lucretii became separate lines, but
their double line and their firm alignment with the Julio-Claudians must
have made them overwhelmingly powerful.

Indeed, it is through these long-lived families that the city's connections with Rome become obvious—first, through the *tribuni militum a
populo* and the flamens of Augustus; second, through the naming of
emperors and emperors-to-be as duovirs and even through the establishment of the cult of Nero following his adoption by Claudius; finally,
through the new flaminate of Vespasian and the interference of his agent
in local elections. These families worked hard to make their and their
city's allegiances clear.

Disappearance

Our second general pattern, perhaps the most typical, is one that I tan-
gentially explored, that of disappearance. This resulted not only from
adoption into another gens and temporary withdrawal to the country
estate but also from three other, more obvious processes. Here belong

---

10. *Apochae* 138.

11. Rawson, "Properties" 89, citing J.A. Crook, *Law and Life of Rome* (Ithaca
1967) 132: "Ancient families surviving for many generations in genetic and
property continuity are not characteristic of Rome." In contrast, however,
S. Treggiari ("Sentiment and Property: Some Roman Attitudes," in *Theories of
Property: Aristotle to the Present,* ed. A. Parel and T. Flanagan [Waterloo,

Fig. 27. Block IX.3 and the house of M. Lucretius

such families as the Gellii and Staii as well as the Mammii and Clodii of
the Augustan Age and the Rusticelii and Terentii of the Claudian. In Augustan days the Gellii appear simply to have not produced a son and to
have married their daughter into the gens Holconia, producing her son,
M. Holconius Gellius. Likewise, apparently the last daughter of the Staii
produced L. Albienus Staius, duovir of A.D. 31–32. The Mammii and the
Clodii, however, seem to have succumbed to financial ruin due to their
extravagance in building and entertaining the Augustan city. More
sober cooperation in such projects, like that of Eumachia and Lucretius
Decidianus Rufus on separate parts of the Porticus Concordiae Augustae Pietatique and, later, that of Cuspius Pansa and Alleius Nigidius
Maius on the amphitheater, meant continued life for a gens as long as
there were descendants—though unfortunately, little is known of Eumachia's. Similar to the Mammii and Clodii, however, were the Claudian Rusticelii and Terentii, although here we cannot speak of families.
Rather, these were individual men who stretched their limited financial
resources too far in the search for improved status and doomed their
own efforts and the chances of any descendants in the process.

    A subcategory can also be discerned. Rather than disappearing en-

---

Ontario 1979] 53–85) discerned (73) that "ancestral lands and houses were in a
different category and might even be regarded as a trust to be passed onto one's
descendants."

tirely, families such as the Melissaei and Istacidii appear to have survived, although not in positions of political prominence. Apparent freedmen of both gentes signed the tablets of Caecilius Iucundus, and a procurator of the Istacidii was apparently in charge of their property, the Villa dei Misteri, during Pompeii's last years.[12] The owners of the Villa dei Misteri, however, can hardly have failed to be prominent; they must in fact have broken all patterns and decided not to pursue politics—at least not during these years at Pompeii.

Ironically, we can talk about the houses of three of Pompeii's disappearing families, if only because they clearly became the properties of newly arriving gentes. The Casa delle Nozze d'Argento (fig. 2)—huge and in the early Second Pompeian style, although later repainted in part—clearly belongs to the time of the Roman colony. Who lived there at that time is unknown, but it was taken over in the thirties A.C. by the Albucii and became the seat of that family thereafter. The houses of Iulius Polybius (fig. 15) and Rustius Verus (fig. 14) also predate their last owners' arrival in Pompeii and must have been vacated by their original builders. All three houses stand as clear reminders of just the sort of disappearance I have been discussing.

Regular Advancement

A long, steady climb to prominence is perhaps the role most widely expected of families in such a highly stratified society as that of Pompeii, and there are indeed families who seem to have achieved such steady advancement. They do not, however, form the most apparent or prevalent pattern in our evidence. The tides of life perhaps run more powerfully out than in, and for a gens—whether or not it was striving for political importance—regularly to have consolidated and built over generations was no mean accomplishment. Such consolidation in fact attests a diligence and steadiness like that of those few distinguished families who were able constantly to husband their resources and so regularly to take part in the political scene. Of families of this sort, we have earlier identified the Cerrinii and Helvii, whose risings are clear, beginning with lowly attestations and working upward through freedmen and adoptions.

Unfortunately, we can summon the house of neither of these families as evidence. That of the Helvii remains unidentified, while that of Cer-

---

12. Della Corte 946.

rinius Vatia, the Flavian representative of his family, perhaps at VI.*Occ*.36, was excavated and then reburied.[13]

Returns

The early prominence of a fourth category of families first faded but then regained luster, probably, however, in new freedman lines. Of these, we can identify the Ceii and Caecilii. Their modest yet comfortable houses (figs. 22 and 23) seem to fit the rising freedman's profile, and Ceius Secundus, many of whose supporters are known, was supported almost exclusively by the city's less distinguished citizens, while he himself in classic fashion supported his powerful superiors.

Here too perhaps belong the Trebii, a family attested in the Samnite city[14] and then not again until Claudian times, in the person of A. Trebius Valens the elder. Whether this was a freedman line is not clear, although had it been long established and freeborn, we would expect a grander, older house than the property at III.2.1 (fig. 7), which is similar in scale to that of Ceius and Caecilius. However, it also compares to that of Lucretius Fronto and may simply be the city property of an estate-based family.

Newcomers

Finally, wealthy newcomers keen to establish their lines appeared without antecedents in the record. Of these, we can distinguish three sorts: freeborn, descendants of local freedmen, and descendants of imperial freedmen.

The evidence allows us to trace at least two waves of the freeborn. First were the Albucii and the Gavii. The Albucii appeared on the political scene in the thirties A.C., the Gavii in the forties or fifties. The Albucii, as we have seen, lived in the Casa delle Nozze d'Argento, and only a well-established gens could have acquired and inhabited this

---

13. Della Corte 20. Cerrinius also seems to have had some connection near block IV.2, where *vicini* posted programma 443 in his support (see Franklin, *Electoral* 29 n. 16).

14. Conway 47 (= Vetter 15), 77.A3 (= Vetter 46), 77.A4 (= Vetter 46a), 77.C27 (= Vetter 47).

massive house. Although we do not know the house of the Gavii, a pro-gramma posted by their neighbors at VI.13.16 indicates that it lies in this older neighborhood not far from the house of the Albucii.[15] Our lack of early record for both these families suggests that they arrived in Pompeii wealthy and prominent. Similar but later were the Suettii, Casellii, and Samellii, whom we saw arrive in Flavian days, but none of whose houses have been identified.

Of local freedmen, the most conspicuous are the LL. Popidii, who obviously controlled vast wealth and were able to support political careers for their sons. We cannot trace their antecedents, although we know of a direct Neronian connection through the elder Popidius Secundus, Augustianus, and of other, freeborn Popidii. Suetonius reports very substantial monetary rewards of four hundred thousand sesterces to the leaders, at least, of the Augustiani, and given their property, we can assume that L. Popidius Secundus—and with him, Popidius Ampliatus—profited financially as well as famously from the imperial favor of his appointment.[16] In contrast to the slowly rising descendants of freedmen of modest properties, the LL. Popidii will have established themselves in the city of Pompeii with substantial sums of money, so that they were able to acquire and knock together the properties that became the huge Casa del Citarista (fig. 21).

Finally, there were the imperial freedmen who, like the Popidii, arrived in town with abundant resources and set about acquiring substantial properties and demanding status and careers for their descendants. This group included C. Iulius Polybius, Ti. Claudius Verus, and their circle. Indeed, as we have already seen, both the house of Iulius Polybius and that of Rustius Verus, like that of the Albucii, were older houses acquired by newcomers, presumably when older families went under.

---

15. *CIL* IV.3460: *Gavium aed(ilem) o(rant) v(os) f(aciatis) / vicini rog(ant)*. Nothing, however, supports the identification of the house on which this notice appears as that of Gavius Rufus, as Della Corte (115) would have it. Even Della Corte (p. 154) rejected the identification of VII.2.16 as property of the Gavii: "L'antica identificazione, *domus M. Gavi Rufi,* e le conseguenti concordi indicazioni della bibliografia sono purtroppo da rigettarsi."

16. Suet. *Ner.* 20.3: . . . *insignes pinguissima coma et excellentissimo cultu, puris ac sine anulo laevis, quorum duces quadringena milia sestertia merebant.*

Pompeis difficile est

In overview, this survey supports several conclusions. First, well established gentes dominated the political scene, absorbing lesser lines and fortunes to their advantage even when childlessness, ostensibly the worst of outcomes, threatened. Lesser families, local and newcomers, appeared and disappeared, rising to aedile or duovir, but the power of the established and locally well-connected families—connected through adoption as well as marriage—must have been impressive. Few families can be shown to have built their resources to rise slowly to power over the years; rather, disappearance due to a variety of factors is the more usual pattern. Those in power dominated too in their appointments on religious fronts, females as *sacerdotes Veneris et Cereris* and males as imperial flamens—if we take the latter as religious, as well as political, officers. By early Julio-Claudian times we can trace at least one apparent son of a freedman, M. Lucretius Manlianus, in local politics, and by the late Claudian and Neronian periods we can see descendants of imperial freedmen playing significant roles, but it is not until the Flavian era that sons of local freedmen can be readily traced in the evidence.

Of descendants of freedmen, the Ceii, the Caecilii, and perhaps the Trebii appear to have slowly amassed resources and to have launched their careers on still moderate fortunes, just as we saw many men of whose antecedents we are unsure do—after which they disappeared—in Claudian days. C. Iulius Polybius and the Lucii Popidii, in contrast, were able to make their highly visible splashes because of massive resources, reflected in their substantial houses. As C. Iulius Polybius in particular demonstrates, moreover, disguising one's ancestry with name changes was not requisite; it was wealth, adequate or abundant, slowly or rapidly acquired, that mattered. Social acceptability, even if not complete—witness Claudius Verus soliciting the Obellii Firmi—regularly followed.

Keep in mind, however, that I have examined only local political prominence in my studies. Some families, such as the Sextilii, whom we know to have been important also in Nola, may well have chosen temporarily not to take part in the electoral struggle or to focus their efforts elsewhere. Indeed, a local political career, although necessary, may not have seemed the most important element to a gens. And we must factor in any Roman grandees who owned property in the area and who must have been extended the privilege of membership in the *ordo*. If such had not been the practice for years, how would Cicero have known of the intensity of the political struggle at Pompeii?

To what degree the evidence from Pompeii can be extrapolated to other cities is unclear, but there is little that would seem to set it apart from that of other cities of similar times and location. Simple acquaintance with human nature would suggest that apart from local enthusiasms centered around Poppaea Sabina, the temporary alliances I have discerned in this survey could be traced elsewhere as well, if only the evidence were extant. And essentially all the impulses that I have here been able to trace originated in local men, distinguished but not particularly remarkable, seeking to align themselves with that awkward power that grew with the slow metamorphosis of Augustus that established the imperial era in Rome. Intelligent self-interest, after all, flourishes everywhere.

What *is* clear is that Cicero was correct. In the face of entrenched families with interconnections that, with the exception of occasional adoptions, we unfortunately still cannot trace, and in light of those alliances, entanglements, and short-lived enthusiasms shared among the candidates and magistrates I have here highlighted, at Pompeii it was difficult indeed.

Appendix: Dated Pompeian Magistrates

14–13 B.C.
  duoviri: M. Melsonius
             P. Rogius Varus
  aediles: N. Paccius Chilo
             N. Ninnius Pollio
                                        (*CIL* X.886)

2–1 B.C.
  duoviri: M. Holconius Rufus
             A. Clodius Flaccus
  aediles: P. Caesetius Postumus
             N. Tintirius Rufus
                                        (*CIL* X.890)

A.D. 1–2
  duoviri: M. Pomponius Marcellus
             L. Valerius Flaccus
  aediles: A. Perennius Merulinus
             L. Obellius Lucretianus
                                        (*CIL* X.891)

A.D. 2–3
  duoviri: M. Numistrius Fronto, died in office
             Q. Cotrius
  aediles: C. Annius Marulus
             D. Alfidius Hypsaeus
                          (*CIL* X.892; *EphEp* 8.316)

A.D. 3–4
  duoviri: M. Staius Rufus
             Cn. Melissaeus Aper
                                        (*CIL* X.824)

A.D. 13–14
  duovir: L. Rusticelius Celer
  aediles: Seius Flaccus
                                        (*CIL* X.894)

A.D. 14–15
duovir: M. Holconius Celer

(*CIL* X.840)

A.D. 22–23
duoviri: M. Holconius Gellius
             L. Aelius Tubero
aediles: C. Vergilius Salinator
             Cn. Lucretius Decens

(*CIL* X.895)

A.D. 25–26
quinquennales: M. Alleius Luccius Libella
                   M. Stlaborius Veius Fronto
        aediles: Q. Pompeius Macula
                   M. Fulvinius Silvanus

(*CIL* X.896)

A.D. 31–32
duoviri: M. Lucretius Manlianus
             L. Albienus Staius
aediles: L. Eumachius Fuscus
             N. Herennius Verus

(*CIL* X.899)

A.D. 33–34
duoviri: M. Lucretius Epidius Flaccus,
             praefectus for Caius Caesar
             (Caligula)
             M. Vesonius Marcellus
aediles: L. Albucius Celsus I
             D. Lucretius Valens I

(*CIL* X.901)

A.D. 40–41
quinquennales: M. Holconius Macer,
                   praefectus for Caius Caesar (Caligula)
                   M. Lucretius Epidius Flaccus
        aediles: C. Adius
                   L. Licinius

(*CIL* X.904)

A.D. 52–53
duoviri: Q. Coelius Caltilius Iustus
             L. Helvius Blaesius Proculus

(*Apochae* 138)

A.D. 55–56
  quinquennalis: Cn. Alleius Nigidius Maius
                           (*Apochae* 148)

A.D. 56–57
  duoviri: Q. Postumius Modestus
           C. Vibius Secundus
  aediles: Q. Bruttius Balbus
           C. Memmius Iunianus
                           (*CIL* X.826)

A.D. 57–58
  duoviri: C. Cornelius Macer
           Sex. Pompeius Proculus
                           (*Apochae* 145)

A.D. 58–59
  duoviri: L. Albucius Iustus
           L. Veranius Hypsaeus
                           (*Apochae* 142)

A.D. 59–60
  duoviri: Cn. Pompeius Grosphus
           Cn. Pompeius Grosphus Gavianus
                           (*Apochae* 143)

The preceding *duoviri* were replaced before 8 May 60 by the following, who remained in office until 30 June 61.

A.D. 60–61
  duoviri: Sex. Pompeius Proculus, *praefectus*
           N. Sandelius Messius Balbus
           P. Vedius Siricus
                           (*Apochae* 144)

A.D. 61–62
  duovir: Ti. Claudius Verus
                           (*Apochae* 151)

·

Inscriptions Cited

Boldface entries refer to inscriptions cited and numbered in the text.

4608	**44;** 68n. 9		7316	**153**
4615	**43;** 66n. 6		7321	173n. 74
4625	**52**		7332	87n. 85
4637	**46;** 68n. 13		7342	**174**
4754*a*	118n. 56		7343	**175;** 162n. 28
4999	**208**		7364	**176**
5229	**144;** 133n. 14		7366	**207**
5364	**117**		7387	**196**
5376	**118**		7429	186n. 129
5914	116n. 51		7454	101n. 3
5915	116n. 51		7456	**146;** 140n. 35
6621	136n. 22		7464	176n. 88
6629	72n. 31		7466	86n. 82, 171n. 66
6678	**51;** 72n. 31		7468	**203**
6682	**130**		7469	174n. 78
6686	75n. 47, 131n. 5		7474	173n. 74
6697	108n. 24		7486	86n. 82, 171n. 66
6817	**104**		7488	**70;** 91n. 94, 151n. 68
6828	**105**		7490	176n. 88
6838	**81**		7502	86n. 82, 171n. 66
6841	**131**		7504	181n. 115
6856	113n. 42		7510	172n. 72
7077	118n. 56		7519	140n. 35
7116	48n. 7		7539	**190**
7128	78n. 59		7556	171n. 64
7134*b*	87n. 85		7564	**182**
7138	87n. 85; 170n. 62		7576	158n. 17
7143	181n. 115		7579	**169**
7146	172n. 72		7580	86n. 82
7160	91n. 94, 152n. 70		7584	158n. 17
7161	173n. 74		7598	86n. 82
7168	**185;** 173n. 74		7605	158n. 17
7175	173n. 74		7609	86n. 82, 171n. 66
7184	**158**		7613	91n. 96
7187	175n. 86, 176n. 87		7614	173n. 74, 180n. 77, 186n. 129
7188	176n. 86		7618	173n. 74, 180n. 77, 186n. 129
7190	189n. 141		7619	186n. 129
7192	175n. 86		7624	180n. 77, 186n. 129
7193	91n. 94, 152n. 70, 176n. 86		7627	186n. 129
7194	175n. 86		7629	86n. 82
7203	158n. 17		7632	173n. 74, 180n. 77, 186n. 129
7210	174n. 77		7633	91n. 94, 151n. 68
7238	171n. 67		7665	173n. 74
7243	121n. 69		7667	166n. 48
7244	86n. 82		7681	172n. 72
7247	121n. 69		7702	173n. 74
7251	176n. 89		7705	86n. 82
7283	55n. 35		7706	173n. 74
7291	74n. 42, 193n. 154		7732	86n. 82
7298	176n. 89		7738	181n. 115

Kockel
N2   **52**
N34   **56**
N39   **187**
S1   **194**
S2   **13**
S4   **28**

NSc
(1890) 333   **72**
(1898) 171   **20**
(1900) 344   55n. 33
(1910) 390   **38**; 165n. 41
(1933) 322–23   **87**

Sabbatini Turnolesi
2   29n. 46
3   **18**
4   29n. 46
6   **84**
9   **73**
10   **74**

12   **127**
15   **163**
18   **140**
22   **172**
25   **179**
26   168n. 54
75   163n. 32

Varone, *Erotica*
91   **211**
92   **61**

Varone, "Tituli"
1   18n. 7
2   165n. 43
3   181n. 114
5   71n. 25

Vetter
22a   167n. 51
30   54n. 79

Index